THE SAYINGS OF JESUS
IN THE CHURCHES OF PAUL

THE
SAYINGS OF JESUS
IN THE
CHURCHES OF PAUL

*The Use of the Synoptic
Tradition in the Regulation
of Early Church Life*

BY
DAVID L. DUNGAN

FORTRESS PRESS
PHILADELPHIA

Library of Congress Catalog Card Number 70–155785

ISBN 0–8006–0056–8

PRINTED IN GREAT BRITAIN   1–56

To
Irvine Mitchell Dungan
and
Gertrude Adaline (née) Peterson
this book is lovingly
dedicated.

Preface

It is commonly observed that the literature of the New Testament outside of the Gospels says little or nothing about the teachings of Jesus. This fact has been given many different interpretations. In our case, it raised the question, to what degree did the early Christians actually live according to the teachings of Jesus? For example, we can see, from such writings as the Pastoral Epistles and the Didaché, that members of the early Church had many regulations and obligations to perform, *as Christians*, in addition to what was required of them as Greeks or Syrians or Romans. But is it possible to see anywhere among these Christian community regulations practices that may be traced back to Jesus' instigation in particular? Thus, it should be made clear at the outset that this is primarily an essay in early Christian *law*, not ethics or ritual. Our concern shall be with certain actually operating, constitutive regulations of the early Church, and their relationship with Jesus' teachings.

If this is the general realm within which our discussion shall move, its concrete beginning was an analysis of the chapter on 'Legal Sayings and Church Rules', in Rudolf Bultmann's *History of the Synoptic Tradition*. It quickly became clear that Bultmann had jumbled together Synoptic material of many different kinds: disputes between Jesus and his contemporaries over the Torah, ethical debates and proverbs, actual legislative pronouncements, and even the debate with the Sadducees over the Resurrection. The chief difficulty seemed to be that there was no control over what should be considered a 'community regulation', in contradistinction to all this other material.

In the course of seeking a way through the problems involved, it gradually emerged that *Paul* could well serve as a control principle to interpret the plethora of the Synoptic phenomena, for, by means of his letters, actual Christian communities could be considered as an integral part of the whole question. This study of Paul's use of two commands of the Lord to regulate the life of his congregation at Corinth (and elsewhere) is the result.

Whatever helpful illumination or further understanding has been achieved is chiefly to the credit of my dissertation advisor,

Krister Stendahl (now Dean of Harvard Divinity School), and to Helmut Koester (Professor of New Testament and Early Church History in the same institution). Their high standards of critical scholarship, careful analysis of the primary texts, and constant attention to methodological problems, were always matched and more than matched by patient assistance and cheerful support. Also playing a key part was the financial assistance of the Higgins Trust Fund of the Presbytery of Chicago, under whose auspices I was a Graduate Fellow from 1964–1967. The many letters of warm encouragement sent by the Reverend Ellis Butler, Secretary to the Fund, will always be especially remembered. I wish also to take this opportunity to thank Dr. Maria Grossman, Director of the Andover-Harvard Library, and Mr. Charles Woodbury, in charge of circulation, for their kind assistance. Nevertheless, the opportunities afforded me from so many sides would have come to nothing more than once, had it not been for the constant encouragement of my wife.

September, 1969   D.L.D.
Knoxville, Tennessee

Table of Contents

ABBREVIATIONS   xiii

INTRODUCTION   xvii
   1. Paul and Jesus; the state of the question.   xvii
   2. The purpose of the present inquiry.   xxix

PART I.   THE LORD'S COMMAND CONCERNING
          SUPPORT FOR APOSTLES

CHAPTER ONE. PAUL'S REACTION AGAINST THE ABUSE OF
THE LORD'S COMMAND CONCERNING SUPPORT FOR APOST-
LES (1 COR. 9.4–18)   3
   1. The proof that Paul as well as the rest of the apostles
      are supposed to be supported by the churches (9.4–12a)   4
      A. 9.4–6 Are Paul and his associates exceptions among
         the apostles?   6
      B. 9.7–12a Several arguments justifying this apostolic
         prerogative   9
   2. Paul boasts that he does not abuse this regulation
      (9.12b)   14
   3. Further arguments supporting this regulation; the
      command of the Lord (9.13f.)   16
   4. Paul emphatically repeats his intention not to make
      use of this authority (9.15–23)   21
   5. Paul's method in this matter the same as his general
      missionary procedure (9.19–23)   25

CHAPTER TWO. PAUL'S BASIC POSITION vis-à-vis THIS COM-
MAND OF THE LORD   27
   1. Paul's financial relations with his churches   28
   2. The relation between Paul's missionary strategy and
      the sayings-of-the-Lord tradition   33

3.   The success of Paul's policy regarding financial support   36

4.   The actual wording of the command of the Lord   40

CHAPTER THREE. THE MISSION INSTRUCTIONS IN THE
SYNOPTIC GOSPELS   41

1.   The original form and contents of the Mission instruc-
     tions   41

     A.   The interrelation of the Synoptic accounts   41
       (i) Luke's so-called Q-block (Luke 10.1–12)   42
      (ii) Luke's so-called Markan block (Luke 9.1–5)   48
     (iii) Matthew's so-called conflation of Mark, Q, and M
           (Matt. 10.1–16)   51
      (iv) The originality of Matthew's entire version compared
           to the other three accounts   59
       (v) Mark's abridgement (Mark 6.7–11)   63

     B.   Conclusion   66

2.   The character of the support to be accorded the disciples
     in the original account of the mission of the Twelve   67

3.   The attitudes of the gospel editors toward this issue   69
     A.   Matthew   69
     B.   Luke   71
     C.   Mark   74

CHAPTER FOUR. PAUL AND THE EDITORS OF THE SYNOPTIC
GOSPELS   76

PART II.   THE LORD'S COMMAND CONCERNING
                    DIVORCE

CHAPTER ONE. PAUL'S INSTRUCTIONS ON MARRIAGE   83

1.   Marriage is recommended for all (1 Cor. 7.1–7)   83

2.   Widows and widowers (1 Cor. 7.8f.)   88

3.   Divorce; the command of the Lord (1 Cor. 7.10f.)   89

4.   Marriage with unbelievers (1 Cor. 7.12–16)   93

CHAPTER TWO. FEATURES OF PAUL'S USE OF THIS COMMAND
OF THE LORD   100

CHAPTER THREE. THE SAYINGS ON DIVORCE IN THE SYNOPTIC
GOSPELS   102

1. The account of Jesus' debate with the Pharisees
regarding divorce (Matt. 19.3–9//Mark 10.2–12)   102

  A. The original order of the story   102

  B. The concluding saying on divorce-remarriage (Matt.
19.9//Mark 10.11f.)   107

  C. The so-called Matthean insertions 'for any cause' and
'except for fornication'   109

  D. The assumptions and horizon of Jesus' answer (Matt.
19.3–9)   115

  E. The originality of Matt. 19.3–9   122

2. The gospel editors' use of this account   125

  A. Matthew   125

  B. Mark   127

  C. Luke (16.18)   129

  D. Conclusions   131

CHAPTER FOUR. PAUL AND THE EDITORS OF THE SYNOPTIC
GOSPELS   132

PART III RESULTS

RESULTS   139

1. Paul's intimate relation with the Synoptic tradition   139

2. Paul's conservatism regarding the tradition itself   141

3. How much of the Synoptic tradition did Paul use?   146

APPENDIX   152

BIBLIOGRAPHY   156

INDICES   171

Abbreviations

Aland et al. *NT*=K. Aland et al. *The Greek New Testament* (1966).

Allo=E.-B. Allo, *Saint Paul. Première épître aux Corinthiens* (1935).

AusCathRec=*Australasian Catholic Record* (Sydney).

Bacon=B. W. Bacon, *The Beginnings of Gospel Story* (1909).

Bauer *Lexicon*=W. Bauer, *A Greek-English Lexicon of the New Testament and Other Early Christian Literature*. Trans. and ed. W. F. Arndt, F. W. Gingrich (1957).

Beare=F. W. Beare, *The Earliest Records of Jesus* (1962).

Billerbeck *Kommentar*=H. L. Strack, P. Billerbeck, *Kommentar zum Neuen Testament*. 6 Bde (1922–63).

Blass-Debrunner-Funk *Grammar*=F. Blass, A. Debrunner, *A Greek Grammar of the New Testament and other Early Christian Literature*. Trans. and ed. R. W. Funk (1961).

Brown-Driver-Briggs *Lexicon*=F. Brown, S. R. Driver, C. A. Briggs, *A Hebrew and English Lexicon of the Old Testament*[2] (1957).

Bultmann=R. D. Bultmann, *The History of the Synoptic Tradition*. Trans. J. Marsh (1963).

BZ=*Biblische Zeitschrift* (Paderborn).

CBQ=*The Catholic Biblical Quarterly* (Washington, D.C.).

ET=English translation.

EvTh=*Evangelische Theologie* (München).

Héring=J. Héring, *La première épître de saint Paul aux Corinthiens* (1949).

HUCA=*Hebrew Union College Annual* (*Cincinnati*).

Hurd=J. C. Hurd, *The Origin of 1 Corinthians* (1965).

JBL=*The Journal of Biblical Literature* (Philadelphia).

JB=*The Jerusalem Bible*.

JJSt=*The Journal of Jewish Studies* (Manchester).

Klostermann *Luke*—E. Klostermann, *Das Lukasevangelium*[2] (1929).

Klostermann *Mark*=idem, *Das Markusevangelium*[4] (1950).

Klostermann *Matt.*=idem, *Das Matthäusevangelium*[2] (1927).

Lagrange=M.-J. Lagrange, *Évangile selon Saint Matthieu*[7] (1948).

Liddell-Scott-Jones *Lexicon*=H. G. Liddell, R. Scott, *A Greek-English Lexicon*. 9th ed. rev. by H. S. Jones (1961).
Lietzmann-Kümmel=H. Lietzmann, *An die Korinther I/II*. 4. Aufl. von W. G. Kümmell (1949).
Lightfoot=J. B. Lightfoot, *Notes on the Epistles of St. Paul* (1895).
Lohmeyer-Schmauch=E. Lohmeyer, *Das Evangelium des Matthäus*. 3. Aufl. von W. Schmauch (1962).
Loisy=A. Loisy, *L'Evangile selon Luc* (1924).
Moffatt=J. Moffatt, *The First Epistle of Paul to the Corinthians* (1930).
Montefiore=C. G. Montefiore, *The Synoptic Gospels*. 2 vols. (1927).
NEB=*The New English Bible*.
NTS=*New Testament Studies* (Cambridge).
NovTest=*Novum Testamentum* (Leiden).
RAC=*Reallexikon für Antike und Christentum. Sachwörterbuch zur Auseinandersetzung des Christentums mit der antiken Welt*. (1962–).
RecSciRel=*Recherches de science religieuse* (Paris).
RefTheolRev=*The Reformed Theological Review* (Melbourne).
RevHistPhilRel=*Revue d'Histoire et de Philosophie Religieuses* (Strasbourg).
RevQum=*Revue de Qumran* (Paris).
RevThéolPhil=*Revue de Théologie et de Philosophie* (Lausanne).
RGG³=*Die Religion in Geschichte und Gegenwart. Handwörterbuch für Theologie und Religionswissenschaft³* (1957–).
Robertson-Plummer=A. Robertson, A. Plummer, *A Critical and Exegetical Commentary on the First Epistle of St. Paul to the Corinthians* (1911).
RSV=*Revised Standard Version of The Holy Bible*.
Scrip=*Scripture* (Edinburgh).
Scripta=*Scripta Hierosolymitana* (Jerusalem).
StTh=*Studia Theologica* (Lund.)
Taylor *Luke*=V. Taylor, *Behind the Third Gospel* (1926).
Taylor *Mark*=idem, *The Gospel According to St. Mark* (1955).
TDNT=G. Kittel, ed. *Theological Dictionary of the New Testament*. Trans. G. W. Bromiley Vols. I–III (1964–).
ThLZ=*Theologische Literaturzeitung. Monatschrift für das gesamte Gebiet der Theologie und Religionswissenschaft* (Liepzig).

TWNT=G. Kittel, ed. *Theologisches Wörterbuch zum Neuen Testament*. Vols. I–VI and continuing (1933–).

VerbDom=*Verbum Domini* (Rome).

Weiss=J. Weiss, *Der erste Korintherbrief*[2] (1910).

ZAW=*Zeitschrift für die Alttestamentliche Wissenschaft* (Berlin).

ZNW=*Zeitschrift für die Neutestamentliche Wissenschaft* (Berlin).

ZThK=*Zeitschrift für Theologie und Kirche* (Tübingen).

Introduction

1. *Paul and Jesus; the state of the question*

In his book *Paul and Rabbinic Judaism*[2] (1955), W. D. Davies discusses at some length the question whether and to what extent Paul was familiar with and used the teachings of Jesus. Although willing to grant that much of Paul's parenetic traditions derived from Jewish sources, Davies nevertheless concludes that 'it was the words of Jesus Himself that formed Paul's primary source in his work as ethical *didaskalos*.'[1] The chief argument for this conclusion according to Davies, is the vast number of parallels between Pauline exhortation and the teachings of Jesus as they are preserved in the Synoptic gospels. Setting forth a number of examples 'where Paul is clearly dependent upon the words of Jesus' from Romans, 1 Thessalonians, and Colossians,[2] and adding the handful of 'explicit references to the words of Jesus',[3] Davies decides that there can be little question whether or not Paul knew the teachings of Jesus. On the contrary, 'Paul is steeped in the mind and words of his Lord . . . unconsciously mingling them with the hortatory material he has derived from other sources.'[4]

Although he does not dwell upon the matter, Davies is perfectly aware that his view is by no means unchallenged in current New Testament research. In the same year that the first edition of his book was published, 1948, Rudolf Bultmann's *Theologie des Neuen Testaments* began appearing in fascicles; within a decade it had become the major work in its field. In it, Bultmann asserts categorically, 'the teaching of the historical Jesus plays no role or practically none in Paul'.[5] What was the basis of such a generalization? Bultmann argues that it was Hellenistic not Palestinian

---

[1] Op. cit. 136.   [2] Ibid. 138f.

[3] Ibid. 140; e.g., 1 Cor. 9.14; 7.10; 11.23ff.; 14.37 (noting later the textual problem involved here, see p. 141, n. 5); 1 Thess. 4.15f.; and, surprisingly, Acts 20.35.

[4] Ibid. 140; see further idem, *The Setting of the Sermon on the Mount* (1964) 341–366.

[5] ET K. Grobel, *Theology of the New Testament* (1951); see I 35; hereafter cited as 'Bultmann *Theology*'.

Christianity to which Paul was first introduced, and 'after his conversion . . . Paul made no effort toward contact with Jesus' disciples or the Jerusalem Church for instruction concerning Jesus and his ministry. On the contrary, he vehemently protests his independence from them in Gal. 1–2'.[1] Thus, according to Bultmann, on Paul's own testimony, he is not only ignorant of, he is also indifferent to the teachings of Jesus; 'in fact, his letters barely show any traces of the influence of the Palestinian tradition concerning the history and preaching of Jesus'.[2]

The debate over the relation between Paul and Jesus has been continuing for more than a century and a quarter. As the two opinions quoted above show, it is far from over.[3] The main issue was posed by Ferdinand Christian Baur in his famous article, 'Die Christus-partei in der korinthischen Gemeinde' (1831). In it Baur claimed that Paul developed his theology in conscious opposition to that of the earliest Jerusalem—scil. Petrine—wing of the Church, and that the theology Paul set forth deliberately ignored the words and deeds of the historical Jesus in favour of a direct relationship with the Risen Christ.

The first major response, a long article by Heinrich Paret, 'Paulus und Jesus, Einige Bemerkungen über das Verhältnis des Apostels Paulus und seiner Lehre zu der Person, dem Leben und der Lehre des geschichtlichen Christus',[4] did not appear until

[1] Bultmann *Theology* I 188. Bultmann's position briefly set forth in section 16, 'The Historical Position of Paul', was worked out more fully in his earlier article, 'Die Bedeutung des geschichtlichen Jesus für die Theologie des Paulus', *ThBl* 8 (1929) 137–151, reprinted in idem, *Glauben und Verstehen* I (1958) 188–213 (page references will be to the latter). In this article, Bultmann builds upon the work of Wilhelm Bousset and Wilhelm Heitmüller; see further below.

[2] Bultmann *Theology* I 188.

[3] Besides the indispensable history of the earlier period of the debate by Albert Schweitzer, *Geschichte der paulinischen Forschung von der Reformation bis auf die Gegenwart* (1911), ET W. Montgomery, *Paul and His Interpreters* (1912; hereafter cited as 'Schweitzer *Paul*'), this introductory discussion is largely indebted to V. P. Furnish, 'The Jesus-Paul Debate: From Baur to Bultmann', *BJRL* 47 (1964–65) 342–381. Typical of the astonishing degree of ferocity which the discussion had attained in Germany by the time of Schweitzer was the violent reception his history was accorded; see, e.g., W. G. Kümmel, ' "Konsequente Eschatologie" Albert Schweitzers im Urteil der Zeitgenossen', in idem, *Heilsgeschehen und Geschichte* (1965) 328–339.

[4] *Jahrbucher für Deutsche Theologie* 3 (1858) 1–85; cited in Furnish 'Jesus-Paul' 343.

1858, after several more articles and one full-length book on Paul had come from Baur's pen developing his position in greater detail.[1] Paret's response is all the more significant because it employed most of the arguments used in one way or another ever since by those disagreeing with Baur and his School: (a) Paul's kerygmatic Christ, i.e., his theology as a whole, presupposes a full knowledge of the events in the life of the earthly Jesus as well as his teachings; (b) Paul's letters do in fact contain information about Jesus' life history and furthermore there are numerous explicit references to and implicit allusions or parallels with the teachings of Jesus in them; (c) the assertion of a 'silence' or 'indifference' on the part of Paul to the facts of the historical Jesus is unfounded not only because we have evidence for only a small part of Paul's whole missionary activity, it also makes the mistake of assuming that Paul's letters are typical of his preaching. On the contrary, his letters must have presupposed his preaching, and in the latter he would have dwelt at length upon Jesus' words and deeds, for kerygmatic as well as didactic purposes.[2] Let us take these three arguments of Paret and use them as foci around which to view the subsequent stages of the debate on this question.

Dominating the centre of the stage for most of the 19th century, at least in Germany (where most of the discussion was taking place), was the first question, namely the issue as to the nature and origin of Paul's theology, or 'religion' as it was usually called.[3] Paul Feine's massive history of Pauline research is devoted to nothing else than evaluating the numerous attempts to describe the nature of Paul's 'religious experience'.[4]

The central question for this approach consisted of an obsession with describing the inner dynamics of Paul's 'Damascus experience', and the results were far-fetched in the extreme. In utterly romantic fashion, and not without a powerful note of the anti-semitism currently popular in academic as well as not-so-academic circles, everything in Paul's thought was made to depend upon this moment of supreme confrontation between the

[1] Furnish 343; Schweitzer *Paul* 12–21.

[2] Furnish loc. cit.

[3] Furnish 378–380; cp. Schweitzer *Paul* 33–40.

[4] *Der Apostel Paulus. Das Ringen um das geschichtliche Verständnis des Paulus* (1927). He takes up in succession the theological (i.e., systematic), the history-of-religions, the eschatological, and the 'religious' (i.e., the psychological), interpretations of Paul's 'experience'.

raging, blood-thirsty Jew and the gentle, slain Lord, whose compassion instantly overwhelmed Paul first with guilt and then tremendous gratitude, transforming the former persecutor of the Church into a devoted apostle, who henceforth abandoned all ties to his Jewish past, preaching instead the unique Gospel of freedom to Jew and Gentile alike. Despite warnings from the conservatives that the Christ Paul met on the road to Damascus was no other than the historical Jesus, the 'Damascus experience' became the favourite homiletical hunting-ground for liberals of every persuasion. It presented a perfect opportunity for driving wedges between the historical Jewish milieu of Paul (and Jesus, too, for that matter) and an idealized, 'up-dated' portrait of Paul more palatable to the modern temper.[1]

This approach received its most thorough elaboration in the work of H. J. Holtzmann, *Lehrbuch der neutestamentlichen Theologie* (1897),[2] but it remained for William Wrede to state it in its most drastic form, seven years later. In his brief book, *Paulus* (1904),[3] Wrede also emphasized the cruciality of Paul's conversion experience, but he explained that what it consisted of was Paul's identification of the figure of a divine, celestial Christ, *in which he already believed*, with the historical Jesus. But this happened in such a way that the figure of the historical Jesus was completely infused with Paul's Hellenistic-Jewish speculations, above all with his full-blown messianic belief. In this exchange, nothing of the historical Jesus was preserved save the bare actuality of Jesus himself, while everything from Paul's Hellenistic-Jewish background and theological impulses was introduced. Therefore, insofar as Paul's synthesis became the indispensable basis for all later Christian theology, says Wrede, 'it follows conclusively ... that Paul is to be regarded as *the second founder of Christianity*'.[4]

Wrede's book, translated into English in 1907, ignited a storm of controversy on both sides of the Atlantic, as numerous books and articles appeared in support of or opposition to his thesis. The very brilliance of his handling of the 'Damascus experience'

[1] The first full-length presentation of this view in America was the book by Shirley Jackson Case, *Jesus. A New Biography* (1927); Furnish 363.
[2] See Schweitzer *Paul* 100–116.
[3] ET E. Lummis, *Paul* (1907).
[4] *Paul* 179; cp. Furnish 'Jesus-Paul' 349f.

and its consequences, however, served to drive one lesson home, and that was the utter lack of objective, scientific controls available to those seeking a psychological basis upon which to interpret Paul's theology. Thus, an article by Wilhelm Heitmüller signalled an attempt to bring the discussion away from its preoccupation with Paul's psyche. In 'Zum Problem Paulus und Jesus' (1912),[1] Heitmüller suggested that the great synthesis claimed for Paul by Wrede may not have been entirely the result of Paul's 'religious genius', at all. Pointing to evidence in Acts and in the traditional material in Paul's letters, he argued that Paul's theology was to be accounted for by the fact that he had been converted by a branch of the Hellenistic Church, in which there was little interest in the contents of Jesus' preaching or deeds, where this synthesis had already been formed.[2]

Thus Rudolf Bultmann, in *Die Geschichte der synoptischen Tradition* (1921),[3] which was dedicated to Heitmüller, accepted Heitmüller's reformulation of the issues, and led the way with Martin Dibelius, *Die Formgeschichte des Evangeliums* (1919),[4] back to a new investigation of the literature of the period, this time paying the utmost attention to the whole question of the role of tradition in the early Church. For the first time the problem was brought clearly into focus how it could be that a Church in which a disinterest regarding the historical Jesus prevailed at the same time preserved so much tradition regarding the life and teachings of Jesus. Or, as Bultmann puts it near the end of his *History of the Synoptic Tradition*,

It is not possible to state sufficiently sharply the contrast in the N.T. Canon with the Synoptic Gospels on the one hand and the Pauline letters and the later literature on the other. It must still be a puzzle to understand why Christianity, in which Pauline and post-Pauline tendencies played so dominant a role, should also have the motives which drove it to take over and shape the Synoptic tradition out of the Palestinian Church. This puzzle can only be solved by recognizing that there were strata of Hellenistic Christianity of which so far little is

[1] *ZNW* 13 (1912) 320–337.
[2] Heitmüller 336. See the critique by H. J. Schoeps *Paul* (1961) 62f.
[3] ET J. Marsh, *The History of the Synoptic Tradition* (1963); hereafter cited as 'Bultmann'.
[4] ET B. T. Woolf, *From Tradition to Gospel* (1934).

known, and on the further working out of which everything must depend.[1]

Since references to the actual details of Jesus' life and ministry are almost completely absent from Paul's writings—except a few which can just as easily be understood to be 'events' within Paul's theological Christ-myth[2]—the second main line of defense against the Tübingen position has been the claim that it can uphold its sharp separation between Paul and Jesus only by ignoring the numerous parallels between their respective teaching, especially in the parenetic sections of Paul's letters. The maximalist 'record' for finding such parallels and allusions is still held by Arnold Resch who, in *Der Paulinismus und die Logia Jesu* (1904),[3] claimed to have 'discovered' no less than 925 allusions to Jesus' teachings in the nine Pauline letters (including Colossians), 133 more in Ephesians, 100 in the Pastoral Epistles, and, for good measure, 64 in the Pauline speeches in Acts.[4] Not content with that, Resch even 'recovered' dozens of heretofore *unknown* sayings of Jesus in Paul's letters.[5]

[1] Bultmann 303; cp. idem 'Die Bedeutung des geschichtlichen Jesus', 189f. Contributing heavily to this view was W. Bousset in such works as *Hauptprobleme der Gnosis* (1907), *Kyrios Christos*[2] (1921), and *Die Religion des Judentums im späthellenistischen Zeitalter*[3] (1926).

The statement of the question quoted above has received the attention of U. Wilckens, who in two recent articles, has tried to show that the original split occurred when the 'Hellenists' (Acts 6.1) were driven out of Jerusalem before they were able to learn very much of the Jesus-tradition ('Hellenistisch-christliche Missionsüberlieferung und Jesustradition,' *ThLZ* 89 [1964] 517–520), and that the two wings of the early Church rejoined later when the Palestinian-Jewish-Christians were driven out of Palestine in 70 and 135 ('Tradition de Jésus et Kerygme du Christ: la double histoire de la tradition au sein du christianisme primitif,' *RevHistPhilRel* 47 [1967] 1–20).

Despite the general realization by now of the fatal pitfalls involved in using *Acts'* *account* of the 'Damascus experience' to account for Paul's theological creativity and apostolic independence, a few still seem unable to resist it, e.g., H. J. Schoeps *Paulus* (1959 ET H. Knight 1961), and J. Munck, *Paulus und die Heilsgeschichte* (1954 ET F. Clark, *Paul and the Salvation of Mankind* 1959).

[2] See Bultmann *Theology* I 188.

[3] *Texte und Untersuchungen* NF 12 (1904).

[4] See Furnish, 'Jesus-Paul' 348 n. 6; further Davies *Paul and Rabbinic Judaism* 137.

[5] Schweitzer *Paul* 42.

A special variation of this approach was initiated by Alfred
Seeberg with his book, *Der Katechismus der Urchristenheit* (1903).[1]
In this work, attention was directed for the first time at the basic
role *tradition* played in the Pauline parenesis. Seeberg attempted
to demonstrate that in the parenetic sections of all of the NT
epistles there is a striking consistency of pattern, and that this
pattern—largely Jewish in origin and contents—shows close
affinity with both the spirit as well as the content of Jesus' teachings
as preserved in the Synoptic gospels. It was his conclusion that
this constituted proof that Jesus' teachings had passed into the
didactic activity of the early Christian Church through its cate-
chisms, and were there preserved, albeit anonymously and mixed
in with current Jewish parenesis. Seeberg's work was received
with qualified approval by both Martin Dibelius and Rudolf
Bultmann,[2] but it seemed to find its most enthusiastic reception
among the Scandinavian scholars (see below) as well as in England,
where it stimulated several other studies along the same paths,
as for example in the work of E. G. Selwyn,[3] Ph. Carrington,[4] and
C. H. Dodd.[5]

But we may be sure, this whole approach was not without its
staunch critics. In 1906, for example, Martin Brückner published
an article entitled 'Zum Thema Jesus und Paulus',[6] in which he
insisted that in all comparisons of this kind, one whole side was an
extremely vague entity due to the cloud of uncertainty hovering
over the Synoptic gospels as a whole and each, individual saying
in particular, as to whether one actually had here the *ipsissima
verba Jesu*. Furthermore, Brückner argued, 'the discovery of

[1] Seeberg developed his research through a series of publications;
Das Evangelium Christi (1905); *Die Beiden Wege und das Aposteldekret*
(1906); *Die Didache des Judentums und der Urchristenheit* (1908);
Christi Person und Werk nach der Lehre seiner Jünger (1910).

[2] See Bultmann *Theology* I 360.

[3] *The First Epistle of St. Peter*[2] (1955) 363–466.

[4] *The Primitive Christian Catechism* (1940).

[5] *Gospel and Law* (1951) 17–20; idem, 'The Primitive Christian
Catechism and the Sayings of Jesus', *Studies in Memory of T. W.
Manson* 1893–1958 (1959) 106–118. Dodd considered this approach
'the soundest method of determining, with the highest degree of
probability which the nature of the case admits, the contents of the
early Christian "pattern of teaching" as Paul calls it' (*Gospel and Law*
17).

[6] *ZNW* 7 (1906) 112–119; cited in Furnish 'Jesus-Paul' 351.

parallels does not necessarily mean that one has thereby proved the *dependence* of one source upon the other'.[1] This objection has the more force since Paul rarely claims such dependence to begin with. Not only that, but the Pauline side of the 'parallel' is the historically earlier writing.

Albert Schweitzer's history of Pauline research, which also appeared about this time,[2] had another criticism to bring against this approach.

It is strange that most of these authors believe that they reduce the acuteness of the problem [of Paul's silence with regard to Jesus' teachings] by pointing out in the epistles as many reminiscences of Synoptic sayings as possible. If so many utterances of Jesus are hovering before Paul's mind, how comes it that he always merely paraphrases them, instead of quoting them as sayings of Jesus and thus sheltering himself behind their authority?[3]

In Schweitzer's opinion, the sayings are not there at all, for Paul was not interested in what Jesus had said during his ministry in Palestine. 'If we had to rely on Paul,' Schweitzer later wrote, 'we should not know that Jesus taught in parables, had delivered the Sermon on the Mount, and had taught his disciples the "Our Father." *Even where they are specially relevant Paul passes over words of the Lord.*'[4]

The third major defense against the Tübingen School's position lay in the argument that its use of the letters of Paul as evidence for the whole activity of the Apostle was inadmissible.

[1] Quoted from Furnish 351.

[2] Mentioned above p. xviii n. 3.

[3] *Paul* 42f. As a remarkable example of the flimsiness and *ad hoc* character of the explanation for this phenomenon given by proponents of this approach, one may cite E. G. Selwyn's comment on 1 Peter: 'We have seen how often *verba Christi* lie just below the surface of this Epistle. . . . If we ask why is it that 1 Peter, despite his partiality for *verba Christi* so often drives home his point by quoting from the Old Testament when a word of the Lord would have seemed more telling, the answer is, no doubt, that the OT passage was already linked in Jewish tradition with the injunctions he was making, and was therefore more familiar to those Christians who had been accustomed to the synagogue' (*St. Peter* 366f.). See further W. Schmithals 'Paulus und der historische Jesus', *ZNW* 53 (1962) 148.

[4] Schweitzer, *The Mysticism of Paul the Apostle* (1931) 173; italics added. See also Bultmann *Theology* I 189.

This objection, as developed by Paret, G. Matheson, J. Weiss, E. Vischer, and A. Deissmann, among others,[1] claimed that Paul's letters obviously presupposed an extensive missionary preaching and instruction. In themselves, as can be seen fron their contents, they are little more than fragmentary discussions of particular issues, frequently taken up in a polemical and therefore one-sided manner, and therefore give, at best, a partial and distorted view of what Paul actually taught in his larger missionary activity. As Eberhard Vischer contends,

One is not permitted simply to identify what stands in his letters with his missionary preaching. So it is possible, indeed probable, that Paul had imparted more about the life of Jesus and his words in the oral proclamation than one is able to infer from his letters. A passage like 1 Cor. 11.23ff. presupposes that the congregations are acquainted with at least a part of the history of Jesus.[2]

This argument has also been attacked on several sides. For one thing, it is essentially an argument from silence. The probabilities claimed for what Paul did in his missionary preaching are merely gratuitous, for we have no direct evidence on typical missionary preaching for this period, Pauline or any other. For another, this argument must overcome the well-nigh fatal objection that it is refuted by Paul himself in Gal. 1–2. Heitmüller insists that there is simply no way to soften Paul's vehement denial of any dependence, whether for his commission as an apostle or for the contents of his 'gospel', upon the Jerusalem leadership. Finally, following Heitmüller again, there is nothing in Paul's letters that *necessitates* our thinking that his preaching was any more concerned with the historical Jesus than his letters are. Paul would have had no use for such preaching since he did not proclaim the message of Jesus but the Hellenistic-Christian kerygma of Christ the Lord. It was to the constant elaboration of this theme that he devoted his energies, both in preaching and in writing.[3]

And so the debate continues, as each side periodically makes additional contributions from within its own presuppositions and, largely, for its own audiences.

[1] See Furnish 'Jesus-Paul' 343f., 354, 362.
[2] Quoted from Furnish 351.
[3] 'Zum Problem Paulus und Jesus,' *ZNW* 13 (1912) 320–337; cp. Furnish 359; further Bultmann *Theology* I 187–189.

B

Something of a new direction has been given the whole discussion in recent decades, however, by the so-called Uppsala School, Anton Fridrichsen and his students. Recognizing that an impasse has been reached due to an over-emphasis upon the purely theological or the purely literary aspects of the problem, Fridrichsen began asking about the evidence for Paul's relationship to the rest of the leaders of the early Church.[1] Operating from a somewhat conservative theological opposition to the conclusions of the Tübingen School,[2] Fridrichsen asserted that the essential issue was, what was Paul's *historical* relation to Jesus?[3] In his brief but influential essay, *The Apostle and His Message* (1947),[4] Fridrichsen sought to demonstrate Paul's solidarity with the Jerusalem leadership. To achieve this, however, Fridrichsen was compelled to account for Paul's disavowal of any dependence upon these Jerusalem 'pillars'. Taking as his starting-point 1 Cor. 15.1ff, he argued that Paul here clearly claims his fundamental unity with the Kerygma as well as the leadership of the early Church. This passage is the necessary counter-weight to Gal. 1–2. Then, in an argument reminiscent of F. C. Baur's division of the early Church into Petrine and Pauline wings, Fridrichsen goes on to argue that there was, on this basis, a dual Apostleship and a dual form of the *interpretation* of the basic Kerygma; the first, Peter's Gospel to the Circumcized (Jewish Christians), and the second, Paul's Gospel to the Gentiles (Hellenistic Christians). In this manner, Fridrichsen could allow for both Paul's vehement claim to theological and apostolic independence as well as his equally plain basic concord with the Jerusalem leadership.

[1] A drawback in Furnish's otherwise helpful and comprehensive study of the history of this debate is his inexplicable omission of the Scandinavian contribution. He gives no more than a cursory glance at one of Fridrichsen's articles, and is completely silent about his pupils. Also missing is sufficient reference to the indispensible contributions of the English at key points in the history of the discussion.

[2] Furnish quite misleadingly compares Fridrichsen with the American fundamentalist scholar and New Testament lecturer at Princeton, J. Gresham Machen; see 360, 368. Fridrichsen's solid philological and history-of-religions' approach belonged to a world foreign to Machen. Not to be denied, however, are Fridrichsen's pious motivations; see, e.g. 'Jesus, St. John and St. Paul', *The Root and the Vine* (1953) 54.

[3] 'Jesus, John, Paul' 37f.

[4] *Uppsala Universitets Årsskrift* 1947:3.

Essential to Fridrichsen's reconstruction of events was extensive utilization of Acts and its portrayal of Paul's close relationship with the Jerusalem leaders. But to make this acceptable, a major reversal of the widespread scepticism concerning Acts' historical reliability was necessary.[1] Thus, although this was not its main purpose, Bertil Gärtner's book, *The Areopagus Speech and Natural Revelation* (1955), contained an extended defence of Acts' value as a primary source for the history of the earliest Christian community.[2]

The year before Gärtner's book came out, another of Fridrichsen's students had focussed attention on an entirely different issue, using new evidence fresh from the just-discovered Dead Sea Scrolls. Rejecting the very popular view of Dibelius and Bultmann that the traditions contained in the Synoptic gospels largely originated in and were circulated among essentially unliterary, lower-class Galilean peasants whose folk-hero Messiah was the object of their numerous miraculous legends and striking sayings,[3] Krister Stendahl, in his book *The School of St. Matthew* (1954), posed the question as to what kind of community or milieu must be presupposed to understand the phenomenon of the Gospel of Matthew, especially its sophisticated manner of using the Old Testament. By comparing Matthew's use of the Old Testament with the style of exegesis of the Qumran *Habbakuk Commentary*, Stendahl laid the basis for the argument that Matthew was the product of a highly-trained, precise and thoroughly tradition-minded Christian (rabbinic) School.[4]

The other shoe was dropped three years later when Harald Riesenfeld, addressing the 1957 Oxford Congress on 'The Four Gospels', proposed that the implications pointed to by Stendahl for Matthew in fact held for all of the Gospels as well as Paul and other writings in the New Testament.[5] His programmatic speech

[1] The initial attack upon the reliability of Acts was also made by F. C. Baur; see the excellent history of the earlier period by A. C. McGiffert, in K. Lake and F. J. Jackson, edd., *The Beginnings of Christianity* II Pt.I (1922) 363–395; for the more recent developments, see H. Conzelmann, *Die Apostelgeschichte* (1963) 4–10.

[2] See especially 26–36; 248–252.

[3] Dibelius *From Tradition to Gospel* 8; Bultmann 4, 6.

[4] *School* 13–19, 30–35 (same pp. in second ed., 1968).

[5] 'The Gospel Tradition and Its Beginnings,' reprinted in *Studia Evangelica. Texte und Untersuchungen* 73 V.R. 18. Also appeared separately; London, 1957 (page references are to the latter). The essay has recently appeared again in a collection of Riesenfeld's articles, *The Gospel Tradition*, Philadelphia, 1970.

was given full-scale development in a book published five years later by Birger Gerhardsson, *Memory and Manuscript. Oral Tradition and Written Transmission in Rabbinic Judaism and Early Christianity* (1961). According to the thesis of Riesenfeld and Gerhardsson, the widespread evidence of the use of technical terms for receiving and transmitting tradition, *especially in the letters of Paul*, demonstrates beyond any doubt that the leadership of the earliest Christian Church included highly-trained transmitters of the Church's official traditions, known as 'the Word of God', which was nothing else than the words and acts of and the teachings about Jesus the Messiah.[1] This group included the Apostle Paul as his letters clearly show,[2] and the point of origin of this chain of carefully memorized and meticulously preserved tradition was *none other than Jesus himself.* He taught his disciples, having them memorize his words in typical rabbinic fashion,[3] as they did their pupils after them, and the result was, in part, much of what we now have in our *four* Gospels, viz., accurate versions of Jesus' words and deeds.[4]

[1] *Memory* 214–245.

[2] Ibid. 288–323.

[3] Ibid. 122–170, 203–207 *et passim*; see also Riesenfeld *Gospel Tradition* 24, 26f.

[4] Riesenfeld 28. Cp. the earlier suggestion of Stendahl: 'There may therefore be an unbroken line from the School of Jesus via the "teaching of the apostles", the "ways" of Paul (1 Cor. 4.17), the basic teaching of Mark and other *huperetai tou logou,* and the more mature School of John to the rather elaborate School of Matthew with its ingenious interpretation of the OT as the crown of its scholarship' (*School* 34); but see his second thoughts in the 2nd ed., p. x.

Besides the classic studies on the problem of Paul's use of tradition by A. Seeberg and others mentioned above, including also the work of O. Moe, *Paulus und die evangelische Geschichte* (1912), there may be mentioned (in addition to the rich bibliographical suggestions to be found in Gerhardsson *Memory*) the following: B. T. Holmes, 'Luke's Description of John Mark', *JBL* 54 (1935) 63–72; C. Lattey, 'How Do You Account for the Lack of Direct Quotations in the Epistles from our Lord's Sayings?' *Scrip* 4 (1949) 22–24; R. E. Balcomb, 'The Written Sources of Paul's Knowledge of Jesus' (Diss. Boston Univ. 1951); L. Cerfaux, 'La tradition selon saint Paul', and idem 'Les deux points de départ de la tradition chrétienne', in *Recueil Lucien Cerfaux* (1954) I 253–264, 265–282; O. Cullmann, 'La tradition', trans. 'The Tradition', in A. J. B. Higgins ed., *The Early Church* (1966) 55–99; T. Lohman, 'Die Verwendung autoritativer Ueberlieferungen im Urchristentum mit besonderer Berücksichtigung der nachpaulinischen Briefliteratur'

As might be expected, such a bold hypothesis aroused instant and vociferous debate and discussion. It is too early to tell what the outcome shall be. In any case, the thesis of Stendahl-Riesenfeld-Gerhardsson is extraordinarily suggestive, and will be taken up again at the conclusion of our study, where we will see how our results tally with it.

Meanwhile other new approaches have appeared. For example, the New Hermeneutik produced a new way to discuss the issues, as can be seen in the recent work of Eberhard Jüngel, *Paulus und Jesus: Eine Untersuchung zur Präzisierung der Frage nach dem Ursprung der Christologie* (1962). W. Schmithals, in 'Paulus und der historische Jesus' (1962),[1] took a fresh look at the problem from the perspective of his recent research into early Christian gnosticism. In 1963, W. G. Kümmel gave the Presidential Address for the annual meeting of the *Studiorum Novi Testamenti Societas*, taking as his subject, 'Jesus und Paulus'.[2] Thus it is amply clear that the discussion of this question is far from over.

2. *The purpose of the present inquiry*

This investigation takes as one of its points of departure the old question of Paul's use of the sayings of Jesus, and as its other, the more recent Scandinavian interest in the question *how* Paul uses this kind of tradition. What is new with this study is the particular selection of material to be addressed in the letters of Paul.

As noted above, much of the discussion in the past concerning Paul's knowledge and use of sayings of Jesus commits several methodological errors which tends to nullify its value. As should have been obvious from the example of Resch, there is no scientific-

---

(Diss. Jena 1952), cp. idem *ThLZ* 79 (1954) 58ff.; N. L. Norquist, 'The Transmission of the Ethical Tradition in the Synoptic Gospels and the Writings of Paul' (Diss. Hartford Seminary Foundation 1956); D. M. Stanley, 'Pauline Allusions to the Sayings of Jesus', *CBQ* 23 (1961) 26–39; K. Wegenast, *Das Verständnis der Tradition bei Paulus und in den Deuteropaulinien* (1962); B. Rigaux, 'Reflexions sur l'historicité de Jésus dans le message paulinien', *Analecta Biblica* 18 (1963) 265–274; J. P. Brown, 'Synoptic Parallels in the Epistles and Form-history', *NTS* 10 (1963–64) 27–48; P. Fannon, 'Paul and Tradition in the Primitive Church', *Scrip* 16 (1964) 47–56.

[1] *ZNW* 53 (1962) 145–160.
[2] Published in *NTS* 10 (1964) 163–181.

ally controlled norm of selection guiding this gratuitous designation of word-correspondences between the text of Paul and the text of the Synoptics (or even thin air, as when Resch began to plumb the depths of *unknown* sayings of Jesus) as Pauline allusions to the teachings of Jesus, especially when Paul himself does not say so. On the other hand, the correspondences so often noted must have some explanation. What is required is a new way to investigate how Paul uses this type of tradition.

We propose that the first step should be to consider those places where Paul cites sayings of Jesus *explicitly*. In these, at any rate, there can be no doubt that Paul is alluding to a saying come down to him in the tradition as a word of the Lord. But then the question arises, what is the relation between this command of the Lord and what we term a saying of the historical Jesus? This brings us face-to-face with the central problem in this whole aspect of Paul's relation to Jesus, a problem which the older discussion of Paul's allusions to the sayings of Jesus didn't even begin to consider. Looking for parallels in the Synoptic material is no help, for it is plain that *they also are records of the words and commands of the Lord* and not what we would term collections of the sayings of the historical Jesus. In this respect, they are not the least bit different than Paul. What *does* distinguish them from Paul in this regard is that in them the Church's profound interest in the time when Jesus was among his followers in the flesh is given expression, while in Paul's letters one sees concern focussed primarily on the Risen Lord's present rule and future victory. This is why there is no incompatibility whatever in Paul's receiving a word, as it were, directly and in the present, 'from the Lord' —e.g. the words of Institution of the Lord's Supper (1 Cor. 11.23ff.), which nevertheless was a saying which we know came to him through the tradition, and which was recorded in the gospels as having been spoken (in some form) at the last supper with the disciples. What the Lord *said* the Lord *says*.[1]

[1] This characteristic of early Christian piety finds its most beautiful illustration in the naive transposition of sayings of Jesus preserved in the tradition as having been uttered before his death to the period after his death, in later redactions; e.g., the Gospel of Thomas and the *Epistula Apostolorum*. But the same motivation is behind the words that close the Gospel of Matthew: '. . . make disciples of all nations, . . . teaching them all that I have commanded you'. (Mt. 28.19f. RSV). Of many that could be mentioned, still an excellent discussion of this

But if this be so, how shall the connection between Paul's allusions to the commands of the Lord and sayings of the historical Jesus be shown? It is to this precise task that the following study is devoted. As will appear, the procedure for arriving at a solution to this question is rather more complex than heretofore realized.

Paul's actual application of these traditional sayings of the Lord in the context of his churches fitted into a general pattern of similar application by other apostles and leaders in the Church. This fact we have determined by a strict consideration of evidence as contemporary as possible with Paul. Of such, we have two kinds at our disposal: what can be reconstructed form-critically out of the Synoptic accounts as having been the early Church's use of various sayings of Jesus to guide its life, and what we can perceive of the Synoptic editors themselves, and their use of them as revealed by the processes of redaction. By comparing these three sets of evidence, we have found that they mutually illuminate each other, Paul proving to be an invaluable aid in determining the historical conditions presupposed by the Gospel editors' way of handling the saying in question, while the Synoptic material helps to clarify what Paul may have had as the actual saying he refers to. In both directions, a common pattern begins to emerge in the way the saying is used.

The clarification of this common pattern produces two other results. By taking the many facets of Paul's *Sitz-im-Leben* as a sort of 'negative' and placing it over the *Synoptic* account, we were able to trace the faint outlines of redactional activity with much greater accuracy and confidence than could ever have been possible with a hypothetically reconstructed *Sitz-im-Leben*, and were thereby able to sift out of the Synoptic accounts with greater than usual sureness the historical saying of Jesus being carried along in the tradition's account, and further concealed by the redactional activity. In fact precisely the way Paul used the command of the Lord provided the critical evidence for determining in the Synoptic material, whether in *either* context we had to do with a saying of the historical Jesus, and, if so, what it may have been. But the evidence from the oral tradition as well as the redactional

---

phenomenon is O. Cullmann's essay, 'The Tradition'; see above, p. xxviii n. 4. Further W. D. Davies *Setting* 341–366. On the relation of the difficult passage in 2 Cor. 5.16 to this phenomenon, see most recently J. Blank *Paulus und Jesus* (1968) 304–326.

activity in the Synoptic accounts was equally illuminating for Paul's context. Indeed, they provided the indispensable basis for realizing what Paul was referring to as the command of the Lord. Here again, by placing the (Synoptic) saying as a kind of 'negative' over the larger context around the place where Paul mentions the command of the Lord, we were enabled to discern heretofore unrecognized aspects of the way Paul was actually using it.

By this means, we achieve two goals at once. On the one hand, we provide a relatively solid basis for asserting that Paul is in these cases relying on a saying of the historical Jesus (although, to be sure, he did not think of it as such), and on the other, we arrive at a number of objectively documented guidelines to follow in further investigation of Paul's use of this type of tradition; specifically, the whole area of his tacit allusions to words of the Lord.

Two legal sayings were chosen for this study; the Lord's command prohibiting divorce (1 Cor. 7.10f.) and another command ordaining support for apostles (1 Cor. 9.14). These two were chosen because in their cases there is no room for doubt that an actual saying of the Lord is being referred to, which is not true of 1 Cor. 14.37 or Gal. 6.2.[1] In the second place, sayings of a legal nature were selected as being especially well suited to the task of throwing into sharp relief precisely how and the extent to which a saying of Jesus fitted into the life of an early Christian community—something not so easily determined by means of a liturgical saying (1 Cor. 11.23ff.), or one from the realm of apocalypse (1 Thess. 4.15f.).

Strange as it may seem, such an investigation has, to my knowledge, never been conducted before regarding these two passages, with a view to seeing what light they may shed on the larger problems involved in understanding Paul's relation to

---

[1] In the case of 1 Cor. 14.37, we apparently have something in the nature of a command 'in the Lord', cp. 2 Cor. 13.3; see G. Zuntz, *The Text of the Epistles* (1946) 139; further W. D. Davies *Paul and Rabbinic Judaism* 141 n.5. Gal. 6.2 seems to be an exhortation to the *imitatio Christi*; so H. Schlier, *Der Brief an die Galater* (1962) 271f.; further, C. H. Dodd, *Gospel and Law* (1951), idem 'Ennomos Christou', *Studia Paulina in Honorem J. de Zwaan* (1953) 96–110. But see E. Burton, *A Critical and Exegetical Commentary on the Epistle to the Galatians* (1921) 329f.

Jesus. For this reason, then, the results of this study may be all the more interesting, as we seek to learn where Paul fits, *vis-à-vis* the editors of the Synoptic gospels and the other leaders of the Church of his day, on the map of early Christian tradition-activity in terms of *this* type of tradition: the commands of the Lord.

PART I

The Lord's Command Concerning Support for Apostles

Paul's Reaction Against the Abuse of the Lord's Command Concerning Support for Apostles (1 Cor. 9.4–18)

'In the same way, the Lord commanded that those who proclaim the Gospel should get their living by the Gospel.' (1 Cor. 9.14 *RSV*)

This verse is frequently mentioned by those seeking to show that Paul knew of and used sayings of Jesus to regulate the life of his congregations. Whether or not this particular reference in fact is dependent upon something Jesus actually said is a question we shall discuss later. For the time being, we should bear in mind what we have discussed above, namely, that Paul himself does not make such a distinction. Jesus for Paul is Jesus the Lord of the Church at that very moment guiding and protecting His people from His exalted position at God's right hand. Thus when Paul refers to a command of the Lord, the obvious implication is that it is a regulation binding upon the Christian community. A *law* in the technical sense of that term. B. Gerhardsson would consider this an excerpt from 'the ecclesiastical section' of Paul's 'Talmud'.[1]

However, no sooner has Paul referred to this command of the Lord than he asserts in the most unequivocal language that he does not and will not obey it. Hardly what one would expect! Those who confidently lump this passage together with other passages where Paul mentions a saying of the Lord to prove that Paul relied on Jesus' teaching have overlooked this strange fact. But not only is Paul found to be customarily disregarding this regulation. Later on in his subsequent correspondence with the Corinthians, after his disobedience has apparently become the focus of a violent controversy, Paul dares to denounce in the most savage way certain other famous apostles (none other than Peter and the brothers of the Lord!) who were proceeding in *accordance* with it. Not only that; what is even stranger, Paul a second time asserts his intention never

---

[1] *Memory and Manuscript,* trans. E. J. Sharpe (1961) 303.

to allow the Corinthians to support him, even though he has to admit at the same time, which must have been most embarrassing, that all the while he had been at Corinth he had been secretly accepting financial support from a congregation in Macedonia! A most peculiar situation. Let us see if we can unravel the tangled threads of this fascinating and confusing story. The best place to begin is with Paul's argument in 1 Cor. 9.

There has been considerable disagreement as to the correct interpretation of Paul's argument in Chapter 9. Therefore, our best course will be to follow his reasoning step by step. This is not to suggest, however, that Paul himself constructed a carefully arranged, logical argument intended to be carefully read by the world at large. As elsewhere in his letters (except for Romans),[1] Paul speaks directly to people he knows well, about subjects of deep concern confronting them. Thus, as in any conversation or letter between people who have a close relationship, many different matters are brought up and discussed, not in any particular order, and much is left unsaid since both sides share a great deal of common knowledge. Of course, all of this large area of common knowledge and mutually understood nuances of wording is now lost to us. Indeed, precisely in this consists the major challenge confronting anyone who would interpret Paul's letters rightly; namely, learning enough about him and his cultural and religious background as well as that of his correspondents so that one is able to read with facility between the lines and accurately discern the full stream of communication going on back and forth around the written words. This takes years of study and patient analysis. But let us see how far we can follow Paul.

1. *The proof that Paul as well as the rest of the apostles are supposed to be supported by the churches* (9.4–12a)

There is a sharp and abrupt turn in the flow of thought after the last verse of Chapter 8. To add to the impression of a complete break between 8.13 and 9.1, our modern editions of the Bible insert a chapter division at that point although no such thing would

_____

[1] The best recent discussion in English of the special place of Romans in the spectrum of Paul's letters is that of G. Bornkamm, 'The Letter to the Romans as Paul's Last Will and Testament', *Australian Biblical Review* 11 (1963) 2–14.

have been there in Paul's actual letter. In fact, it is very misleading. But even without that distraction, some of the older commentators actually concluded that all or part of Chapter 9 originally came somewhere else in 1 Corinthians.[1] However, as J. Jeremias and others have shown, even though there is not a single word in Chapter 9 concerning meat contaminated by having been dedicated to pagan deities at the time of slaughter nor the Christian's freedom simply to ignore the whole pagan cultus thus encountered, subjects which Paul discusses in both Chapters 8 and 10, nevertheless 'this whole chapter, from the first to the last verse, is nothing else than an explanatory digression to illustrate the point of 8.13: Paul holds up [in Chapter 9] before the Corinthians his own conduct, as a Christian able to forego a right due to him (1 Corinthians 13 stands in a similar independent fashion between Chapters 12 and 14)'.[2]

From this point of view, the motivation for the first half of Paul's argument (vv. 4–15) becomes readily understandable: far from being an attempt to establish this regulation among the Corinthians for the first time, as D. Daube has suggested,[3] Paul is simply proving that 'to live at the expense of the congregations is, technically speaking, his right—just as incontestable as the right of the Corinthians to eat of the meat sacrificed to pagan idols'.[4] Similarly, the point of 9.1–3 is to establish Paul's status as an apostle to bring this 'explanatory digression' into a parallel logical structure with the beginning point of the argument in Chapter 8 regarding the 'strong', i.e., 'we all have knowledge'. The importance of this similarity in structure between Paul's

[1] See J. Weiss 231f. For other representatives of this position, see Allo 208. More recently, W. Schmithals, *Die Gnosis in Korinth*[2] (1965), 81–93; Héring 10f.

[2] 'Chiasmus in den Paulusbriefen', *ZNW* 49 (1958) 156. See further J. J. Collins, 'Chiasmus, the "ABA" Pattern and the Text of Paul', in *Analecta Biblica* 18 (1963) 573–583; Lietzmann-Kümmel 39; Robertson-Plummer 176f.; H. Preisker, *TWNT* IV 702; E. Käsemann, 'Eine paulinische Variation des "Amor Fati" ', in idem *Exegetische Versuche und Besinnungen* II (1964) 237f.; C. K. Barrett, 'Things Sacrificed to Idols', *NTS* 11 (1964–65) 138–153; Moffatt 114; Allo 211f.

[3] *The New Testament and Rabbinic Judaism* (1956) 395f.; see below.

[4] G. Didier, 'Le salaire du désintéressement (1 Cor. 9.14–27),' *RecSciRel* 43 (1955) 228f.

argument in Chapter 9 and Chapter 8, as being integral to his effort to explain and defend the position stated in Chapter 8, is not usually noticed.

On the other hand, this recognition should not blind us to the possibility that Paul may be trying to settle another problem as well. That is, there seems to be a certain defensiveness about Paul's argument in Chapter 9. As we can see from v. 5, Paul and his associates are being compared with Peter, the brothers of the Lord and other apostles, and some of the Corinthians must have been confused as to why Paul's group had not accepted their financial support as they had. Was it because Paul was some sort of 'sub-apostle?' Paul takes this opportunity to kill two birds with one stone. He argues, concerning meat sacrificed to idols, why that legitimate right ought not to be observed when it would be injurious to the weaker brethren, and, at the same time, he takes as an illustration his own practice of not observing a certain legitimate authority of apostles, when to do so would be injurious to the Church. But let us consider his argument in greater detail.

A. 9.4–6 ARE PAUL AND HIS ASSOCIATES EXCEPTIONS AMONG THE APOSTLES?

By means of a series of rhetorical questions (v. 1f.), Paul states the obvious: 'I am without doubt an apostle.' In the second series (vv. 4ff.), he narrows the discussion to that specific apostolic authority he and Barnabas share with the other apostles, namely, the authority they are not using, and begins to show that this is not because they are substandard apostles of some sort. To paraphrase what he says through v. 5: 'Don't apostles have the authority to receive support? Does anyone think I am not accepting it because I don't have the right to it? Do these people also conclude that I am not married like Cephas and the brothers of the Lord and other apostles because I don't have the *right* to get married?'[1] The rhetorical questions pile up upon one another.

[1] Paul is not here referring to whether the women accompanying the brothers of the Lord, Cephas, and the other apostles, may also receive the support of the community. He is not referring to the wives of these men *accompanying* them at all, as is commonly thought. As J. B. Bauer, 'Uxores circumducere 1 Kor. 9.5', *BZ* N.F. 3 (1959) 94–102, has shown, Paul is merely referring to being married as such. Bauer collects examples to show that that can be the meaning of *periagein*.

'Or is it that Paul and Barnabas are exceptions? Do you think we work for a living because we—in contrast to the other apostles—do not possess this apostolic right?'

Let us pause for a moment to notice that we have just passed by one of those very points in Paul's letters where, in a brief aside, he mentions something that would be of extraordinary interest to us to know more about: who were these 'brothers of the Lord' going around with Cephas (i.e. Peter)? What were they doing in Corinth? We can only wonder, for Paul never mentions them directly again. It is possible, however, that their visit was not entirely friendly, from Paul's point of view. Indeed, to judge from Paul's letter to the Galatian churches, his relations with precisely this group of apostles was badly strained at Antioch not long before. And if we look ahead to what Paul eventually says in 2 Cor. 10–13, it seems to be the case that the presence of precisely this band of Jerusalem apostles in Corinth marks an ominous turning point in Paul's relationship with his people there. In fact, this side-glance at the customs of other well-known apostles in v. 5 should make it clear to us that Paul is fully aware of the differences between the course they follow and the one he has chosen. Naturally, the Corinthians would be only too aware of this also. Indeed, they seem to have split up into several factions behind one or another apostle, perhaps for just such reasons as these (1 Cor.

In the second place, Jewish apostles were never accompanied by their wives on official journeys, and it would be quite unlikely that this group of Jerusalem apostles would differ in that particular respect. But most important, the real motivation for Paul's turning to marriage at this point may simply have been through an association of ideas. In v. 4 he asks, 'Do we not have authority to eat and drink?' He thus names the first two actions of a very common, popular triad of human actions often associated together: 'eat, drink and make merry' (or some other euphemism for sexual intercourse as Uriah's question to David makes explicit: 'The ark and Israel and Judah dwell in tents; and my lord Joab and the servants of my lord are camping in the open field; shall I then go to my house, to eat and to drink, and to lie with my wife?' 2 Sam. 11.11; cp. further, 1 Sam. 30.16; 1 Kings 4.20; Luke 12.19). For pagan parallels to this phrase, see Klostermann ad Luke 12.19; Bultmann *TDNT* II 774 n. 38. Paul himself returns to this association of ideas at 1 Cor. 10.7 where he quotes Exodus 32.6: 'The people sat down to eat and drink and rose up to dance.' Thus, in 9.4f. he is simply asking the Corinthians, 'Have we not the right to eat and drink and have a wife?'

C

1.11f.). Before we go any further it might be helpful to get a better idea of how widespread this practice of Paul's was, wherein he admits he has deliberately adopted a course different from that of Peter, the brothers of the Lord, and the rest of the Jerusalem leadership.

In the first place, Corinth was not the first city where Paul had refused to allow the local congregation to support him. He had already used the same approach elsewhere. In the second place, this was not a matter of Paul's own individual practice, but that of several (if not all) of his chief assistants as well. In fact, what Paul mentions here to illustrate his argument concerning idol-meat *is a general practice current among the top levels of the entire Gentile mission that appears to be in flat opposition to the custom of the Jerusalem apostolate.* For example, Barnabas clearly belongs to this group (1 Cor. 9.6), as does Titus (2 Cor. 12.16–18). Two other close associates, Silvanus and Timothy, worked with their hands alongside Paul at Thessalonica, rather than have that congregation support them (1 Thess. 2.9). Then these same three travelled to Corinth in the first missionary journey to that city and there repeated this procedure.[1] On the other hand, it is not clear whether the apostle Apollos belonged to this group.

Just listing the number of apostles in Paul's immediate entourage does not give an adequate idea of the magnitude of this departure from the norm, however. Many other assistants besides these four should probably be included.[2] Furthermore, we must take into account the several congregations which had accepted

---

[1] J. Weiss 238; Moffatt 118; Robertson-Plummer 188.

[2] The list of Paul's fellow-apostles and co-workers includes Epaphras, Mark, Aristarchus, Demas, and Luke (Phile. 23), possibly Philemon himself (Phile. 1). If the letter to the Colossians be genuine, as is quite possible (see P. Feine, J. Behm, rev. W. G. Kümmel, *Introduction to the New Testament,* trans. A. J. Mattill, Jr. (1966), 240–244), these same individuals (except for Philemon) are mentioned there again as fellow-workers, including also Tychicus and Jesus Justus (1.7; 4.7, 10, 14?). Prisca and Aquila are also to be included within this number (Rom. 16.3), and possibly the deaconess Phoebe (Rom. 16.1f.).

It may well be that Paul was one of the instigators of this innovation, in which case his associates would naturally have been expected to follow his halakhic example, cp. on this Gerhardsson, op. cit. 293f.; for a description of the rabbinic parallel in this regard, see 181–187.

this relationship.[1] On the other hand, merely belonging to a large body of apostles following this new procedure was not enough to keep Paul from falling into bitter controversy because of it. Indeed, Paul eventually came almost to the breaking point in his relationship with the Corinthian congregation because of certain misunderstandings arising as a result of his way of handling the matter of support.

Why did Paul and the others adopt this new course? Why did they feel required to dispense with the current practice endorsed by the Jerusalem apostles? Was the Pauline entourage alone in abandoning the established course of action, or were there even others among the apostolate who acted in the same manner? These are all important questions, and will be taken up in due time.

B.   9.7–12a SEVERAL ARGUMENTS JUSTIFYING THIS
APOSTOLIC PREROGATIVE

Continuing the stream of rhetorical questions, Paul makes it clear that this was a completely unquestionable right. He first appeals to common sense, a style of argument familiar in rabbinic texts as the testimony of *derekh eretz*, 'the way of the world': 'Who works for nothing?' The use of the language from the sphere of workman/wages is natural, it having been a common metaphor in the early Church for apostles and evangelists of various types.[2] The analogies here introduced in Paul's favorite diatribe-style[3] all stem from this workman metaphor.

[1] There has not been, to my knowledge, in recent N.T. research an attempt to delineate precisely the full size, power, and distinguishing characteristics of the 'Pauline regime' in the Gentile-Christian mission zone. Still the most serviceable description is that of A. von Harnack, *The Mission and Expansion of Christianity in the First Three Centuries*, trans. and ed. J. Moffatt (Harper Torchbook 1961), 77–80. Helpful studies around the subject are A. Fridrichson, *The Apostle and His Message* (1947); H.-J. Schoeps, *Paul* trans. H. Knight (1961), 63–74; Hurd 240–270; C. K. Barrett, 'Cephas and Corinth', *Festschr. O. Michel* (1963), 1–12; idem, 'Christianity at Corinth', *BJRL* 46 (1963–64) 269–297; in general see K. Stendahl, art. 'Kirche II. Im Urchristentum' *RGG* III[3] (1959) 1297–1304.

[2] D. Georgi, *Die Gegner des Paulus im 2. Korintherbrief* (1964) 49ff., 235ff.; H. Koester, 'The Purpose of the Polemic of a Pauline Fragment (Phil. 3), '*NTS* 8 (1961–62) 320; see further below.

[3] R. Bultmann, *Der Stil der paulinischen Predigt und die kynisch-stoische Diatribe* (1910) 93, 97.

The Torah is next brought to bear: 'These may be only human comparisons, but does not the Law itself say the same thing?' (*JB*)[1] Surprisingly enough, what Paul turns to in the Torah is a trivial regulation providing that farmers should not put muzzles on oxen while they are threshing grain (Deut. 25.4). But let us be wary, for its seems Paul does not consider this passage actually to be concerned with oxen at all. That is the point of the rhetorical question at the end of v. 9 and beginning of v. 10: 'Is God thinking here about cattle? Or is he speaking purely for our sakes? Assuredly for our sakes!' (Moffatt) Paul's exegesis may seem strange to us, but as a matter of fact, a survey of contemporaneous Jewish use of this passage shows that it was a favorite—especially among the Pharisees—for defending the principle of a fair return for a workman's labor.[2]

Next, Paul briefly elaborates upon the Torah just cited.[3] It is possible to rearrange the punctuation of the Greek in such a fashion that Paul seems to be quoting a phrase from some writing: 'the plowman should plow in hope and the thresher thresh in hope

---

[1] The text should be emended, as G. Zuntz shows, *The Text of the Epistles; A Disquisition upon the 'Corpus Paulinum'* (1953) 98 n.2 (and cp. the conjecture of Bowyer in Nestle's apparatus), to read *tautá* not *taûta*. D. Daube, consistently with his theory that Paul is here attempting to justify for the first time the regulation that apostles should receive financial support from the Corinthian congregation, refers to Paul's rhetorical question here in v.8a, 'Do I say this on human authority?' (*RSV*), as being a clear give-away of Paul's uneasiness. That is, Daube argues that *Me kata anthropon tauta lalo?* is a stock Pauline and rabbinic apology-phrase for entertaining arguments which, even if only theoretically considered, 'without such an apology, might be considered near-blasphemous' (viz., teaching for money; *New Testament* 394f.). Although it is admittedly true that Paul uses this phrase as an apology elsewhere (Rom. 3.5; 6.19; Gal. 3.15; cp. Blass-Debrunner-Funk *Grammar* 495 (3)), the cliché part of it is only *kata anthropon* as the wide variety of other verbs occurring with it proves; see Bauer *Lexicon* s.v. *anthropos* 1. c. for examples (to which add: *zen* Ign. Trall. 2.1; Rom. 8.1). As for Paul's alleged establishing this regulation for the first time at Corinth, see below.

[2] Billerbeck *Kommentar* III 382–384; all examples of discussions of this particular phrase. Josephus makes similar use of this passage (*AJ* 4.233). Gerhardsson's comment, that 'typically enough, [Paul] interprets the statute allegorically; he cannot use the Scriptures as straightforward *nomos*!' (317)—is especially wide of the mark.

[3] A 'homiletical expansion'; Bultmann *Stil der Diatribe* 89, 95f.

of a share in the crop' (*RSV*), but this is not likely.[1] Paul is simply dwelling on the quotation from Deuteronomy in his best sermonic style, using typical current Christian missionary-language, as v. 11 shows. For what Paul actually means by the contrasting terms in v. 11: 'spiritual things/material things', cp. Rom. 15.27 where he contrasts the coming of the Gospel to the Gentiles and the return of money to Jerusalem.

Finally, Paul asks: 'if others share authority[2] over you, shouldn't we even more?' (v. 12a). We may recall here his earlier chiding remark: 'For though you have countless guides in Christ, you do not have many fathers, for it was I who begot you in Christ Jesus through the Gospel' (4.15 *RSV*). Paul rightfully held a pre-eminent place among the other apostles and teachers who had labored at Corinth.[3] What is so significant about Paul's rhetorical question in 9.12a, however, is that it clearly indicates that the practice of supporting apostles financially was already well-known and in practice at Corinth.[4]

It is true that one could get the impression from this vivid series of rhetorical questions that Paul is attempting to establish this regulation for the first time among the Corinthians, possibly against a certain resistance. Many commentators have understood Paul in this way. Thus, for example, D. Daube explains Paul's

[1] The phrase *gar egraphe hoti* has led some to suggest that Paul is quoting a lost apocryphal work as Scripture, e.g., J. Weiss 237; Lietzmann-Kümmel 41; further references in Allo 218. This is incorrect, however, since the *gar* belongs with the *di' hemas* and *egraphe* refers to what was just cited, viz. Deut. 25.4. The *hoti* then is merely explanatory (Allo 218), and should be translated as follows: 'Clearly this was written for our sakes *to show that* the plowman should plow in hope', etc. (*JB*).

[2] Not '*this* authority', as nearly all commentators and official translations have it, apparently under the influence of the immediately following 'this authority' in v. 12b. To be sure, sharing authority in general included receiving support; that is the point. For the style of argument here and above at v. 8, see J. Bonsirven, *Exégèse rabbinique et exégèse paulinienne* (1939) 317.

[3] Lietzmann-Kümmel cautiously identify 'the others' as Cephas and Apollos (42). But what of 'the brothers of the Lord?' Actually, Allo is probably much more on the right path: 'The "others" are . . . all those who might receive a recompense from the Christians, no matter who' (219).

[4] Lietzmann-Kümmel 40; von Campenhausen *Begründung* 25; Georgi *Gegner* 237f.

use of the Torah as the first main argument rather than the command of the Lord, which only comes last in a rather anti-climactic fashion, on the grounds that Paul is doing this deliberately since there were at Corinth certain 'Jewish traditionalists' who would have been highly incensed at Paul's suggestion that they should pay him, a teacher of the Word of God, for carrying out his calling. Such an idea was diametrically opposed by current Pharisaic teaching.[1]   However that may be, apart from

[1]Although Daube's interpretation of Paul's argument in 1 Cor. 9 requires some modification, he does bring attention to a much more fundamental problem which has not received the attention it deserves: how did the early Church come so early and so widely to accept this practice of supporting its leaders financially in spite of the virtually unanimous (recorded) Pharisaic opposition to such recompense? On this whole subject, see G. F. Moore, *Judaism in the First Centuries of the Christian Era* (1962) II 96f.; *E*. Schürer, *The History of the Jewish People in the Time of Jesus Christ*, trans. S. Taylor and P. Christie (1885), II[1] 317ff. The explanation of D. Georgi, *Gegner* 234–241, may include the necessary and well-known information regarding the possible influence of the Greek wandering mystagogues who dispensed their lore for money. Georgi sees these hellenistic religious traditions behind the figures of Paul's opponents in 2 Corinthians. But what about Paul himself? He also accepted financial support. Not only that, but where did he come by this very elaborate argument in 1 Cor. 9.7–11? Where did this 'command of the Lord' come from? Or what about the other leaders of the Church? Are we to believe, for example, that such apostles as Peter and the Jerusalem leadership—among whom were no doubt some still-observant Pharisees (cp. Acts 15.1)—accepted this financial support once they departed from familiar Pharisaic jurisdiction and were in the wide-open Gentile mission-field?

This question is all the more interesting and difficult since the Pharisaic testimony is not unambiguous, and their views on this issue underwent substantial changes at just this same time; see now E. Urbach, 'Class-status and Leadership in the World of the Palestinian Sages', *Proceedings of the Israel Academy of Sciences and Humanities* II 4 (1965) 1–37 (trans. I. Abrahams); and for the whole question see G. Allon, *The History of the Jews in Palestine during the Period of the Mishnah and the Talmud* (in Hebrew) I (1953). For translating generous portions of the latter as well as numerous helpful suggestions, I am deeply indebted to Rabbi Ben-Zion Gold of Hillel House, Harvard University.

One reason why this issue has been obscured is due to Billerbeck's commentary. It is one more case of an anachronistic 'parallel'. At Matt. 10.10 (the saying about a workman being worthy of his food, to be discussed below), Billerbeck cites without any explanation a writing he calls *Tanchuma* 119a to the following effect: 'Wer sich mit der Tora

the fact that Daube must invoke out of thin air these 'Jewish traditionalists' in Paul's audience, vv. 12a and 15 show that this regulation was already familiar to them and indeed in effect, at Corinth and elsewhere.

As a matter of fact, in view of the two sharp refusals actually to abide by this regulation that he is about to express (in vv. 12b, 15), it is strange that Paul's real posture as he makes these points, has not been more commonly recognized. It is not really positive at all. As von Campenhausen says, 'the whole elaborate marshalling of arguments has only one purpose—to serve as the foil for the vehement renunciation which he expresses.'[1] In view of Paul's long-standing disregard of this regulation as far as the Corinthians were concerned, it is obvious that all Paul can be doing in this context, von Campenhausen continues, is to 'set forth his well-known decision not to accept support from his congregations in a new, explicitly "pedagogical" interpretation.'[2] It is this 'pedagogical' intention, I believe, which partly accounts for the argumentative tone throughout, which lies behind the curious pun at the conclusion (v. 18), but most importantly of

---

beschäftigt hat von ihr seinen Lebensunterhalt' (*Kommentar* I 569). It seems that the edition of this writing used by Billerbeck, according to J. Z. Lauterbach, *Jewish Encyclopedia* XII 46 s.v., was *Tanchuma* C—i.e., an edition first published at Constantinople in 1522. That edition was a conflation of two earlier works, *Tanchuma* and *Yelammadenu*, plus miscellaneous material out of the vast stream of medieval Jewish homiletical Midrashim (cp. Moore *Judaism* I 161–173; on *Tanchuma* see 169f.). An edition from various MSS was compiled by S. Buber (Wilna 1885), which Lauterbach designates as *Tanchuma* A, and which he suggests contains material that may go back as far as the fourth century to the namesake: Rabbi Tanchuma b. Abba, a Palestinian Amora of the fifth generation. But it is not the latter edition that Billerbeck cites at Matt. 10.10 (although he does seem to know of it, see *Kommentar* I vii). That is, the reference at Mt. 10.10 is to the older *Tanchuma* C, which means that it is most likely a rather late tradition, possibly from the middle ages; hardly a very illuminating 'parallel' for a mid-first century Palestinian milieu. Of course, Billerbeck does not claim that it is. He clearly set no rigid historical boundaries for his exhaustive collection of texts. But the unwary who do not check the dates of his references may be misled (see, among others, Klostermann *Matt.* 87).

[1] *Begründung* 24.
[2] Ibid. 11 n.15.

all as far as this study is concerned, which is the real reason why
Paul offers no concrete explanation for not obeying the explicit
command of the Lord (in v. 14).

2. *Paul boasts that he does not abuse this regulation* (9.12*b*)

After Paul persuasively demonstrates the full validity and
potential applicability of this apostolic prerogative, he asserts
proudly, 'But we have not made any use of this authority!' In the
next verses he goes on to name two more reasons for its validity
and then declares a second time that he does not want to make use
of this regulation (v. 15). We should not be insensible to the
possible presence of rhetorical artifice here. This antithetical
climax—if that is what it is—is quite effective: 'Look at all these
reasons which prove how valid this right is! But even so, I have
not made use of it. It is even commanded by the Lord! Never
mind. I have not used it and am not writing all this to ask it of you
now.'

Paul explains that he (and many others) have 'put up with
anything rather than obstruct the Good News of Christ in any
way' (*JB*). What is Paul referring to as an 'obstruction?' This is
not explained, and it might be appropriate at this point to see
whether we can discern Paul's meaning from elsewhere in his
letters. One thing is certain; it must have been something of
major proportions. G. Stählin notes that not obstructing the
Gospel's progress would have to be 'the supreme concern of
Paul'.[1] The question of Paul's meaning takes on additional
importance in view of the fact that it is this 'obstruction' which
causes Paul to disregard, among other things, an explicit command
of the Lord.

To learn the actual circumstances summarily referred to by
the term *egkope*, 'hindrance, obstruction',[2] commentators have
combed Paul's letters for places where he explains his reasons for
not accepting financial support. Several suggestions have been
brought forward. Lietzmann-Kümmel point to Paul's desire to
avoid an appearance of selfishness,[3] as do Robertson-Plummer,[4]

[1] *TDNT* III 857.
[2] Bauer *Lexicon* s. v.
[3] Op. cit. 42.
[4] Op. cit. 186f.

and J. Weiss.[1] Weiss adds that Paul did not want to be a financial
burden on the poor (see especially 2 Cor. 12.13). G. Stählin joins
these two reasons together.[2] H. Windisch decided that Paul
wanted clearly to disassociate himself from certain apostles who
'peddled the Word of God' (2 Cor. 2.17), as well as from the
typical wandering pagan preachers who sold their mysterious
teachings for whatever they could get.[3] All of these suggestions
are correct to some degree. In his most explicit passage, Paul has
this to say to the congregation at Thessalonika, another church
where he had refused financial support.

We [i.e., Paul, Sylvanus and Timothy] have not taken to preaching
because we are deluded, or immoral, or trying to deceive anyone; it was
God who decided that we were fit to be entrusted with the Good News,
and when we are speaking, we are not trying to please men but God,
who can read our inmost thoughts. You know very well, and we can
swear it before God, that never at any time have our speeches been
simply flattery, or a cover for trying to get money; nor have we ever
looked for any special honor from men, either from you or from anybody
else, although we could have imposed ourselves on you with full weight
as apostles of Christ. Instead, we were unassuming. . . . Let me remind
you, brothers, how hard we used to work, slaving night and day so as
not to be a burden on any one of you while we were proclaiming God's
Good News to you. (1 Thess. 2.5–10 *JB*).

Paul here indicates quite clearly that he considered this
regulation a definite apostolic prerogative not lightly to be set
aside. This must be kept in mind to protect us from all too-one-
sided interpretations of Paul's comments in various contexts
against actually making use of this right. On the other hand, this
passage also shows that Paul did not hesitate to forego financial
support when, in his estimation, to demand it as an apostle could
have caused hardship and resentment, bringing the Gospel into
disrepute. In short, it seems that everything depended upon the
financial strength of each particular congregation.

However, none of these explanations is to be found here in
Chapter 9. In fact, Paul does not give an *explanation* of any kind.
He simply argues the position that this right is totally valid for

---

[1] Op. cit. 238.
[2] *TDNT* III 857.
[3] *TDNT* III 604f.; Georgi *Gegner* 234–241.

apostles, but that he and his associates would rather put up with any privation than obstruct the Gospel. A glance at the pattern of argument in Chapter 8 reveals what is happening. There Paul cites, as the reason for not making use of a legitimate Christian authority: 'you sin against Christ' (8.12). Parallel to this in Chapter 9 is: 'obstructing the Gospel'. What is missing in Chapter 9, however, is the brief explanation of the concrete circumstances involved.

Not everyone knows this [viz., that idols have no real existence, see above v. 4]. There are some who have been so accustomed to idolatry that even now they eat this food with a sense of its heathen consecration, and their conscience, being weak, is [made guilty] by the eating. . . . Be careful that this liberty of yours does not become a pitfall for the weak! (8.7–10 *NEB*).

This is a clear, practical explanation and it provides a specific content to the categorical offense: 'By sinning against your brothers, you sin against Christ' (8.12 *RSV*). In Chapter 9, however, all Paul mentions is the categorical offense; he, Paul, will never injure the Corinthians nor obstruct the Gospel! Thus we have had to search through the rest of his letters to get a better idea of what his 'boast' actually meant!

3. *Further arguments supporting this regulation; the command of the Lord* (9.13f.)

Do you not know that as men who perform temple-rites get their food from the temple, and attendants at the altar get their share of the sacrifices, so the Lord's instructions were that those who proclaim the Gospel are to get their living by the Gospel? (9.13f. Moffatt).

Despite the demurrer in v. 12, Paul continues to list arguments justifying this regulation. The image he picks up in v. 13 is a new one. It is an analogy between the early Church's leadership and the staff of the Jerusalem temple.[1] To be sure, it, like the work-man-metaphor, was also a common idea in the early Church, i.e., that it was the new spiritual Temple (replacing the old, physical

[1] Paul is not referring to pagan temples as J. Weiss 238, and Allo 219, suggest. See further below.

one in Jerusalem). The historical background of this conception has recently received a flood of light from the Dead Sea Scrolls, where similar ideas were found.[1] Paul seems to have been quite familiar with it, as his references to it in this letter show (3.16; 6.19). Indeed, he seems to have considered himself a priest in this spiritual Temple (Rom. 15.16).

In any case, what is behind this new line of argument? Why this analogy, with its command of the Lord dangling so strangely at the end? If one looks carefully at the Greek (and Moffatt's translation brings this out well), the command of the Lord is introduced in a most peculiar, off-hand fashion; not at all what we would expect.

Indeed, there is hardly any agreement concerning the role this command of the Lord plays in the context of all these other arguments for this regulation. Most commentators merely observe that Paul rounds off his argument, as it were, by a final clinching appeal to authority.[2] But some are more subtle. D. Daube, for instance, notes that Paul has waited until the very end to introduce this word of the Lord, and decides that this was because Paul was *afraid* to mention it any earlier.[3] B. Gerhardsson, on the other hand, is certain that all of the earlier stages of Paul's argument had little more than illustrative value, whereas only at the end, in the command of the Lord, does 'Paul finally state, briefly and precisely, what is the real basis of the apostles' right to be supported. This is independent of arguments which can be advanced on its behalf; the Lord has laid down. . . that those who deliver the Gospel shall live by the Gospel. This the decisive argument.'[4] Robertson-Plummer explain the wordy and redundant character of Paul's speech by implying that the Corinthians were somewhat

[1] On the possible points of contact between Essene and Pauline thought here, see J. M. Allegro, 'Fragments of a Qumran Scroll of Eschatological Midrashim', *JBL* 77 (1958) 350–360; D. Flusser, 'The Dead Sea Sect and Pre-pauline Christianity', *Scripta* 4 (1958) 215–266, esp. 227ff.; O. Bentz, 'Felsenmann und Felsengemeinde', *ZNW* 48 (1957) 48–77; B. Gärtner, *The Temple and the Community in Qumran and the New Testament. A Comparative Study in the Temple Symbolism of the Qumran Texts and the New Testament* (1965).

[2] Bultmann *Stil der Diatribe* 103.

[3] For the reasons behind Daube's interpretation, see above, p. 11 f.; further, *New Testament* 396.

[4] *Memory* 317f.

feeble-minded: Paul adverts to the Temple analogy because it was 'a higher and closer analogy than that of the soldier or of the different kinds of husbandman. The other analogies may have escaped their notice, but surely they must be aware of the usages of the Temple!'[1] Allo, in good Gallic fashion, explains Paul's intention by suggesting that he wanted first to insult his enemies before clearing the matter up for his friends: 'It appears that this last argument, the most direct of all, Paul added only at the end after he had already set out the full contents of the "defense" which he needed to compile in order to stop the mouth of his detractors.'[2]

None of these explanations is based on a clear awareness of the basically rather simple reason Paul has for bringing up the whole subject of financial support in Chapter 9 in the first place. As a result, there is a general tendency to over-interpret the passage. Least appropriate of all is Daube's view. Not only does he omit in his discussion any attempt to place Paul's remarks within their larger context but also his view that Paul 'first' argued from Torah, and then 'only at the end' brought in a quotation from Jesus, makes distinctions between these two that are utterly foreign with Paul, whatever may have been the case with the Corinthians.[3]

Gerhardsson, on the other hand, is prey to a confusion of a different kind. He does not notice that the appeal to Torah in this passage is as conclusive as the reference to the command of the Lord; no more and no less. How can it be otherwise if Paul can close off his 'chain of proofs' already by v. 12a and renounce this authority—before he even comes to the 'decisive' basis of it? It looks rather as if Gerhardsson's argument is based more upon a theological distinction between Christ and Torah than it is upon the actual evidence in this passage.

Allo comes much closer with his sensing of the polemic in the air. Paul is definitely exercized by the sight of those who are making use of this authority when he is not, and he sharply criticizes them. Who might this be? V.5 strongly suggests that

---

[1] Op. cit. 187.

[2] Op. cit. 219.

[3] An exceptionally lucid discussion of this difficult problem is given by C. H. Dodd, '*Ennomos Christou*', *Studia paulina in honorem J. de Zwaan* (1953) 96–110. Further, W. D. Davies, *Torah in the Messianic Age* (1952).

it was the Jerusalem apostolate visiting in Corinth. People were comparing them with the Pauline band, to the latter's disadvantage, and so Paul sets the record straight. Incidentally, it is not at all unlikely that just as they differed from Paul in accepting the financial support of the Corinthian church, they also disagreed with his view regarding the right of certain Christians to eat polluted meat, i.e., meat contaminated by having been consecrated to pagan divinities.[1] This just serves to illustrate the well-known fact that there were many deep divergences in practice and belief in the leadership of the early Christian Church. In this particular case, we probably have the first stages of the conflict that later reached grave proportions of bitterness and invective, as we can see from 2 Cor. 10–13.

We shall look into that in the next chapter. But first let us return to the present question of the role of the command of the Lord in the context of Paul's arguments regarding support. H. von Campenhausen has the best solution.

The rather unemphasized way in which the infallible Word of the Lord is here 'also' finally mentioned at the end is striking and can be explained indeed only in the light of the, as it were, theoretical character of the discussion. The entire exposition exhibits in fact a more or less spontaneous and rhetorical character. The sequence, individual weight and reciprocal relationships in which the individual members of this 'parade of proofs' stand to each other should not be—even as elsewhere in Paul—all too strictly analyzed and interpreted.[2]

Von Campenhausen's interpretation rests upon a clear awareness of Paul's didactic concern in the context as a whole, viz., Paul has one purpose in 'parading these proofs' before the eyes of the Corinthians: to show that he possessed as an apostle an identically 'incontestable' (Didier) authority as that possessed by the 'strong'

[1] In fact, the whole early Church was deeply divided over this particular question. For example, one of the major unsolved mysteries of early Church history is to explain the origin and basis of the strange report in Acts 15 which tells of an early, top-level conference in Jerusalem that issued a series of regulations binding upon the Gentile wing of the Church, which included a prohibition of eating idol-meat, *and that Paul consented to promulgate this decree in his churches* (see Acts 16.4). On this whole issue, see W. L. Knox, *St. Paul and the Church of Jerusalem* (1925); further bibliography in Hurd *Corinthians* 250ff.

[2] *Begründung* 25; cp. 11 n.15.

in Chapter 8. The many proofs thus all add up to the same thing. Hence, the supposedly unimportant location and muted character of the command of the Lord, lost as it were in the midst of all these other proofs, is puzzling to us only because we are looking at the passage in the wrong way.

Nevertheless, even if there is nothing behind what appears to us as a peculiar location and manner of introduction of a command of the Lord, what is the reason for Paul's apparent unconcern at setting aside a command of the Lord explicitly ordering him as well as the other apostles to accept financial support?

It is remarkable that this has been overlooked by so many commentators. J. Moffatt is one of the rare men who has noticed it and he expresses considerable puzzlement over the fact that Paul appears to be so free from any sense of obligation toward this command of the Lord's. 'Paul's departure from the common practice of Christian apostles on a point for which there was an explicit word of Jesus is significant and puzzling. He seems to have had no hestitation in taking the word as permissive, instead of feeling bound to any merely external imitation of what was laid down by the Lord.'[1]

B. Gerhardsson has also noticed the problem, and devised an ingenious solution. 'It is interesting to note that Paul classified Jesus' commandment as a permission (*exousia*, Heb. *reshuth*) for the Apostles, not as an obligation (*opheilema*, Heb. *ḥobhah*). Paul is therefore free to abstain from what is here laid down.'[2] What Gerhardsson neglects to explain (and Moffatt, too, for that matter), is why Paul felt free to 'classify' this *direct command* as a discretionary privilege? Paul certainly did not 'classify' the Lord's Supper in such a way that he was 'free to abstain' from it! The Lord's prohibition of divorce was not handled in this fashion! There is an exceedingly interesting phenomenon at work here, and it will not do to muddle things up with sleight-of-hand distinctions like these.[3]

[1] Op. cit. 118.
[2] *Memory* 319.
[3] A major shortcoming of most discussions of this problem is the inability or unwillingness of commentators to avoid special pleading on behalf of Paul. See, e.g., most recently J. Blank, *Paulus und Jesus. Eine theologische Grundlegung* (1968) 200, where he also sets up a typical *ad hoc* distinction to the effect that Paul's 'apostolic freedom' enabled him to disregard a command of the Lord. A second error that

Another important problem to be considered is what the actual wording of the Lord's command was. As Gerhardsson rightly observes, Paul 'does not quote a saying of Jesus, he produces a halakah [i.e. regulation] based on such a saying'.[1] A clue to the answer here might well consist precisely in the curious way the Lord's command is introduced as if it were simply deduced from Temple regulations concerning priests and Levites. But we will consider these things in due time.

At this point, however, Paul ends arguing the incontestability of the apostles' right to receive financial support and repeats that he has not and will not make use of this authority—thereby setting a good example for the 'strong' who are not supposed to use their authority to eat meat sacrificed to idols.

4. Paul emphatically repeats his intention not to make use of this authority (9.15–23)

But I have not used any of these reasons[2] nor am I writing them now in order to begin using this authority. I would rather die than—no one is going to debase what I am proud of!

Paul repeats the boast he first uttered in v.12b., and these two together are the parallel to the sweeping assertion he makes at the

---

frequently occurs is the failure to distinguish properly between 'obligation' and 'right'. One cannot 'waive' an obligation without disobeying it. Rights or privileges may be waived or renounced, but not obligations or laws. Privileges conferred by decree or legislation may of course be waived, but we must observe that this does not apply here. Paul clearly states the Lord's command as a direct obligation upon all apostles. That he has *altered the status* of this obligation into a discretionary privilege is precisely what must be carefully explained. When my Chancellor states, 'All who teach in this University will use offices provided in the University buildings', but I decide to set up an office in the town somewhere, I am not renouncing a privilege bestowed upon me by the Chancellor but disobeying a regulation of his and thereby causing a certain slippage in my status and public image as a faculty member. This is precisely what happened with Paul.

[1] *Memory* 318.

[2] *Ego de ou kechremai oudeni touton ouk egrapsa de tauta* etc. For some reason, the official translations all take *houtos* in the first clause to refer to the authority itself, and not, as the parallelism between *touton* and *tauta* indicates, these *proofs* Paul has just written defending it.

end of Chapter 8 regarding idol-meat: 'If food be the downfall of my brother, I will never eat meat any more, for I will not be the cause of my brother's downfall' (8.13 *NEB*).

This point of contact with the structure of the argument in Chapter 8, moreover, raises another point that must be most carefully considered. Paul is not against using this authority as such, i.e., in principle, even as he is not in principle opposed to eating meat which has been consecrated to an idol. The affirmation in 8.13 is prefaced by a conditional clause: '*if* food be the downfall of my brother. . . .' Consequently, there can be no doubt that if it seemed to Paul that such a terrible consequence would not ensue, he would not hesitate to eat such meat, even as he says later (1 Cor. 10.25ff.). The same thing was true of Paul's use of this authority to be supported financially. As a matter of fact, at the very time he was writing this passage, he was probably receiving financial aid from another congregation in Macedonia, as he later admits (2 Cor. 11.7ff.). Vehement asseverations notwithstanding and claims that he is enduring anything rather than burden the Corinthians there may be, the fact is all the time Paul is receiving some assistance from another congregation. True, it is strange that Paul does not mention this. However, this is not the first time Paul has acted in this curiously deceptive manner. In his earlier letter to the Thessalonians, we read the same proud boast that he and his assistants had 'worked day and night' rather than take any financial support from them (1 Thess. 2.9). And yet, although he doesn't say so to the Thessalonians, the Philippian congregation (which he had just left prior to coming to Thessalonika) was supporting him while he was there![1]

One thing is clear. The impact of Paul's proud boast would have been greatly reduced among the Thessalonians had they learned or known of the aid coming in to him from Philippi. Furthermore, it is not difficult to see why, when several of Paul's congregations finally got together and compared notes, he was accused of being a very cunning swindler (2 Cor. 12.16). It will be

---

Thus: 'I have not used any of these *reasons, arguments,* nor did I write them . . . etc.' The translation, 'I have not used any of these rights' (*RSV, JB,* Moffatt, Héring) is inaccurate if for no other reason because Paul is speaking of only one right anyway. Cp. Lietzmann-Kümmel 42; Allo 221; *NEB*. For a discussion of the textual problem in v. 15, not affecting our conclusions, see, e.g., Robertson-Plummer 188f.; Lietzmann-Kümmel 43.

[1] See Phil. 4.16 and further below, pp. 28f., 36ff.

necessary to get as full and balanced a picture of Paul's activities as possible before this peculiar aspect of Paul's method can be properly assessed.

However, it can readily be seen at this point that his sweeping, categorical repudiations should not be taken literally. They are all intended to apply only to the Corinthians, and on top of that, exude a certain rhetorical melodrama concerned primarily with making the point regarding idol-meat. It is from this that his argument gets its one-sidedness, I believe. After all, it was a legitimate authority. Paul never attacked the regulation itself. Using it in such a way that the Gospel was obstructed was what Paul strenuously avoided. This was the real locus of Paul's boast, and not always turning down financial aid whenever it was offered to him. On the other hand, it must be admitted that many aspects of his words here are peculiar and highly misleading.

Finally, Paul turns jocular for a moment, and gets off a little pun. After pointing out that he is not like the regular kind of workman who voluntarily performs his task, since he has no choice whether he will preach the Gospel or not, he goes on to say that therefore he has no basis upon which to claim any wages. Then facetiously asking, 'What are the wages of someone who is not entitled to any?' he answers, 'Why, to do the work for free!' Unfortunately, whether the Corinthians ever got his joke or not, it has largely been wasted on centuries of sober-sided Christian exegetes.[1] If Paul had made a similar pun at the end of Chapter 8

---

[1] This passage has been the focus of considerable disagreement. A brief clarification of some of the major terms may assist the interpretation of the passage as a whole. The meaning of the term *kauchema*, 'boast', refers to his conducting his mission in such a way that no obstacle is laid before the Gospel. It is curious that Bultmann, in his description of the 'apostolic self-boast', considers that there is only one occasion when Paul 'speaks with emotion of his *kauchesis*, namely, 1 Cor. 15.31' (*TDNT* III 650f. s.v.). But Paul's emotion seems rather prominent in this verse (v. 15) as well, a point that has a direct bearing on the correct nuance to assign to *katachrenai* (v. 18, see below, next note).

There is also disagreement as to what Paul is referring to in his phrase *ananke moi epikeitai*. Robertson-Plummer (189) and Allo (222) think he is referring primarily to his Damascus conversion and the forcing from a road of persecution into the new calling of apostleship. However, Moffatt (120f.) and C. Maurer correctly point out that such a self-understanding is Luke's, and not Paul's. Paul envisioned his

D

for the benefit of the 'strong', it would have been something like this: 'Brothers, do not exploit[1] your authority to eat idol-meat. Better to "eat" the unwounded consciences of your weaker brothers.'

---

apostolic calling as having been prepared for him from before his birth (Gal. 1.15). Thus 'necessity' here stands for his very apostleship as such; see Maurer, 'Grund und Grenze apostolischer Freiheit. Exegetisch-kritische Studie zu 1 Kor. 9', *Antwort. Festschr. K. Barth* (1956) 630–641; further E. Käsemann, 'Eine paulinische Variation des "Amor Fati",' in idem, *Exegetische Versuche und Besinnungen II* (1964) *passim*. Hence, the proper translation of *epikeitai* is 'presses upon' (Robertson-Plummer 189) or 'constrains' (Moffatt 120), not 'is laid' (*RSV, JB*). 'I cannot help myself' (*NEB*) is ludicrously misleading. This being the case, then, the terms *hekon-akon* 'voluntarily-involuntarily', in v. 17 are to be understood in the same terms, i.e., Paul is doing a 'job' which he did not give to himself.

The greatest disagreement concerns the term *misthos*. The traditional Catholic exegesis, but including other commentators as well, e.g., W. Wrede and A. Schlatter, understood Paul to refer to his heavenly reward; for a history of the Catholic exegesis, see G. Didier, op. cit. above p.5, *passim*; cp. W. Wrede *Paul* (1907) 16; A. Schlatter, *Paulus der Bote Jesu* (1934) 278. It is of course true that Paul did look forward to his heavenly *misthos*, but that is not what the term refers to here. As E. Käsemann explains, ' "payment" here does not mean the wages to which he is entitled, as if it were a case of an accomplishment worthy of "a payment which is deposited with God" (Gutjahr) [that Paul will collect later]. It is not the heavenly and eschatological reward at all'; 'paulinische Variation' 228. Most recent commentators agree that Paul is speaking of a present *misthos*. What is it? In v. 18, 'with a characteristic love of paradox, the Apostle declares that precisely this abstention from his proper right is his payment' (Käsemann, loc. cit.). Cp. also Georgi *Gegner* 237; Maurer 'Grund' 636f.; H. Preisker *TWNT IV* 699–710 s.v. *misthos*.

[1] Most commentators hold that Paul here means to use *katachrenai* only in the so-called intensive sense, as at 7.31; so Bauer *Lexicon* s.v. It cannot be proven, but it seems to me more likely that Paul means the term differently; not 'use fully' but 'abuse'. The reason is that there seems to be an antithetical parallelism between this term in v. 18 and the plain *chrenai* in v. 15 (cp. *KJV*); his whole point is, in certain cases *any* 'use' is an 'abuse' of this authority.

5. Paul's method in this matter the same as his general missionary procedure (9.19–23)

So though I am not a slave of any man I have made myself the slave of everyone so as to win as many as I could. I made myself a Jew to the Jews, to win the Jews; that is, I who am not a subject of the Law made myself a subject of the Law to those who are the subjects of the Law. To those who have no Law, I was free of the Law myself (though not free from God's law, being under the law of Christ) to win those who have no Law. *For the weak I made myself weak.* I made myself all things to all men in order to save some at any cost; and I still do this, for the sake of the gospel to have a share in its blessings (9.19–23 *JB*).

Paul now suddenly widens the scope of his discussion, and in a ringing passage declares that the same basic strategy he is advocating regarding idol-meat (italicized portion), and which he is himself following regarding the apostolic right of support, characterizes his entire procedure as a missionary. It guides him in his everyday walk through the maze of different customs and taboos making up contemporary Jewish and Gentile life. Paul could not express in more profound terms the full breadth of his 'freedom'. He was beyond the Jew-Gentile distinction. For the sake of the Gospel, he could enter into either community, adopting for the moment whatever regulations and customs prevailed, in order to win as many as possible.

What is fascinating to observe in this passage, however, is that Paul has indirectly answered one of our most interesting questions, namely, how he could, in Gerhardsson's phrase, 'classify Jesus' commandment as a permission'. *Paul's missionary strategy consists of a dialectic comprehensive enough to enable him freely to set aside a direct command of the Lord, or regulation from the Torah, or accepted custom of the churches, or cherished observance from any pagan cultus, or anything else, if to follow it scrupulously would hinder the entry of anyone into the Lord's salvation.*

At this point we reach the end of the material in Chapter 9 of relevance for our study of this apostolic regulation.[1] Now we

---

[1] For the rest of the chapter, see especially D. Daube, *New Testament*, 336–341 (against G. Bornkamm, 'The Missionary Stance of Paul in 1 Cor. 9 and Acts,' *Studies in Luke-Acts* (1966) 194ff.); further Didier 'Salaire' 237–251; H. Chadwick, 'All things to all men', *NTS* 1 (1955) 261–275.

must see if the loose ends can be brought together, and a balanced picture of Paul's attitude toward and use of this apostolic authority be attained. Hopefully, in the process we will find some answers to the many perplexing questions that have come up in the course of our investigation thus far.

CHAPTER TWO

Paul's Basic Position *vis-à-vis* This Command of the Lord

To summarize our results up to this point, we have shown that Paul's argument in 9.4–15 proves that the regulation concerning the duty of congregations to support apostles working in their midst was in general effect in the early Church and well known to the Corinthians. At the same time, it was equally clear that Paul and his associates had for some time been setting aside this regulation. Our first task now will be to try to achieve a balanced picture, as much as it can be recovered from his letters, of when he used this regulation as well as when he set it aside, and his reasons for doing so in each case (if given). Only with a thorough grasp of this overall picture will it be possible to venture answers to some of the other much more complex questions and issues that have appeared.

For example, we need to examine carefully the master-strategy enunciated by Paul in 1 Cor. 9.19–23. We discovered that he there voices a dialectical missionary strategy in terms of which he is able to disregard a vast array of religious ordinances, Jewish or Gentile, and that interestingly enough, this particular command of the Lord seemed to be included among the things which Paul could observe or not, depending upon how it affected the progress of the Gospel. The full implications of this remarkable phenomenon need to be drawn out more precisely, especially as it relates to the larger question of how Paul handles sayings of the Lord in general.

Secondly, many questions came up having to do with the reaction to Paul's statements and practices regarding financial support. That is to say, we found that, although Paul made several categorical assertions in 1 Cor. 9 about never making use of this apostolic prerogative, this seemed motivated more by the immediate requirements of his argument in the context of Chapters 8–10 rather than reflecting his whole feelings on the matter, especially in view of the fact that he was at that very time taking financial aid from another congregation. We also noted that Paul had done precisely the same thing before with the Thessalonian congregation. Then, as it appears, word somehow got around about this strange behaviour of Paul's and the Corinthian congregation (or certain spokesmen in it) angrily accused Paul of dishonesty.

To be sure, a strategy like this must have been confusing to many, nor would the justification of it in 1 Cor. 9.19–23 always have met with ready approval. On the contrary, there is clear evidence that a great wave of distrust suddenly rose in Corinth against Paul. Thus, in this section, we shall probe the various reactions to Paul's missionary procedure. In a way, we shall inquire how successful he was in actually avoiding placing obstacles before the Gospel.

Finally, it was pointed out that, concerning the command of the Lord itself, Paul just refers to it; he does not actually quote its contents. Our last section will seek to answer the question what this saying actually was that Paul (and presumably the Corinthians) knew of concerning support for apostles.

1. *Paul's financial relations with his churches*

Considering Paul's over-all activity as an apostle, there can be no doubt that he received many kinds of assistance, many little material encouragements and gifts, and hospitality everywhere, such as being the house-guest of a certain Gaius while staying in Ephesus (Rom. 16.23).[1] In this, Paul would not have differed at all from the honors and hospitality accorded Jewish apostles (*shelichim*) visiting the local synagogue from distant parts on official business.[2] However, it is certain that Paul, and the regulation, concerns something quite different from hospitality. What is meant specifically, as Paul proves by his references to working (e.g., 1 Cor. 9.6 besides others), is money given to him so that he will not have to earn his own support; in short, a salary. This is the point at issue. This is precisely the thing involved in the command of the Lord: 'Those who preach the Gospel should get their living by the Gospel' (*RSV*).

---

[1] This assumes that Rom. 16 was a letter (or part of one) to the church at Ephesus, not Rome. On this whole question, see P. Feine, J. Behm, rev. W.-G. Kümmel, *Introduction to the New Testament*, trans. A. J. Mattill (1965) 222–226.

[2] See E. Urbach, op. cit. above p. 12.

Paul mentions only one congregation which gave him financial support in sufficient amount so that it could be termed a salary, and that was the Philippian church.[1] They helped him substantially: several payments at Thessalonika,[2] several more at Corinth,[3] and once while he was in prison (presumably in Ephesus).[4] No other major financial aid is mentioned by Paul in the letters we now have. As far as the Philippian assistance is concerned, Paul expresses only the warmest gratitude and love for them and appreciation for their generosity. This is important to place beside the passage in 1 Cor. 9, for it shows that Paul could, at least in this one case, welcome the use of this regulation wholeheartedly.[5]

[1] Phil. 4.15–17. For a suggestion as to the possible history-of-religions background of the phrase *Koinonein eis logon doseos kai lempseos* (Phil. 4.15) but without giving evidence, see Georgi, *Die Geschichte der Kollekte des Paulus für Jerusalem* (1965) 47. On the use of *koinonein* to mean financial sharing in Paul's vocabulary, see Rom. 15.27 (cp. 1 Cor. 9.11); Gal. 6.6; Phil. 4.15. It is interesting to note an exact Latin equivalent in Cicero, *Laelius de amicitia Liber* 16.58 (cited in Wettstein, *Nov. Test.* II 280; cp. also Liddell-Scott-Jones *Lexicon* s.v. *dosis*). Utterly far-fetched is the suggestion of B. H. D. Hermesdorf, 'De apostel Paulus in lopende rekening met de gemeente te Philippi', *Tijdschr. v. Theol.* 1 (1961) 252–256, that Paul opened a bank account with a member of the Philippian congregation and got several loans. See instead O. Glombitza, 'Der Dank des Apostels. Zum Verständnis von Phil. 4.10–20', *NovTest* 7 (1964) 135–141. On the important questions of the unity of Philippians, and the original purpose of 4.10–20 see W. Schmithals, 'Die Irrlehrer des Philipperbriefes', *ZThK* 54 (1957) 306ff.; B. D. Rahtjen, 'The Three Letters of Paul to the Philippians', *NTS* 6 (1960) 173; Georgi *Kollekte* 46–51, 47 n.160; and in general F. W. Beare, *A Commentary on the Epistle to the Philippians* (1959) 4, 149–157.

[2] See Beare Philippians 150ff.; Goergi Kollekte 47ff. L. Morris, 'KAI HAPAX KAI DIS' *NovTest* 1 (1956) 205–208, demonstrates on philological grounds that Paul here refers to *several* gifts of money sent to him at Thessalonika. In view of this, C. Maurer's remark playing down Paul's financial dependence upon the Philippian congregation is hardly surprising in view of the one-sidedness of his whole discussion; see 'Grund' 640.

[3] 2 Cor. 11.8f. [4] Phil. 2.25–30.

[5] It is strange that so many of the discussions of 1 Cor. 9 fail to take notice of this positive side of Paul's attitude toward this regulation; see e.g., E. Käsemann 'Paulinische Variation'; C. Maurer 'Grund'; D. Georgi *Gegner* 235ff.; G. Didier 'Salaire'; Y. Congar, 'Die Kasuistik des heiligen Paulus', *Festgabe für F. X. Arnold* (1958) 16–41. The

On the other hand, numerous passages in his letters indicate the strength, both in polemical contexts as well as when the air is not full of bitterness and strife, of Paul's reluctance to make use of this regulation. For example, in his letter to the Thessalonians, written from Corinth,[1] he makes an emphatic point of the fact that he and his associates had preached the Gospel among them without charge, that is, they had worked for their livelihood rather than ask for any financial assistance. We have discussed at length his similar statements in his second letter (our first[2]) to the church at Corinth, written several years later from Ephesus. What was it about these churches that caused Paul not to make use of his apostolic prerogative and they concur in this course of action?

There seem to have been two main problems, closely related to one another.[3] First, Paul, in claiming support would have worked a financial hardship on the people, would have been 'burdening' them as he says in both his letters to the Thessalonians and to the Corinthians.[4] In plain terms, these two congregations were, in Paul's judgment at any rate, just too poor for him to abide by this regulation.[5] Was he then going to go elsewhere? No, better the Lord's commandment be temporarily disregarded so that they could hear the message of salvation. Meanwhile, he and his assistants would support themselves.

---

result is a seemingly endless belaboring of the real or imagined theological nuances of Paul's argument in 1 Cor. 9, with hardly any recognition of the one-sidedness of his comments there in view of his whole attitude. It is no accident, then, that these commentators hardly mention the fact that Paul eventually got into serious difficulties by the way he handled himself, nor does it even seem to occur to them that it was, after all, Paul's *opponents* who could appeal to the command of the Lord and the regular practice of all the churches in support of their position. Instead, the whole discussion floats upon generalities. For example, Y. Congar's 'four motives why Paul refused support' (19–21) are never related concretely to Thessalonika or Corinth in *contradistinction* to Philippi.

[1] P. Feine, J. Behm, W.-G. Kümmel *Introduction* 182–184.

[2] Paul refers to his first letter in 1 Cor. 5.9. On this whole subject, see J. C. Hurd, *The Origin of I Corinthians* (1965).

[3] See also above, pp. 14f.

[4] 1 Thess. 2.6, 9; 2 Cor. 11.9; 12.14.

[5] One might recall Paul's remark in 1 Cor. 1.26: 'For remember when you were invited to be Christians, brothers. Not many of you were wise, according to worldly standards, not many were powerful, not many came from the nobility. . . .'

On the other hand, if he had claimed his prerogative, and they had decided to support him despite their poverty, this could provoke the comment, 'The Word of Grace comes dear these days!' Thus, the feeling could arise that the Gospel was no more than the means to satisfy Paul's greed (as he says in 1 Thess. 2.5). Both eventualities were abhorrent to Paul. 'At least we do not go round offering the Word of God for sale, as some do' (2 Cor. 2.17 *JB*). Such apostles brought the Gospel into disgrace, effectually turning people away from it. The end result was much worse than if they had never heard it in the first place.

The evidence indicates that the problem was essentially financial. The financial capacity of the congregations at Thessalonika and Corinth was such that Paul could not feel confident in asking for financial support. Although there is nothing explicitly supporting this, we may assume, I believe, that just the opposite was the case with the Philippian congregation.[1] In any case, we can see that Paul's 'boast' in 1 Cor. 9.12b was meant quite literally. He did act in such a way that the course of the Gospel was not hindered, by preaching in places which could not afford to support him. Furthermore, we may note a phrase in his letter to the Philippians which indicates that precisely the same motivation was operating in their case *when he accepted their support.*

As you know yourselves, Philippians, in the early days of my mission, *when I set out from Macedonia* you were the only congregation that were my partners in payments and receipts;[2] for even at Thessalonica you contributed to my needs, not once but twice over[3] (Phil. 4.15 *NEB*).

[1] Is it just coincidence that this was also Paul's *first* missionary church? That is, might it be that Paul considered this type of relationship sufficient when established with one church, rather than piling up financial ties as he went along, or working a new one out with each new mission congregation he established? Such questions must remain open. For a discussion that the phrase *en archei tou euangeliou* indicates that Paul began his mission work in the Greek homeland at Philippi, see M. J. Suggs, 'Concerning the Date of Paul's Macedonian Ministry', *NovTest* 4 (1960) 60–68. Apparently Philippi was a prosperous 'county-seat' with a large contingent of Roman soldiers settled in the immediate area after the battle of Actium; see P. E. Davies, 'The Macedonian Scene of Paul's Journeys', *BibArch* 26 (1963) 91–106.

[2] See above, p.29 n.1.

[3] For a more accurate translation of this Greek phrase, see above, p. 29 n.2.

The significant thing about Paul's comment is that he apparently did not accept financial support from the Philippian church until after he had left and was working elsewhere. That is to say, even in the one case we know of where he did make use of this apostolic authority, he seems to have done so in such a way that it would clearly aid, as Georgi says, 'in achieving further missionary work'.[1] It is possible to see even here Paul's caution that this money not be construed as something Paul enjoys for himself while taking life easy in Philippi. In short, it seems that we can document the concrete implementation of Paul's dialectical missionary strategy *in both directions* regarding his financial relationships with his churches.

Within this general, formal coinherence to his overall missionary outlook, however, must be reckoned a rather one-sided trend. Paul's positive obedience to the Lord's command was matched and more than matched by abstention from obeying it.[2] That is to say, even within Paul's dialectic we must recognize a prevailing reserved or cautious attitude toward this regulation. It is just here that we must look for the reason why Paul initially turned this regulation into a permission—assuming he made such a decision at all; it is quite possible that he simply inherited this alteration ready-made. But whether Paul's or not, this alteration is based on the realization that this regulation was no longer appropriate in every case. Thus it was 'classified' as a permission, not an obligation, to be used when appropriate.

If Paul actually did participate in the revision of the status of this regulation, or if he simply inherited it from his elders among the apostles, in either case it was no longer necessary to justify it by the time he wrote 1 Corinthians. By that time it was quite familiar both to Paul and to his correspondents. It is, however, just this familiarity with the short-cut around the older regulation that explains why, after he has finished the long series of inter-

[1] *Gegner* 236.

[2] Thus Y. Congar's remark that Paul 'knows very well that the apostle should normally . . . accept his support-money' ('Kasuistik' 21), misrepresents Paul's prevailing reserved attitude. On the other hand, the parallel adduced by Gerhardsson of personally more strict observance of certain halakoth under special circumstances by the rabbis (see *Memory* 319) is not relevant here. As the examples Gerhardsson gives show, Paul is not observing Torah more *strictly*, he is not observing it at all.

related justifications for this regulation followed by the un-
restrained advocacy of disregard for it, he creates a startling
impression of willful disobedience to an explicit command of the
Lord. And this impression is all the more intensified by the realization that what Paul's argument actually comes down to is the
claim that acting according to the will of the Lord abuses the
Church!

But of course, Paul is not intending to say any such thing. In
fact, as we pointed out, he is not really arguing one way or the
other about this regulation as such. He is simply trying to place
in an exemplary light his already well-known practice of renouncing this apostolic prerogative in order to press home his argument
to the 'strong' regarding their eating of idol-meat. In the process,
we saw that he has said some very misleading things, things that
must be understood from the perspective of his whole attitude
toward and use of this regulation if they are to be interpreted
correctly.

2. *The relation between Paul's missionary strategy and the sayings-of-the-Lord tradition*

As we noted at the conclusion of our discussion of 1 Cor. 9.1–23,
Paul introduced a vital clarification of his advice regarding the
'strong's' behavior toward the 'weak', as well as his own illustration
from his practice of not accepting financial support, when he lifted
the entire discussion on to the level of his general strategy as a
missionary, and claimed that the apostle of Christ is free to adapt
himself to any surroundings in such a way that the Gospel can
advance unimpeded. Among Jews he can observe all the requirements of Torah, among Gentiles he can dispense with Torah,
among the weak he can avoid meat consecrated to idols. Thus, for
the sake of the unimpeded proclamation of the Gospel (1 Cor.
9.22f.) and unity in Christ (1 Cor. 8.11f.; Rom. 14.17–19), Paul
relativized many sacred obligations and institutions.

It would distract from the main purposes of this study to
undertake at this point a full elaboration of the actual boundaries
and dimensions of Paul's relativization of religious norms within
the structure of the Gospel, but it was far more comprehensive
than is usually recognized. It took in, at least theoretically, not
only many basic religious differences between Jews and non-

Jews, but also basic cultural categories, and even the fundamental sexual differentiation.[1] What was the origin of this astonishing sense of transcendence? Where did the alarming idea come from that he could be 'all things to all men so that by all means [he] might have some' (1 Cor. 9.22)? Is this the proud boast of a Peregrinus, both capable and yet apparently also driven to adopt one after the other a protean succession of self-identities in the course of a half-triumphant, half-desperate search for apotheosis? Is this an apocalyptic visionary speaking, whose consuming sense of impending catastrophe makes dwarf-like the all-too-important structures and institutions of this world, and whose heart, yearning after the gloriously perfect society of the saints, has long-since grown cold toward the world of men? Or is it the radical relativism of a Diogenes the Dog, where life has been reduced to such minimal requirements that the customs of men are a matter of indifference? Or is it just a kind of tolerant Epicurean universalism, rooted ultimately in *ennui* over against the Hellenistic world's upheaval and turmoil, its welter of conflicting religious claims and conventions? Whatever the source, it can immediately be seen that Paul's 'distancing' of himself from the cherished beliefs and institutions of his countrymen, both Jewish and Gentile, put him radically out of step with them, which inevitably led to friction and misunderstanding. Thus, although in this section we shall suggest the importance of this outlook for the whole mission-dynamic of the Church, in the next we must ask about the other

[1]'All baptized in Christ, you have clothed yourselves in Christ, and there are no more distinctions between Jew and Greek, slave and free, male and female, but all of you are one in Christ Jesus' (Gal. 3.27f. *JB*). Paul clearly thought that this extraordinarily extensive breakdown of normal human distinctions (as understood in his age) was the way it should be in the Church, as his many statements to this effect testify; see, besides the above, Rom. 10.12; 1 Cor. 7.17–24; 12.13; and Gal. 5.6; 6.15. But even Paul himself fell short now and then; women were to keep silent in church, apparently for no other reason than that they were women (1 Cor. 14.33b–36). It should not be concluded, on the other side, that *everything* could be included within Paul's dialectic. This is what makes tracing the actual boundaries of Paul's scheme so difficult. If he could say, on the one hand, 'food is for the belly and the belly for food',—echoing a slogan of the Corinthians which led to the conclusion that it was unimportant what one ate—he drew a sharp line before its corollary: 'the body is for sex and sex is for the body'; see 1 Cor. 6.12ff.

side, specifically, the bitter conflict with some of the Corinthians.

The importance of the fact that Paul includes within the limits of his dialectic a specific and explicit command of the Lord cannot be overestimated. The implication is dazzlingly clear: this command of the Lord, and no doubt many others regarding we don't know what subjects, was *relativized, i.e., obeyed or not depending upon how this affected the progress of the Gospel and the unity of the Church.* Paul's missionary dialectic was emphatically not merely a theoretical possibility, for we observed in our analysis above that his concrete behavior conformed *in detail* to the principle enunciated in 1 Cor. 9.19–23.

As a matter of fact, there are signs all through his letters of this relativization under the Gospel. Rom. 14 is a classic passage. There he seeks to transcend all religious distinctions, Jewish or pagan, regarding kinds of food. 1 Corinthians contains case after case where Paul places in his larger dialectic all sorts of distinctions which the Corinthians had made between superior and inferior Christians (and many of which Paul agrees with!).

The freedom Paul displays over against this command of the Lord (and therefore presumably others as well) is of decisive significance in furthering our understanding of how the early Church handled such traditions. We must remember that Paul was followed in this practice of not accepting financial support by a large number of associates as well as several churches. This indicates a large group within the early Church for whom regulations, whether based on Torah, on local (or general) custom, or even on sayings of the Lord, were treated dialectically—i.e., in the way Paul describes in 1 Cor. 9.19–23. This meant that whenever a significant conflict or dispute or problem arose in the Church over its regulations, and the possibilities for such disagreements would be innumerable considering the extraordinarily pluralistic religious territory covered by the early Church, the decisions made ultimately seem to have favored whatever course best promoted the further flowering of the Gospel and encouraged Christian harmony, at least as they understood these things.

This realization should not surprise us, of course, after two generations of form-critical investigation of the Gospels. We have long since become accustomed to the constant appeal to hypothetical reconstructions of this or that *Sitz-im-Leben* in order to explain the alterations and modifications of various

Synoptic pericopes when viewed in their interrelationships. However, it is one thing to postulate such activity on the part of the early Christian community, or the editors of the Gospels; it is something else again to see someone from that very community *actually enunciate and then put into practice such deviation from the received tradition of the sayings of the Lord, precisely within a 'Sitz-im-Leben-der-Kirche'*. This is the actual significance of Paul's 'defence' of his practice in 1 Cor. 9, as far as the history of the Synoptic tradition is concerned, for there he makes it perfectly clear that he could set aside a law in effect in the early Church, founded upon an explicit command of the Lord, and that what made this possible was his firm grasp of the freedom to maintain the unimpeded progress of the Gospel within a context of the harmony of the Church. As we shall now observe, however, there was, at least temporarily, a wide gulf between what Paul intended and what he actually achieved among the Corinthians.

3. *The success of Paul's policy regarding financial support*

It is difficult to answer this question with any confidence, for we simply do not know anything about the great majority of Paul's financial arrangements with his congregations. For example, we have no clear idea how he maintained himself during his long stay in Ephesus. And unfortunately, regarding all of his congregations except the one at Corinth, no mention of the issue on the part of the members themselves is visible in Paul's letters. We might make the general summary that, as the discussion in the first chapter showed, from Paul's point of view the Gospel was not impeded in the way he handled this regulation. For his part, then, his policy was a success, insofar as we can reconstruct it from his letters. As for the opinions of the members of his churches, however, we must remain largely ignorant.

In the case of one church, however, matters are different. There we have quite a bit of evidence regarding the reaction of his church-members to his policy. It seems to be the case that, whereas at first everything went all right, suddenly Paul's habit of not accepting support from them became the focus of bitter resentment. What happened? Let us turn first to Paul's passionate defence of himself and listen carefully to his words.

Did I commit a sin by lowering myself when I preached without payment the Gospel of God to you in order that you might be lifted high? I robbed other churches, getting money from them to be a minister to you! As long as I was there I never burdened anyone when I lacked something. It was the brothers from Macedonia who gave me everything I needed, and I'm going to keep from burdening you in the future the way I have in the past. As the truth of Christ is in me—I swear that this reason to be proud will not be stopped as long as I work in the area of Achaia! You ask me why do I do this? Do you think it's because I don't love you? God knows I do! It's because what I do— and I am going to go on doing it—shuts up some people who are trying to pretend they are as good as we are, those fakes! Such apostles are treacherous workmen. They deck themselves out as apostles of Christ and it's no wonder people are fooled. If the Devil himself can appear to be an angel, I'm not surprised if his ministers can appear to some to be ministers of righteousness. But they'll get what's coming to them! (2 Cor. 11.7–15).[1]

This is Paul at his angriest. It seems that certain apostles on a tour through the Greek churches, namely, Peter and the brothers of the Lord and some others (the same group mentioned in 1 Cor. 9.5),[2] came to strengthen the Corinthian congregation as well. While they were there, they may have shown some surprise that the founder of the Corinthians' church had never accepted their financial support as was customary. Perhaps at this point we have to date the writing of 1 Corinthians, where, in Chapter 9, Paul deals with this by the way, while arguing a more important problem. When this letter arrived, it may have happened that Peter and the rest felt moved to tell the Corinthians that, regardless of what Paul said in the letter, they knew that while he was at Corinth he received financial support from another congregation. This kind of information would certainly be known to someone as

[1] My translation.
[2] There is no need to enter into the debate now going on as to the identity of Paul's opponents in 2 Corinthians; on this whole subject, see most recently D. Gorgi, *Die Gegner des Paulus in 2. Korintherbrief* (1964). My opinion is that they were precisely the group mentioned in 1 Cor. 9.5 (against Georgi); see on this, C. K. Barrett, 'Christianity at Corinth', *BJRL* 46 (1963–64) 269–297. Gal. 1, 2 makes it perfectly clear that Paul is not in the least intimidated by these kinfolk of Jesus (are the *adelphoi tou kyriou* in 1 Cor. 9.5 the same group as the *tines apo Jakobou* in Gal. 2.12?) or Peter.

important as Peter and his companions, especially if they had
come to Corinth by land, the way Paul had, namely, via Philippi
and the coastal route through Athens. In any case, as we can see
from the passage quoted above, where Paul re-uses words and
phrases that we first read in 1 Cor. 9, the Corinthians must have
been stung to the quick by this news and hurled Paul's now rather
hollow-sounding boast back in his face. It does seem that Paul
was indeed trapped by his own words, for it is interesting to note
that here Paul says nothing about 'working night and day' in order
not to burden them, but rather admits that money had come from
elsewhere. It must have been most embarrassing.

In fact, Paul's reaction does not seem to have been wholly
straightforward even here. Not long after this passage he comes
back to the matter of support and exclaims sarcastically: 'Name one
way in which your church is inferior to the rest of the churches
except that I myself have not financially burdened you? Forgive
me that injustice!' (2 Cor. 12.13). The impression which clearly
seems to be intended is that the Corinthian church stands alone
as being the place where Paul worked for nothing. Now we know,
and he certainly knew, this was not true. This attempt at conceal-
ment makes Paul's other boast of not being a burden (in his letter
to the Thessalonians), while not mentioning the fact that he was
being partly subsidized, look very dubious. Perhaps we are
misreading his words. In any case, Paul is very angry, and things
spoken in anger are rarely worthy of careful scrutiny.

It is interesting to note that both in this passage as well as the
one quoted at length above Paul mentions *several* congregations as
helping him out. Actually in 2 Cor. 12.13 Paul implies that *all* the
other congregations *except* the Corinthian were helping to support
him. This must be placed next to his statement in Phil. 4.15
where Paul makes it clear that when he first began in Greece, only
one congregation was giving him support. Did the support of
Paul gradually grow up to be a multi-congregational affair? It is
quite possible.

As the several letters which go together to make up our 2
Corinthians show, Paul soon made a reconciliation with the
Corinthians. The matter was somehow settled—we don't know
how—and Paul was no longer suspected of being a swindler: 'You
say I personally put no pressure on you, but like the cunning
fellow that I am, I took you in by a trick? So we exploited you . . .?'

(2 Cor. 12.16 *JB*). But the peculiar thing that emerges from all this is the fact that the success of Paul's over-all missionary strategy seems to have depended, at least in some measure, upon Paul's ability to keep his different congregations from learning too much about the way he had arranged things elsewhere! Once his congregations got together and began to compare notes, then the fat was in the fire. On top of that, given the presence of other apostles who had no great admiration for him, such a passage as Paul wrote in 1 Cor. 9.19–23 could be turned by them into a weapon of deadly effectiveness against him. Accusations of inconsistency, deceitfulness, confused thinking—Paul laid himself wide-open to attack in that passage.[1]

One last point. We should not fail to notice that nowhere in the entire context of the attack upon Paul, whether conducted by the angry Corinthians or by the Jerusalem opposition, is he charged with *disobeying the command of the Lord*. This is, I think, more than a mere argument from silence. Paul himself raised the opportunity for this charge to be brought against him in the context of his discussion in 1 Cor. 9, but no one seems to have made use of it. This suggests that what upset the Corinthians so much was only a matter affecting their pride; Paul was spurning their legitimate right to help him—even while he was secretly being helped by another congregation. Thus they drew a natural conclusion: he didn't really love them! But all this means that this command of the Lord seems to have already passed into a certain state of eclipse as far as the Pauline churches were concerned. This is worthy of notice, and we shall examine, in the next chapter, what evidence there is to verify this question, i.e., whether this particular command of the Lord actually did pass into disfavor in the rest of the early Church, as we can see it did with the Pauline congregations.

[1] See the discussions of this sort of reaction to Paul in Hurd 128; further especially H. Chadwick, 'All things to all men (1 Cor. 9.22)', *NTS* 1 (1954–55) 261–275. It is undeniable that such a reaction to Paul is rather justified. For example, the advice Paul gives when he tries to speak dialectically to an actual problem frequently comes out sounding inconsistent and confused; see, e.g., two notorious passages such as 1 Cor. 7.20–24 (which is so difficult it can hardly be translated confidently) and 1 Cor. 10.25–31.

E

4. *The actual wording of the command of the Lord*

This general resumé of our findings and discussion of issues arising out of them now concludes with one final question. We have noticed that Paul does not actually quote the saying of Jesus directly, but only gives a summary of it when he mentions the command of the Lord. What was this saying itself? Furthermore, is it possible for us to determine whether Paul is referring to a saying which actually did go back to Jesus himself, or is it rather a saying which originated in the early Church? One thing seems clear, at any rate. This regulation was widely known in Paul's day, and must have belonged to a central core of sayings of the Lord in circulation among many congregations.

This suggests where we should look for an answer to our question. Beyond this one reference to it, Paul nowhere else mentions this saying of the Lord, or gives any indication as to what its actual wording may have been. Hence, we must seek elsewhere for the solution to this problem, and where better than in the early Church's compilations of sayings of the Lord—the Synoptic gospels. Perhaps by examining the saying in them on this exact subject: Jesus' instructions to his disciples regarding mission, we may be able to determine what Paul and the Corinthians may have known as the command of the Lord regarding support for apostles.

CHAPTER THREE

The Mission Instructions in the Synoptic Gospels

We have two main questions to ask concerning the Synoptic gospels' versions of the mission instructions: (a) what was the original[1] form and contents of those instructions, and (b) what can we discern about the gospel editors' own attitudes toward them? Our purpose is to determine whether we can cast any light on the actual content of the saying of the Lord which Paul presupposes in 1 Cor. 9.14, and secondly to see by the way the gospel editors use and modify their sources whether they reveal the same kinds of tensions we found in Paul's attitude toward this regulation.

1. *The original form and contents of the mission instructions*

None of the extra-canonical gospels we now have preserve anything like Jesus' instructions to the Twelve (or the Seventy-two), although we shall note a distant echo in a passage from the Gospel of Thomas of a saying now appearing in Luke. Turning exclusively to the canonical material, then, there is, regarding the relevant portion of the mission instructions, viz., Matt. 10.1–16// Mark 6.7–11//Luke 9.1–5//Luke 10.1–12, a general consensus concerning the main issues involved. The straightforwardness and simplicity of this consensus, however, is largely a result of a shallow acquaintance with the evidence and its complexity. Our first task, then, will perforce be a critique of the received interpretation of this pericope.

A. THE INTERRELATION OF THE SYNOPTIC ACCOUNTS

As just noted, there is very little disagreement among New Testament commentators concerning the interrelationships of the four versions of the mission instructions. Thus, for example, the

---

[1] That is, the most original version we can discern. Obviously, there is a slipperiness in the methodology at this point; see below, p. 61 n. 2.

opinion of B. H. Streeter on Matthew's version is still typical: 'the discourse part of Matt. 10 opens . . . by conflating a Mission Charge from the three sources, Mark, Q, and M.'[1] Luke, on the other hand, supposedly keeps his source material separated into blocks, according to the view of Streeter and others. Hence, he has two accounts. To quote Streeter again, 'when Mark and Q overlap [i.e., when both independently preserve the same story], Matthew carefully conflates the two . . . as contrasted with Luke's presentation of the same material as two distinct episodes.'[2] Finally, Mark is considered to be an abridgement of some sort. As we shall see, opinion is split as to whether Mark abridged Q[3] or some other account.[4] Now if we stand back to consider this array of positions for a moment, it is immediately clear where we must begin in order to seek an answer to our first question: since Luke 10.1–12 is supposedly pure Q, and all the other versions are in some way less authentic, we shall examine it first to see if it really is the most original we have.

(i)   Luke's so-called Q-block (Luke 10.1–12)

As noted, the common critical opinion is that in this passage, one encounters the Q version of the Synoptic mission instructions more or less intact. However, some have noticed that this episode's

[1] *The Four Gospels*[2] (1930) 263; cp. 187, 211, 254, 273f. See further, G. Strecker, *Der Weg der Gerechtigkeit*[2] (1966) 194; R. Bultmann 325; Klostermann *Matt.* 84f.; W. L. Knox, *The Sources of the Synoptic Gospels* (1953) II 48, 50; G. D. Kilpatrick, *The Origins of the Gospel According to St. Matthew* (1950) 26f.; F. Hahn, *Mission in the New Testament*, trans. F. Clarke (1965) 41; F. W. Beare 82. But against see Lagrange 196; B. C. Butler, *The Originality of St. Matthew* (1951) 13–19.

[2] *Four Gospels* 211. Further C. G. Montefiore II 146, 445, 460; Taylor *Luke* 153; W. L. Knox *Sources* II 48, 54.

[3] Montefiore I 120.

[4] Streeter 190, reversing his earlier opinion, see idem, 'St. Mark's Knowledge and Use of Q' in Wm. Sanday ed. *Studies in the Synoptic Problem* (1911) 170f. According to W. L. Knox, Mark is here drawing upon his (written) 'Twelve Source'; *Sources* II 48, cp. I 21ff. V. Taylor's opinion is typical of the obscurity prevailing in critical opinion as to the identity of Mark's source: 'the narrative itself is redactional. . . . The sayings . . . were derived either from oral tradition, or more probably from a primitive collection *comparable to* Q and M' (*Mark* 302 italics mine).

location in the outline of the career of Jesus comes neither from Mark, nor even from Q, but is obviously the result of Luke's own editorial activity.[1] What must have been in Q, namely Jesus' mission instructions to his twelve disciples, has here been recast by Luke as a second mission speech by Jesus to Seventy-two[2] 'others', apparently because he wanted a gospel account prefiguring the Gentile mission (there being 72 nations in the world according to common reckoning).[3]

Other problems emerge. The first verse of the instructions, namely, the saying about the harvest and the workers, may have been first in Q's version. Matthew has this saying in another place, at 9.37, and some consider him to have inserted it there to introduce the call and subsequent listing of the disciples' names.[4] On the other hand, as we shall see in a moment, Luke has in fact broken up the pericope at this point in order to insert the next saying concerning 'lambs in the midst of wolves'.[5] Thus he may also have brought in the harvest saying as a good introduction to his new set of instructions for the Seventy-two.

The saying concerning lambs in v. 3 is intimately connected with Luke's unique interpretation of the next verse, v. 4, where Jesus tells the disciples not to take provisions with them when they leave. This verse has been widely misunderstood. Since it plays such a crucial role in all of the versions of the mission instructions, perhaps we should pause here for a closer examination of it, to see if we can discover its correct meaning.

Vincent Taylor, following T. W. Manson, has suggested that the close parallel between the items here prohibited and those which must be left behind by anyone who desires to enter the Temple precinct, viz. staff, sandals, wallet, and dust upon the feet (Mish. Ber. 9.5), means that 'the mission is meant to be regarded as a specially sacred undertaking'.[6] While the similarity in items

[1] Beare 156; Knox *Sources* II 49.

[2] See now K. Aland et al. *NT* for MSS evidence on '72'.

[3] Cp. Gen. 10 LXX and see Klostermann *Luke* 113. For references to non-Jewish use of these numbers, see Knox *Sources* II 49 n. 2. For Jewish use, see B. M. Metzger, 'Seventy or Seventy-two Disciples?' *NTS* 4 (1959) 299–306; further, Billerbeck III 48ff. The possible influence of *Aristeas* is discussed in S. Jellicoe, 'St. Luke and the Seventy-Two' *NTS* 6 (1960) 319–321.

[4] Knox II 51; cp. Bultmann 98.

[5] But see Hahn *Mission* 44; Beare 82.   [6] *Mark* 304.

mentioned is striking, Jesus' mention of such other things as *bread* (Luke 9.3) and *two tunics* (clearly in Q, see below), indicates that something else is meant here—something not even remotely related to Temple prohibitions.

By far the most common interpretation is that Jesus is advocating an ascetic renunciation of worldly goods. On this assumption, then, it is customary to compare the several versions of this part of the mission instructions to find which one has the strictest degree of 'asceticism required of the disciples',[1] it naturally being so that the strictest will have been the original. When inquiry is pressed as to possible reasons why Jesus might have urged such an ascetic regimen upon his disciples, this entire line of interpretation suddenly begins to appear rather flimsy. C. G. Montefiore takes these 'severe injunctions' to mean that the disciples were not to waste time worrying about material possessions since the End was so near.[2] According to F. W. Beare, Jesus was ordering the disciples to 'travel light, without staff or sandals or even a change of clothing . . . . There was no time to spare'.[3]

Spare for what? Jesus is not ordering his disciples to leave behind their sums of extra money, extra supplies of food, and numerous bags for extra clothing and other gear! He ordered them to carry *no* money whatsoever, *no* food at all, and *no* clothes except what they had on. One might well view this as traveling 'exceedingly light' (Manson)! As a matter of fact, no one travels this light, except a lunatic. In other words, the point of the instructions must lie somewhere else than in the mere verbal prohibitions themselves. As Hahn and others correctly observe, the 'object of all these stipulations is that the disciples be completely without means in their service and venture, and therefore remain completely dependent on other people for everything

---

[1] Knox II 48.

[2] *Synoptic Gospels* II 148; cp. T. W. Manson, *Sayings of Jesus* 76; Taylor *Mark* 304.

[3] Beare 156. It is willingly granted to this interpretation that it has the clear support of the last phrase in Luke 10.4: 'greet no one along the way.' Not found in any of the other accounts, Luke may well have inserted it to suggest the need for swiftness—'like Gehazi of old [who greeted no one along the way] on his mission of life and death (2 Kings 4.29)'; Taylor *Mark* 302. Fanciful is Hahn 45f.; so also is A. O'Hagan, 'Greet no one on the way' (Luke 10.4b), *StudBibFrancLibAnn* 16 (1965/66) 69–84.

down to the last detail.'[1] The disciples are to take nothing along *since they can have anything they need from those with whom they stay.* We shall see in a moment that there is clear evidence in the surrounding verses of both Matthew and Luke to prove that this is how they also understood this saying. First, however, let us pause to take note of a remarkable, independent parallel and confirmation that this is indeed what is in view. Josephus describes an identical custom prevailing among the Essenes.

They [the Essenes] occupy no one city, but settle in large numbers in every town. On the arrival of *any of the sect* from elsewhere, all the resources of the community are put at their disposal, just as if they were their own. . . . Consequently, *they carry nothing whatever with them on their journeys*, except arms as a protection against brigands. In every city there is one of the order expressly appointed to attend to strangers, who provides them with raiment and other necessaries. . . . *They are, moreover, freely permitted to take anything from any of their brothers without making any return.* (*BJ* 2, 124–127 Thackeray, italics added).

Besides illuminating the point of Jesus' advice to his disciples, this passage also reveals another very interesting aspect, namely, the type of Essene traveller here mentioned is not necessarily an official of the community. Rather, Josephus stresses that it was a general custom of total hospitality to all traveling brothers. Thus, if Jesus did send his closest associates out on such a trip as this with these instructions, he may have meant nothing more complicated than the Essene hospitality. To be sure, the later Church understood this as ordaining the means of support for its elite corps, the apostles. But as the Essene practice shows, no formal elite is necessarily in view in such instructions as these.

Thus, this part of the instructions was no more than a reminder that his disciples would lack nothing while they are away on their trip. Luke later makes this explicit during the Last Supper scene, when he has Jesus refer back to these instructions and ask, 'When I sent you out without purse or haversack or sandals, *were you short of anything*? *No, they said.*' (*JB*) This little interchange, missing in the other gospels, is taken by H. Conzelmann to be a major clue to the entire theological conception underlying the framework of Luke-Acts.[2] For example, it is on the basis of this

[1] *Mission* 45; see further Bacon 66; Montefiore II 148.
[2] *The Theology of St. Luke,* trans. G. Buswell (1960) 13, 80ff., 233f.

clue that Conzelmann makes the brilliant deduction that Luke's motivation for inserting the saying in v. 3 into the context: 'Behold, I send you out as lambs in the midst of wolves', is to make precisely the opposite point this saying expresses in Matthew. Pointing out that this saying comes at the end of the mission instructions in Matthew (see Matt. 10.16), Conzelmann argues that Luke has transposed it to the front of the instructions precisely before Jesus' assurance to his disciples that they will not need to take anything by way of equipment for their trip. The result is amazing. Conzelmann says, 'In Matt. 10.16 the emphasis [of the saying] is on the threats to which the disciples are exposed. . . . In Luke, on the other hand, the emphasis is on the *protection which they will enjoy in the midst of danger*. For whereas in Matthew the meaning appears in 10.16 itself, in Luke [the meaning of the lamb/wolf saying comes out] *in the directions which follow concerning equipment*. Luke states their significance explicitly in 22.35: they represent [Luke's view of] the absolute peacefulness of the period of Jesus.'[1] It is a fascinating example of how the two gospel editors have taken a saying of Jesus to mean two diametrically opposite things.

To return to our analysis, then, considerable evidence has accumulated against the usual view that Luke 10.1–12 is a pristine copy of the Q version of the mission instructions. In the remainder, vv. 5–12, the evidence of Luke's editorial activity is no less abundant. For example, although the orders about bestowing 'Peace' and accepting hospitality (vv. 5–7a) may be from Q, the prohibition of door-to-door begging (v. 7b) is very doubtful. It fits a later condition in the Church perfectly, when wandering missionary-apostles had become a bane (cp. Didaché 11–13), and is highly out-of-place in this Palestinian-Jewish milieu. The same thing is true of the next verse: 'Whenever you enter a town and they receive you, *eat whatever is set before you*' (Luke 10.8 *RSV*). This order also applies perfectly to conditions in the later Church, namely, the food problems that arose in the Gentile mission area. There is, for instance, almost a verbatim parallel to this phrase in the part of Paul's discussion concerning idol-meat that we have just been examining: 'If an unbeliever invites you to dinner and you are disposed to go, *eat whatever is set before you* without raising any question on the ground of conscience' (1 Cor. 10.27

---

[1] Ibid. 106; see further 106 n.1.

RSV).[1] That Paul has here slipped in one of the maxims of the Gentile-area missionaries seems corroborated by a passage in the Gospel of Thomas as well.

If you go into any land and wander in the regions, and if they receive you, *eat what they set before you,* heal the sick among them. *For what goes into your mouth will not defile you.* (Log. 14 ed. Guillaumont et al.)

If we glance over and compare Matthew's version of the mission instructions, we see that it presents a sharp contrast to Luke at this point, since in it there is nothing whatever by way of guidance concerning the kinds of food the disciples might be allowed to eat. In this respect, his version seems closer to the conditions in Jesus' original milieu. This is all the more likely, if the injunction at the head of Matthew's account is original, which warned the disciples not to go into Gentile territory anyway. Conversely, the secondary character of these sayings in Luke's version is all the more understandable, since Luke 10 is supposed to be a prefiguring of the mission precisely to the Gentiles. In fact, Luke's concern for this particular problem does not stop here, but rises to major prominence in the story of Peter's vision of the banquet of unclean foods followed by the meal with the centurion (Acts 10).[2]

To return to Luke's account of the sending of the Seventy-two, the interpolation of these sentiments into his source has resulted in a rather awkward passage. As B. C. Butler notes, 'the disciples are first brought to a house [where they are to eat and drink], and then reference is made to their arrival at a city, and they are then to "eat" in a "city".'[3] It almost sounds as if Jesus expects

[1] Greek: *pan to paratithemenon hymin esthiete* 1 Cor. 10.27; cp. *esthiete ta para tithemena hymin* Luke 10.8.

[2] There seems to be an inner link between the problem of unacceptable food being offered to a Christian missionary, and the problem of apostle-support. That is to say, it seems more than merely accidental that both in the Lukan context as well as in 1 Cor. 8–10 both are discussed together. Of course, one can easily see how both problems might arise at the same time, i.e., given a Gentile milieu. In any case, this is one more indication of the close association of ideas in 1 Cor. 8 and 9. Paul's 'explanatory digression' (Jeremias) is not motivated merely because it was a similar case of forbearance.

[3] *Originality* 18.

the disciples to be provided with something like 'public entertainment'.[1]

The end of Luke 10's version of the mission instructions continues to show signs of editorial reworking. We have seen quite enough, however, to show how mistaken the usual opinion is, that Luke has done nothing more than carefully insert a block of Q here. On the other hand, the similarities between this account and the one in Matthew makes it clear that Luke is not following Mark's version, but rather is independently revising Q according to his own purposes. Thus, despite the heavy reworking, a general outline of the Q account is still visible: after the introductory gathering of the disciples,[2] and giving them authority to heal and announce the Kingdom, there comes the encouragement that personal necessities will be no problem. Next followed instructions on how to act toward receptive communities, and how to act toward hostile communities. When we discuss Matthew's version, this scheme will be elaborated more fully, for, as will appear, he also preserves its basic structure faithfully, indeed more faithfully. However, in order to prevent the impression that I have simply modelled my reconstruction of the Q account around Matthew, as Hahn uncritically does around Luke 10,[3] let us turn now to a consideration of Luke's other version of these instructions, namely, the charge to the Twelve (Luke 9.1–5). There we will find aspects corresponding neither to Mark 6 nor to Luke 10 but only to Matthew's version. In this way we shall seek to demonstrate that Matthew's version most faithfully preserves the full Q account.

(ii) Luke's so-called Markan block (Luke 9.1–5)

It is a part of the received opinion that it is Luke's custom in copying from his sources consistently to use one and then the next, only rarely conflating them as Matthew usually does.[4] To

[1] Knox *Sources* II 52; cp. Beare 155.

[2] It is possible that the Q account did not specify which disciples. 'In Mark, the Charge was addressed to the Twelve; in "L" it was addressed to the Seventy. Since the "Q" material has been combined with the Marcan Charge to the Twelve by Matthew, and with the "L" Charge to the Seventy by Luke, it would seem that the hearers were indicated vaguely in "Q" or else not indicated at all' (Beare 155).

[3] *Mission* 43.

[4] Streeter *Gospels* 211, 275.

prove this generalization, commentators are especially fond of
these two passages in Luke. For example, F. W. Beare writes,
'Luke has used the whole of the brief Marcan Charge in his own
version of the Charge to the Twelve, and does not draw on it [in
Chapter 10].'[1] So also W. L. Knox: 'Luke preserves the Marcan
charge in its original place at 9.1ff. and inserts the Q version at
10.1ff.'[2]

As in the previous case, however, the received opinion withers
under a close scrutiny of the evidence involved. A few commentators have noticed, for instance, that Luke is hardly following Mark
here at all. They have even felt impelled to invoke the existence
of a special source to explain Luke 9.1–5![3] This chronic reflex,
unfortunately so common in current scholarship, is hardly justified,
since at those points where this account differs with Mark and
Luke 10 it agrees with Matthew's version. Thus we may simply
take these to be fragments of Q (See APPENDIX). Let us look
more closely at some of these special agreements.

The most important agreement between Matt. 10 and Luke 9
over against the other versions is the similarity between Luke 9.2
and Matt. 10.7f. Mark seems to have something like this saying
elsewhere (see Mark 3.14), where it is indubitably his own formulation. Luke 10.9 seems to be another echo of this verse, and there
also it is secondary.[4] Thus the correspondence between Luke 9.2
and Matt. 10.7f., in terms of content and location in the context,
is difficult to explain in any other way except that this is a fragment
of the Q account.[5]

Secondly, there are two points of contact in Luke 9.3 and Matt.
10.9f., missing entirely from either Mark or Luke 10, namely, the
mention of silver (money) and the staff. To be sure, Mark does
mention the staff, but in such a way that Matthew and Luke agree
against him! They prohibit what he allows—hardly a coincidental

[1] *Earliest Records* 155.
[2] *Sources* II 48; further Hahn *Mission* 41; Beare 155.
[3] Streeter *Gospels* 248.
[4] See below, p. 59.
[5] So Klostermann, 'Luke narrates [the account in Chapter 9] with
many little divergences from Mark in which he corresponds with
Matthew, obviously depending, as also Zahn believes "upon a tradition,
be it oral or written, which appears also in Matt. 10" ' (*Luke* 103). Of
course, there is another completely different way to account for the
phenomena; see below, p. 66 n. 2 and p. 71 n. 2.

independent correction of Mark's text! These points of correspondence between Luke 9 and Matt. 10 show that Luke has some
Q material here that he has omitted in constructing the charge to
the Seventy-Two.

We have, however, only begun to notice the full extent to
which this version is independent of Mark. Let us now collect all
the agreements between Luke 9.1–5, Luke 10.1–12 and Matt.
10.1–16 against Mark. By referring to the Chart in the
APPENDIX, we can see that:

(1) Matthew and Luke (in both versions) record the instructions not to provide equipment for the trip in direct speech, while
only in Mark is part of them (6.8f.) in report-form and part
(vv.9f.) in direct speech.

(2) Matthew and Luke (in both versions) quote Jesus as having
given a blanket recommendation to leave everything behind.
Mark alone reports that Jesus made exceptions, recommending
that the disciples leave behind everything except sandals and
staff. These they were apparently to take on the trip.

(3) Most important of all, in astonishing contrast to the three
other versions, Mark's account is totally stripped of all references
to the fact that the disciples' whole purpose was to announce the
Kingdom of God. Instead, Mark's version describes little more
than an incidental side-excursion of the disciples to extend the
scope and impact of Jesus' miraculous healing power. Well
might Streeter have once called this 'a mutilated excerpt'.[1]

Other lesser correspondences between the three against Mark
might be brought up, but inasmuch as they are merely the side-
results of the massive editing here described, we need not spend
further time on them.[2] Enough has been seen, however, to show
that Luke 9.1–5 cannot possibly be understood as largely Markan
material.[3]

[1] 'St. Mark's Knowledge and Use of Q,' in Wm. Sanday, ed.,
Studies in the Synoptic Problem (1911), 175.
[2] See the careful discussion of the evidence in Streeter, op. cit.
previous note. He concludes: 'Q therefore contained substantially all
that Mark gives in much the same language, and in addition six sayings
which are intimately connected with them. Again, therefore, Mark's
version is a mutilated excerpt of Q' (175).
[3] Streeter retracted his earlier position in his magnum opus, *The
Four Gospels. A Study of Origins*[2] (1930). There he contended that
Mark did not know Q. Consequently, his view also changed on this

On the other hand, a glance at the Chart (see APPENDIX) makes it equally obvious that there is an almost identical structure in both Mark's and Luke's charge to the Twelve, as well as some points of verbal similarity. How can this strange similarity-within-opposition be explained? For Luke 9.1–5 is a curious but thorough conflation of Q material and Markan structure. In other words, this is not only not a *Markan* block, neither is it a Markan *block*.

(iii) Matthew's so-called conflation of Mark, Q, and M (Matt. 10.1–16)

Matthew's account of the mission of the Twelve is not located in the Markan order of the events of Jesus' career. In Mark, Jesus sends out the Twelve immediately after the rejection at Nazareth. Matthew records the sending much earlier. According to Matthew's view of Jesus' ministry, the sending out of the Twelve initiates a climactic turning-point in Jesus' public activity in Galilee. Matthew's way of emphasizing the importance of this event is shown most clearly by the fact that Jesus' mission instructions to his disciples on this occasion are by no means limited to the few remarks Mark or Luke 9.1–6 record, but continue on and on for *thirty-seven verses*, and is, in fact, a major oration covering a wide variety of subjects. The first such oration is of course the Sermon on the Mount, delivered to the disciples and the crowds. It is Jesus' 'messianic inaugural speech' (Baur).[1] This is followed

---

pericope, so that he attempted to understand it as Luke's dependence upon Mark, not Q. The result is hardly acceptable. Luke 9.3–5 'is mainly from Mark, but its differences from Mark seem to arise from conflation with the same Q discourse as that best preserved in Luke 10.4ff.; Luke 9.3–5 . . . seems to retain *a word or two from Q*' (*Gospels* 248, italics added). For Klostermann's list of agreements between Luke 9 and Matt. 10 against Mark, see *Luke* 103. It is especially important to remember, when compiling lists such as these, what W. R. Farmer calls 'the concatenation of agreements' of Matthew and Luke against Mark; see *The Synoptic Problem,* New York (1964) 138; cp. Streeter *Gospels* 245. In this case, that would be precisely the total excision of all references to a mission to preach the Kingdom of God's imminent arrival. This drastically separates the *entire* account of Mark from the other two, and demands explanation as such.

[1] F. C. Baur, *Kritische Untersuchungen über die kanonischen Evangelien, ihr Verhältniss zu einander, ihren Character und Ursprung* (1847) 460.

by a series of accounts of various healings among the people, so that Jesus' fame spreads far and wide. Thus Matthew builds toward Jesus' next major step, namely, at the right moment to send his 'Twelve disciples' (10.1) out among the Jews 'to gather the harvest' (9.38). This second phase of Jesus' ministry is begun with a second major oration, this time to his own disciples alone, regarding the momentous task now laid before them. Preceeding both orations is an identical summarizing comment (9.35, cp. 4.23), clearly from Matthew himself, that serves to mark the transition from one part of the larger narrative to the next.

This artificial setting of Matthew's version of the mission instructions, therefore, indicates that, as with the Sermon on the Mount, Matthew is consciously bringing together into a unified construction various bits and pieces of tradition previously unrelated to each other. For example, the names of the Twelve which Matthew pauses to enumerate in 10.2-4 clearly breaks up the context. Let us take a closer look at the rest of the account, and see if other fragments can be thus isolated.

As 10.1 indicates, a unified series of instructions begins at 10.7. Whether any of the intervening material also originally belonged to it cannot any longer be determined with certainty, especially since parallels with Luke are lacking[1]. On the other

[1] The prefatory charge in Matt. 10.5f.: 'Go nowhere among the Gentiles and enter no town of the Samaritans, but go rather to the lost sheep of the house of Israel', presents an interesting problem in this regard. V. 6 is a saying found again in the story about the Syrophonecian woman (15.24) where it is generally considered Matthew's insertion (but see Strecker *Weg* 194f.). Hence this is the original setting. The question then is, did this come as a part of the original mission pericope Matthew received, or is this an interpolation of his own?

Anything resembling this saying is missing in the other gospels, especially the very strange: 'go nowhere among the Gentiles'. Since it is lacking elsewhere, many consider this an insertion by Matthew from his special material; Knox *Sources* II 49, Kilpatrick *Originality* 27, Streeter *Gospels* 255, Klostermann *Matt.* 86. What is not often enough observed is the precision of the scope of the journey here ordained. 'The mission is practically limited to Galilee, as between Galilee and Judaea comes Samaria'; Montefiore II 146; cp. Knox II 50. By the same token, the warning to stay out of Gentile towns is also significant, inasmuch as Galilee was at this time more than 60 per cent Gentile, the Jewish inhabitants living in scattered villages and enclaves amongst the predominantly Syrian population. In this case, then, the

hand, Luke 9.1ff. and 10.1ff. pick up parallel to Matt. 10.7ff. and continue with Matthew until 10.16 (or through v. 16) at which point all go on in different directions. Thus we may limit our consideration of Matthew's version to 10.7–16.

The message the disciples are to bring to the people is briefly stated in v. 7b. In addition, they are authorized to perform works authenticating their message: 'heal the sick, raise the dead, cleanse lepers, cast out demons' (Matt. 10.8a *RSV*). Then comes a sharp transition into the question of money: 'You received without charge, give without charge' (v.8b *JB*). With this saying, we enter directly upon that segment of Matthew's long missionary discourse that pertains to this study.

---

third group mentioned in this saying might also have a definite signi-ficance; the 'lost sheep' may well be the *ame ha-aretz* (Beare 81; Montefiore II 146). That Galilean Jews were regarded with con-siderable scorn—at least as a stereotype (much like the modern 'nigger') is difficult to deny. The 'people of the land' were considered as no better than the racially mixed (and therefore permanently polluted) Samaritans (Mish. Dem. 3.4), their very name was an epithet synony-mous with 'sinner' (Mish. Sheb. 5.9). In fact, in one place it is for-bidden to help them (Mish. Git. 5.9). The blanket condemnation by Hillel is notorious (Mish. Ab. 2.6; cp. 3.13); see further Moore *Judaism* I 60; II 72f. Opposed to this whole view, however, is Montefiore II 141f.; see further the long essay by I. Abrahams in ibid. 647–669.

Although the question as to the historicality of the mission of the Twelve is not directly relevant to this study, the general reliability of Matthew's account over against the other three versions is. Hence, the question as to whether this saying may not in fact be impossible to understand *except* as having come from Jesus is pertinent. Thus Knox's comment is apropos: 'a wider appeal to his kinsmen in Galilee would have been inevitable at some period' (II 54 n. 2). Not only that, but an appeal precisely to the rejected and disenfranchized would be quite consistent with what we know otherwise about Jesus' assessment of the various factions in Palestine at the time. Furthermore, if this limitation *were* in the original version of Q's mission instructions, it would be obvious why all later accounts would leave it out. In fact, it is peculiar even to find it here, in view of Matthew's own outlook so clearly laid before us in Matt. 28.19. In other words, it would be quite unlikely that missionary instructions having in view such a ludicrously minimal scope of territory would be inserted at a *later* date, even if the groups mentioned had been somehow allegorized. 'These are archaic ideas unlike the editor's own pro-gentile theology; therefore, they stood in Q^{mt}'; J. Pairman Brown, 'Mark as Witness to an Edited Form of Q', *JBL* 80 (1961) 35; so also Beare 81; Knox II 51; Strecker *Weg* 194 (tentatively).

The first thing that must be said concerning this opening saying is that there could not be a more authentic expression of typical, early-first-century Judaean sentiment regarding the matter of payment for religious duty. For example, Zadok, the son-in-law of Shammai, who was nevertheless also an intimate friend of Yochanan ben Zakkai (a Hillelite) and after him Gamliel II, the Nasi of Yavneh,[1] is remembered as saying: 'Make not of [the Torah] a crown wherewith to aggrandize thyself nor a spade wherewith to dig. And so also Hillel used to say, "He who makes worldly use of the Crown [of the Torah] shall waste away". Hence thou mayest deduce that whoever derives profit from the words of the Law is promoting his own destruction.'[2] In fact, the actual phrase Matthew has has been found elsewhere in a Tannaitic saying: 'It is written, "Behold, I have taught you statutes and ordinances, even as the Lord my God commanded me" (Deut. 4.5)—[this means] even as I have taught you *gratis*, so should you teach others *gratis*.'[3] If this view is found among the Pharisees contemporaneous with Jesus, the same no doubt obtained among the Essenes as well, particularly in view of their attitude toward personal property.[4] Furthermore, it is important to observe that the Pharisees shift their views on this subject after the destruction of Jerusalem in A.D. 70 and the subsequent establishment of the Center at Yavneh. During that period they begin to swing over in favor of minimal support for those performing religious duties,

[1] Strack, *Introduction to the Talmud* 110; R. Travers Herford, *Pirke Aboth. The Ethics of the Talmud* (Schocken ed. 1962) note at 4.7.

[2] *Kal hannehneh midbarē hatōrah nōtēl chayyaw min ha'ōlam* Mish. Ab. 4.5 ed. Blackman. The insertion into the text by Blackman of 'Torah' is possibly incorrect. Hillel may have meant instead the Name of God; cp. Ab. de R. Nathan 12, 'Whoever makes use of the Tetragrammaton has no share in the world to come' (ed. Goldin). Goldin comments (ad loc.), following G. Scholem, *Major Trends in Jewish Mysticism*[3] (Schocken ed. 1961) 358 n.17, that this was a typical form of the prohibition of the use of the Divine Name in black magic. That more could also be understood, however, see the story recounted about Tarphon in bNed. 62a.

[3] bNed. 37a (Soncino). G. Dalman quotes the same passage from the Palestinian recension as follows: ' "As I for nothing, so ye for nothing", says God' in connection with the teaching of the Law; pNed. 38c. He adds bBech. 29a as another occurrence of this idea; *Jesus-Jeshua* (1929) 226.

[4] See 1QS VI. 19, 22.

especially for those connected with Yavneh.[1] This means that not only does the initial saying in Matthew's version introduce a sentiment totally authentic to both Pharisaic as well as Essene piety in Jesus' milieu, it also is a sentiment which, to judge from the early rabbinic literature, is losing ground in the period after A.D. 70 (after which the Essene community also no longer occupies Qumran). Exactly the same thing seems to have been happening in the Church, also. Thus, by the time Matthew was written, prevailing opinion was tending in the direction opposite to this saying's view. Hence, it could well be an original part of this whole pericope.[2]

As we noted above, the next saying: 'Provide yourselves with no gold or silver, not even with a few coppers for your purses, with no haversack for the journey or spare tunic or footwear or a staff, for the workman deserves his keep' (Matt. 10.9f. *JB*), is also perfectly expressive of an idea found in Jesus' contemporaneous Judaea, namely among the Essenes.[3]

---

[1] See for instance the context of the saying quoted above p.54 in bNed 37a. Note also the bitter reproach of R. Gamliel II by R. Yehoshua (fl. 80) soon after the establishment of Yavneh to the effect that the latter (as Nasi) had not been providing enough money to his assistants with the result that they had to work doubly hard to earn their living while also carrying out their official duties at the Center (bBer 28a). We should not conclude from this that Gamliel was providing no support for his associates. There is considerable evidence that this same Gamliel sent 'apostles' (*shelichim*) out into the Diaspora to collect money (the Temple Tax now going to Rome), at least part of which was to be used in maintaining the Center and its staff; Schürer, *History* II[2] 290; Büchler *Jewish Encyclopedia* s.v. 'apostoli'; M. Avi-Yonah, *Geschichte der Juden im Zeitalter des Talmud* (1962) 52–61; E. Urbach, op. cit. above on p. 12, 19f., 23f. See above, p. 12 n. 1, p. 12 n. 1.

[2] A careful history of this development, both among the Christian as well as among the Jewish communities, has not yet been written, although many misinformed assertions have been made about the matter. On the Pharisaic side, however, see most recently E. Urbach, op. cit. above n.20. One peculiarity of Urbach's presentation is his claim that the pre-Yavneh period saw only an informal, entirely gratuitous method of carrying out their various official functions by the Pharisees which does not seem to take into account the many examples he himself cites of such Pharisees holding highly-paid positions in Herod's administration (e.g., Hillel!) and various official posts after Herod's death straight down to the establishment of Yavneh. Furthermore, one would hardly expect the Romans to pick as their puppet government a group which had had no experience in governing.

[3] See above, p. 45.

F

The saying which concludes this verse, 'because the workman deserves his keep' (or 'food' as the Greek says), was not discussed above when we examined Luke 10.4 because Luke does not have it there. It should be clear, however, how perfectly it expresses the meaning of the so-called prohibitions regarding equipment for the journey. One might expect such a clear explanation (on Matthew's part) of the preceding word would make impossible such a wrong-headed interpretation of Matt. 10.9//Luke 10.4 as is usually found, namely, that Jesus is here actually *prohibiting* his disciples from having certain things. He is actually saying just the opposite! You can get anything you want—as you go! Such a mistaken interpretation seems to have arisen mostly because the text was broken into pieces, and Matt. 10.10b (the workman saying) was considered in isolation from its context. When that occurs, then Matt. 10.9–10a do look like prohibitions. However, splitting 9–10a from v.10b must first be justified, for it fits the preceding perfectly, precisely as its clarification. That Luke has it elsewhere has already been partly explained through our observation that the so-called prohibitions are given their original significance in the verse that *precedes* them, so he is free to use this saying later; but on this question more in a moment.

Next comes Jesus' instructions on how the disciples should behave in the villages they will pass through (vv. 11–15). The careful, even cautious, tone in these instructions concerning the Blessing (v. 13) is directly related to the second action the disciples are commanded to perform wherever they are *not* welcomed: 'If anyone will not receive you or listen to what you say, then as you leave that house or that town shake the dust of it off your feet. I tell you this: on the Day of Judgment it will be more bearable for the land of Sodom and Gomorrah than for that town' (Matt. 10.14f. *NEB*). The action Jesus here requires of his emissaries is nothing less than the eschatological curse. This is the meaning of wiping off the dust of the town's streets: 'we want no part of you, even the dust from your streets, *for you are to be utterly destroyed!*' What is being laid on the shoulders of the disciples is nothing less than the task of 'harvesting' (Matt. 9.38) the crop of the elect. Along with their authorization to pronounce the eschatological curse they will bring eschatological blessing.

It is remarkable how widespread is the opinion that vv. 12f.

is just the usual Semitic greeting-custom.[1] That something quite different is afoot is shown by the restriction of this 'greeting' solely to the 'worthy' (who are they?), even more by *calling it back* from the 'unworthy' (unheard of regarding mere greetings), but above all by this action being a parallel to what is explicitly an eschatological curse (v. 14 cp. Luke 10.10–12).[2]

It is fascinating to consider the assumption obviously lying behind these words of Jesus. Precisely in the reaction accorded his emissaries *and then openly effectuated in the concrete/symbolic gestures they give in return—stands the primordial, inscrutable election of Heaven.* Going from village to village, the disciples will flush out into the open, as it were, the concrete lineaments of the Final Decision regarding the actual individuals they meet. It will be a sort of rolling 'realized predestination'.[3] What is so interesting is the obvious assumption that this separation will take place, become visible, immediately. In other words, it almost seems as if the message of the nearness of the Kingdom *is a rallying cry for which a sizable number of Jesus' kinsmen were waiting.* Was there perhaps some sort of already-formed community with Jesus at its head? Might it have resembled the Essenes' in structure, 'living in camps' amongst the towns of Israel?

Whatever the answers to these questions might be, the full significance which this version, at any rate, accords their journey begins to emerge, and it becomes perfectly clear why they are required to be so cautious, even guarded, in their behavior. They are to make God's own eschatological judgment.[4] If this seems

---

[1] See, e.g., B. H. Throckmorton, *The Interpreter's Dictionary of the Bible,* art. 'Peace in the *NT*'; W. Foerster *TDNT* II s.v. *eirene.*

[2] A good illustration of this 'peace' comes from the Essene literature: the Time of salvation for the sons of truth 'will be healing and great peace in a long life, multiplication of progeny together with all everlasting blessings, endless joy in everlasting life, and a crown of glory' 1QS IV 6f., ed. Wernberg-Møller. See further E. Vogt, 'Peace Among Men of God's Good Pleasure (Luke 2.14)', in K. Stendahl, ed., *The Scrolls and the New Testament* (1957) 114–117.

[3] S. Holm-Nielsen finds an identical, surprisingly direct (one is tempted to say, naively concrete) understanding among the Essenes: precisely in being accepted into membership in the sect is proof of one's election among the Sons of Light; see *Hodayot. The Psalms of Qumran* (1960) 282 n.17, 284.

[4] In Matthew, this aspect of the activity of Jesus' disciples comes to light again in the heretofore widely misunderstood saying recorded at

impossible or even repugnant to modern ideas, it was not so unusual in Jesus' day. For example, certain leaders within the Qumran community had precisely the same task, as the following passage shows.

He [the Guide[1]] shall weigh the sons of righteousness according to their spiritual qualities. He shall keep hold of the chosen of time according to God's will as He commanded. He shall give everybody the treatment which is due to him according to his spiritual quality. He shall admit him according to his cleanness of hands [i.e. moral rectitude] and bring him near according to his insight. In this way (shall be guided) his love [approval] and his hatred [disapproval].[2]

As with Jesus, so now in a widening circle throughout the countryside, the eschatological Crisis, the Hour of Separation, *has come*. The disciples make present by their proclamation, by their blessings and by their cursings, God's impending yet primordial Decision. V. 16, which may be a saying added in the context by Matthew to make a transition to the following instructions, nevertheless well conveys both the sense of crisis as well as the tremendous requirement now laid upon the disciples: 'Behold, I send you out as sheep in the midst of wolves; so be wise as serpents and innocent as doves' (*RSV*).

Matt. 4.19 (Mark 1.17): 'Follow me, and I will make you [scil. in the context, Simon and his brother Andrew] *fishers of men*.' Since the discovery of the Qumran scrolls, the precise eschatological significance of this phrase has at last been determined. Cp., for example, 'Thou gavest me my dwelling among mighty fishers, they that spread their nets on the surface of the water, and *such as hunt the children of iniquity*' —in order to throw them into the Pit of eternal destruction! (1 QH V 8 ed. Holm-Nielsen). It is an image lifted from the store of arcane apocalyptic Judaism. On the whole subject, see now W. H. Wuellner, *The Meaning of 'Fishers of Men'* (1967); further, the unpubl. diss. (Harvard University 1963) by Robert J. Maddox, 'The Son of Man and Judgment', which demonstrates the close correlation in outlook between Matthew's special material (especially his Son of Man sayings) and the material in the Similitudes of I Enoch, where the major function of the Son of Man is precisely to bring eschatological Judgment.

[1] A. Dupont-Sommer, *The Essene Writings from Qumran* (Meridian ed. 1962) 95 n.1.
[2] 1QS IX 14f. ed. Wernberg-Møller; cp. V 20b–24. Further H. Ringgren, *The Faith of Qumran* (1963) 208ff.

(iv) The originality of Matthew's entire version compared to the other three accounts

If we consider Matthew's version as it compares with the account in Luke 10, the following points emerge. To begin with, the saying at the very end of Matthew's version (v. 16) appears at the beginning of Luke's, in v. 3, where it has been given a radically different meaning precisely by the transposition.[1] Next, working backward through Matthew's account, Luke has the material dealing with behavior in houses and towns in a different order than Matthew. Furthermore, it is considerably expanded. Also, as Klostermann notes, neither of Luke's versions (nor Mark's either, for that matter), contain any mention of the disciples' need for caution; instead, they are apparently told to stay in whatever house they happen to hit first, which seems very strange.[2] Then comes the double-saying about eating discussed above,[3] which in its present form is undoubtedly from Luke himself.

Now we must go further. Two other parts of this section seem to be expansions by Luke, vv. 9 and 11b. Klostermann explains that the use of direct speech in v. 11: ' "Even the dust of your town that clings to our feet, we wipe off against you",' is Luke's attempt to make more intelligible to a (presumably) Gentile audience an obscure Semitic curse-gesture. Interestingly enough, Matthew's account merely assumes this understanding. The continuation of v. 11 in Luke: ' "Nevertheless, know this, that the Kingdom of God is at hand" ', is not found in Matthew's version at all. Klostermann's opinion is that this is an intentional contrast to v. 9, to the effect: 'the Kingdom of God has come near, i.e., only *near*—it has not come *upon you*!'[4] I suggest, on the contrary, that this passage simply reflects Luke's missionary outlook, as elsewhere. The eschatological curse may indeed be at the very gates, but 'nevertheless,[5] . . . the Kingdom of God is also still at hand, i.e., open for those who will enter.'[6]

---

[1] See above, pp. 45f.   [2] Klostermann *Matt.* 87.
[3] See above, pp. 46f.   [4] Klostermann *Luke* 116.

[5] *Plen touto ginoskete hoti engiken he basileia tou theou.* On adversative *plen* see Bauer *Lexicon* s.v. 1 b: 'only, nevertheless, however, but, etc.' It is a conjunction which adversatively breaks off one point to emphasize what is really important. This shows that Luke is switching to a new thought to emphasize *over against* the Curse just pronounced.

[6] Precisely the same kind of alteration is visible elsewhere in Luke. In his account of the Parable of the Great Banquet (Luke 14.15–24//

In view of these things, therefore, I am inclined to consider
the whole of Luke 10.5–12 a thoroughly reworked version of the
account that is better attested in Matthew. This includes moving
the workman-saying from its original location in the non-prepara-
tion saying (Matt. 10.9f.) in order to place it in an 'eating' context
(Luke 10.7).[1] As for the opening saying in Matthew's version:

Matt. 22.1–10 The Parable of the Marriage Feast) Luke inserts a
second invitation to the originally uninvited 'poor, maimed and blind'
since after the first 'still there was room' (Luke 14.22). The original
parable told only of a decisive rejection of the original guests and one
invitation of the unworthy; J. Jeremias *The Parables of Jesus*[2] (1963) 64.
Thus the parable originally rested upon a powerful sense of imminent
crisis effectuating itself throughout Israel, after which it was too late.
Luke's explicit additional invitation must therefore be attuned to the
open-endedness of the then current Gentile mission. Conzelmann,
Theology of St. Luke 107, fails to discern the point of Luke 10.11b.

[1]As neither of these two claims is obvious, let us consider the
evidence for them. As to the original wording of this saying, there is
considerable uncertainty which is to be chosen. D. Daube points out
that 'Jesus' pronouncement . . . in Matthew appears in a far more
restrained version than in Luke: Matthew mentions a right to meat
only, Luke one to hire'; *New Testament* 396. Thus Klostermann
wonders if Matthew's 'restriction' is an intentional editorial change
directed against abuses caused by wandering prophets in the Church
(*Matt.* 87), such as are warned against in Didache 13. This implies, of
course, that Luke's is the original, and, indeed, Bultmann claims—
without any evidence—that the saying in Luke's formulation was a
current secular proverb picked up by the Church for use in its pro-
mulgation of the support regulation; *History of the Synoptic Tradition*
103. Preisker's finding with respect to the history of the usage of the
word 'wages' (*misthos*) supports Bultmann's claim to the extent that
Luke's version is the more natural as far as typical Jewish and pagan
workman/wages language of the period is concerned—even for sacred
'work'; *TDNT* IV 698f. s.v.

However, although the evidence is much too slim to warrant any
firm decision, I am inclined to oppose this view for three reasons.
First, Luke's location of this saying suggests that he had Matthew's
saying in his source. That is, Matthew's 'food' may lie behind Luke's
using the saying in an 'eating' context. The obvious retort to this
is, however, why then would Luke change the wording to 'wages?'
Second, we have observed editorial activity all through Luke's account,
and relatively little in Matthew's; therefore the balance of favor lies
with Matthew's version of the saying. This however is only a general
argument; the fact is, both sayings fit their present contexts equally
well. Hence, either could be original; cp. B. S. Easton *The Gospel
According to St. Luke* (1926) 160. Third, Daube's comment needs

'Freely you received, freely give,' we noted above how perfectly it expresses Pharisaic rejection of payment for the performance of religious duties.[1] It must be granted that, as such, it could be from Jesus (perhaps uttered on some other occasion), from the Jewish wing of the early Church (from which Matthew otherwise has so much material), or even from Matthew himself—simply one more indication of his familiarity with and preference for Pharisaic piety reformed along 'Christian' lines.[2] The difficulty

---

consideration. In view of Matthew's opening warning not to take *payment*, Luke's wording would be virtually unthinkable with its mention of 'wages'. Of course, the obvious answer to this is that Matthew simply changed the wording to 'food', and so we are back at the beginning. Furthermore, this reply is the more forcible in view of the likelihood that Matthew himself is responsible for the warning against payment (see below).

Of these three reasons, I feel the first two are the most persuasive. Some, however, raise the possibility that both versions were in circulation at the same time, e.g., H. Koester *Synoptische Ueberlieferung bei den apostolischen Vätern* (1957) 213. In any case, it appears that both versions meant more or less the same thing. Clearly, Matthew's did not originally restrict the disciples to food as its context shows, nor did Luke intend for 'wages' to be paid to the disciples. One further item of evidence remains to be considered, however, and that is the testimony of Paul; see below, p. 79.

[1] See above, pp. 54f.

[2] This is an appropriate point at which to express a certain sense of frustration produced by this entire analysis, but which our results regarding this particular saying bring to a head. By employing form-critical methods, we inevitably succumb to its chief defect—namely, its inability to pierce through 'the community'—whether Palestinian Jewish, or early Christian—to the individual probabilities of the historical Jesus. Although for this particular saying we may reach a conclusion as to its inauthenticity in our subsequent discussion, the fact is this 'inauthenticity' is logically limited solely to the context of the most original version of this account that we can form-critically reconstruct, and it indeed says nothing about the actual historical roots, either about the individual saying, or about the entire account as such. Here we must acknowledge the criticism of the peculiar bias of the form-critical method as a whole against *specific* historical occasions and individuals first brought forward by E. Fascher, *Die formgeschichtliche Methode* (1924). Cp. the discussion in V. Taylor, *The Formation of the Gospel Tradition*[2] (1935). Serious consideration must be given to the problem of finding a correlative method for breaking through this generalized 'community' toward specific occasions and individuals, once the broad-scale judgments have been clarified form-critically.

is, the saying as a rejection of *payment* clashes fundamentally with its context, for in the very next saying Jesus speaks about hospitality in such a way that all thoughts about pay or salary are simply out of the question. They are not even possibilities. We shall go into the reasons for this more fully in the next section. Suffice it for the present to point out that it is most puzzling to see Jesus strictly warn his disciples to take nothing (in payment) for what they are about to do, and then add in the very next breath that anything they need will be given to them—money, clothes, food, equipment. The two are in obvious tension.

In general, however, the conclusion is warranted that, as regards the accounts in Matt. 10.1–16 and Luke 10.1–12, Matthew's is definitely the more original. An outline of his version, as being that belonging in Q, would be something like the following:

(a) Charge to proclaim the nearness of the Kingdom and to heal, as visible proof the nearness of the Kingdom.
(b) Assurance that the brothers will see to all the disciples' needs.
(c) Injunction to stop over only among the worthy.
(d) Instruction to pronounce the eschatological blessing upon the worthy.
(e) And to pronounce the eschatological curse upon the unworthy.

This outline of the Q account is important, for it settles immediately the question as to the relative originality of the two other accounts, in Mark 6.7–11 and Luke 9.2–5. Once again, we must seriously question the received tradition as to Matthew's dependence upon Mark's version. As stated above, it is commonly held that Matthew's version is a conflation of Q with Mark plus some special material added by Matthew. Against this view, we are in a position to insist that in every respect: (a) location in the general outline of Jesus' 'career',[1] (b) grammatical structure, (c) the presence of Semitisms,[2] (d) the arrangement of the material within the pericope, and (e) in basic conception of the event itself,[3] Matthew is totally independent of Mark. Stated differently, where there are points of similarity between the two, there is not

---

[1] Beare 80; Lagrange 194; Streeter *Gospels* 274.
[2] See M. Black, *An Aramaic Approach to the Gospels*[3] (1967) 53, 100f.
[3] See above, p. 50 point (3).

one significant point of correspondence with Mark where Mark does not show that it is a heavily edited, or even 'mutilated' (Streeter), version of a more original account.

In short, Matthew's version best attests an account of very early origin, probably based upon certain actual events in Jesus' public activity, describing how on a certain occasion he sent his disciples on a flying tour through the farms and towns of Galilee to proclaim the Kingdom's imminence. Luke 10's version corresponds closely to Matthew's, but we found signs all through of editorial rearrangement, expansion, and interpolation. Luke 9's version is simply an abridgement of the Q account, apparently to conform to Mark's size and scope. The last named still remains to be considered, however. What prompted the author of Mark to make such drastic revisions of this account?

(v) *Mark's abridgement* (*Mark* 6.7–11)

As pointed out at the outset, there is general agreement that Mark's version of the mission instructions is an abridgement of an earlier longer account. The question is, what did he have in this longer account? In view of the similarity with the larger version in Matthew and Luke, many consider this to be an 'extract from Q.'[1] The more sophisticated, however, argue that Mark did not have access to Q,[2] and consequently speak here of an 'overlap'

---

[1] B. C. Bacon 65; cp. Montefiore I 120; in general J. P. Brown, 'Mark as Witness to an Edited Form of Q', *JBL* 80 (1961) 29–44.

[2] See, e.g., Streeter *Gospels* 186f., 242f., 305f. The real reason for the view that Mark did not know of Q is rarely stated. It does not stem so much from any actual evidence, but rather from the realization that if one did assume Mark had Q when he wrote, one would be unable to escape an insoluble, hopelessly complex riddle: *why did Mark omit so much of Q?* It is hopeless and insoluble for the simple reason that it is impossible scientifically to ascertain the contents of Q—much less go on to decide in case after case why Mark omitted certain passages in it; on this see especially the brilliant article by Stewart Petrie, ' "Q" is Only What You Make It,' *NovTest* 3 (1959) 28–33. The result is an extraordinarily cumbersome hypothesis of source relationships. The only reason some Synoptic critics still insist Mark had Q is simply because they never go beyond examinations of isolated passages here and there in the gospels, and work out in detail the full implications of the theory they have saddled themselves with. Incidentally, the same problem besets the Ur-Markus hypothesis. Both of them are essentially futile hypotheses, however attractive they may be for isolated sections of the text.

between the Q account and another one in Mark's special sources. B. H. Streeter, for instance, suggests that since 'Luke 10.1–12 (not being conflate with Mark) represents Q, the differences between Mark and Luke are so great and the resemblances are so few that they favour the view that Mark's version is independent, not derived from Q. *If Mark did use Q, he must have trusted entirely to memory and never once referred to the written source.*'[1] Another who does not think that Mark actually had Q itself before him is R. Bultmann. 'The missionary charges were very early or originally[2] formed into a connected group from which Mark has made excerpts, while Luke 10.2–12 *accurately reproduces it according to Q*, and Matt. 10.9–16 joins Mark and Q, and in the course of doing so Luke like Matthew adds all kinds of similar material.'[3] Of course, Bultmann here assumes the view he has elaborated earlier, namely, that these regulations are a creation of the Church to supervise its missionary activity,[4] but it is quite clear that both he and Streeter agree that Mark abridged an account closely resembling what we have reconstructed as the Q account. The upshot is that not much separates the disputants on this issue except the larger problem of Mark's knowledge of Q: one side claims Mark actually had the Q account, the other that he had another account very much like it. Hence, we may simply proceed with our reconstruction (see above p. 62) as a basis of comparison for what now stands in Mark.

Why such a shortened, 'mutilated' excerpt? Bultmann's

---

[1] *Gospels* 190 italics added. This ancient and honorable loop-hole begs for someone's critical scrutiny. With it, of course, virtually anything can be explained—*away*. For example, V. Taylor turns to it when he must account for the inexplicable, massive presence of Q material in Luke 9, where Luke is supposed to be faithfully following Mark. Well, says Taylor, what probably happened was that 'a few words and phrases [were] carried over by the memory' (*Luke* 87).

[2] 'Very early or originally'—note once again the fundamental slipperiness of the form-critical method when it comes to pin-pointing specific historical events. See above, p. 41.

[3] The italics have been added to indicate a faulty translation in the edition of J. Marsh, *The History of the Synoptic Tradition* 325. Marsh translated 'während Luke 10.2–12 *sie* genau nach Q bringt', 'while Luke 10.2–12 accurately reproduces Q', which completely obscures the fundamental distinction Bultmann makes between Q and the different, special material, whatever it was, upon which Mark drew for his version.

[4] Op. cit., previous note, 146.

explanation is that Mark, 'as an Hellenistic evangelist, . . . well knew that these instructions no longer applied to the mission in the *oikumene* [the wider Gentile world].'[1] Unfortunately, he does not attempt to elaborate further. It would be interesting to know what specifically Bultmann had in mind as having been omitted by Mark. For example, was he thinking of the remarkable transformation and limitation of the purpose of the Twelve's mission as such? One of the few commentators who has noticed something strange about Mark's version is V. Taylor.

Mark has no real appreciation of the immense importance of the event itself in the story of Jesus. . . . He records that the Twelve went out to preach, but does not relate their message apart from the phrase 'in order that they might repent' [in 6.12], and he has only vague ideas concerning their experiences and the results of the Mission. As Mark relates it, the incident is merely an extension of the teaching ministry of Jesus.[2]

Indeed, it is not even that, since Jesus' 'teaching ministry' was, as everyone knows, basically concerned with the advent of the Kingdom of God—but Mark has neatly cut away every trace of this particular theme. Taylor should have said that this 'incident' was merely an extension of Jesus *healing power* as Mark portrays it.

As a matter of fact, there does not seem to have been much attention paid to the question of whether Mark's abridgement is intelligible *as such*. Why did he preserve and omit what he did? The truth is, assuming that the version of these instructions which Mark had in his source more or less resembled our reconstruction, it becomes apparent, as Bultmann suggested, that Mark generally omitted anything hard to understand in the Gentile mission area.[3] For example, he kept the part of the opening charge concerned with healing (Matt. 10.7–8a//Luke 9.2), went on and

[1] Ibid. 145.
[2] *Mark* 302.
[3] With the possible exception of the basic transformation regarding the omission of any reference to the Kingdom of God; this does not look like such a simple emendation. Neither do I agree with Taylor that it is a result of Mark's insensitivity to 'the story of Jesus'; precisely the opposite. It is too pivotal an alteration for that. Rather, one must, in my view, look in the direction of a fully intentional, programmatic alteration, understandable only in terms of and furnishing a clue to the theological outlook of Mark's redaction as a whole.

used fully Jesus' suggestion to the disciples not to prepare for the journey,[1] continued with a brief instruction about staying in houses (Matt. 10.11a//Luke 9.4), omitting the Blessing instruction (Matt. 10.12f.//Luke 10.5f.) no doubt because it was unintelligible, and concluded with the advice on how to cope with hostility (Matt. 10.14//Luke 9.5; 10.10-11a) but leaving off the obscure reference to Sodom (and Gomorrah, Matt.) at the end (Matt. 10.15//Luke 10.12). The result is to be sure a 'pared down' (Hahn) mission charge, but it is not any the less intelligible for that. It is especially interesting to observe, for instance, how fully preserved the section dealing with non-provision of traveling necessities is. In fact, it is even expanded slightly—a clear sign of its importance in the eyes of the editor.

B.   CONCLUSION

This brings to a close our investigation of the relative originality of the four versions of the mission instructions preserved in the Synoptic gospels. We have tried to show that as regards Q, both in terms of structure and contents, Matthew's account is a much more accurate replica, and not Luke 10, as commonly thought. Luke 9 turned out to be mostly a revised copy of Q, apparently to bring it down to Mark's formal outline. In other words, it seemed to be a conflation of Q with Mark (in a rather peculiar way), and not a Markan block in Luke's outline—again as commonly thought. As regards Mark 6, on the other hand, our conclusions coincided with the usual view, namely, that Mark's is an abridgement of an account very similar (if not identical) with Q's. The most important new item gained concerning Mark's revision was a clear recognition of the radical transformation of this account so that it leaves out all mention that the Twelve's mission was to announce the nearness of the Kingdom of God.[2]

[1] In the process, he makes two 'corrections' and changes the whole into Indirect Discourse. Mark's editorial activity was not however, altogether successful grammatically; 'note the imperfect adjustment of the Greek of v.9 to indirect discourse' (Bacon 66; cp. Taylor *Mark* 304f.; further M. Black, *Aramaic Approach*[3] 216f.

[2] Although this entire discussion has been conducted within the framework of the classic Two-Document Hypothesis, and is not intended as a partisan contribution to the discussion of the Synoptic Problem recently resumed, it is, nevertheless, interesting to observe

We thus reach a conclusion to the first main question brought up at the beginning of this chapter, namely, what were the original form and contents of the account lying behind the Synoptic versions of the mission instructions. Before going on to the second main question, namely, what can be discerned about the editors' reaction to it by the way in which they have severally emended or altered the account, it might be a good idea to pause briefly and fix as precisely as possible what is actually said regarding support (as well as what is not said) in the original account.

2. *The character of the support to be accorded the disciples in the original account of the mission of the Twelve*

On the basis of our examination of the four versions of the mission instructions in the Synoptic gospels, we have isolated what appears to be the account underlying all four versions, most faithfully preserved in Matthew. As noted in the summary of it given above, it is an account of what appears to be a concerted effort on the part of Jesus to make visible the number of the elect, i.e., those prepared to welcome the Kingdom of God. Integral to, but obviously not standing out in, the account were a few words explaining how the disciples were to be cared for as they went along their journey.

Focusing only upon the latter, two facts seem obvious. First, it is basically nothing more than a matter of kinsman-hospitality: as they go through the Jewish communities of Galilee, they may expect board and room to be offered by the faithful. I think the

---

that this pericope fits perfectly the Griesbachian hypothesis. Matthew is original. Luke took the account from Matthew and made a shortened excerpt for the Mission of the Twelve since, in his architectonic scheme, it was merely a historical event with no further significance. He saved most of the material for a second account, the Mission of the Seventy-Two, carefully revising, clarifying, and updating it to speak to the needs of the Gentile Mission. Finally Mark, for reasons we will clarify in a moment, selected the shorter version in Luke, rewriting even that. For those uninitiated in the mysteries of Griesbachian interpretation of the Synoptic accounts, see especially W. M. L. Dewette, *An Historical Introduction to the Canonical Books of the New Testament*, trans. F. Frothingham (5th German ed., 1858); and more recently, W. R. Farmer, *The Synoptic Problem* (1964) 199–283. On this pericope, see further F. C. Baur, *Kritische Untersuchungen* 46of., 469f., 543.

Essene parallel is precisely the same idea, nor is this just a coincidence. Second, and here we refer to the 'non-provision' passage, the journey is apparently to be so brief and so small in geographical scope—no doubt limited just to Galilee[1]—that Jesus confidently assures the disciples that *whatever* they need, the brethren will take care of them. This also follows from Josephus' description of the Essene custom of freely providing for every need of the traveling brethren.

Therefore, *completely excluded is any notion of salary*. That is to say, nothing in the original account envisions anything like remuneration for performing the mission, or remuneration for wages lost while performing the mission. The eschatological fervor so visible in the instructions themselves, the informal basis of the housing and feeding of the apostles, but above all, the once-for-all character of this trip, all these factors make it impossible that anything like the institution of a salary for the apostles is in view. By the same token, the original account did not include any warning against abusing the hospitality offered to them, nor instructions concerning the foods that might be given them, nor injunctions against begging from door to door. All such warnings stem from a later period, when the Church encountered various problems as it tried to make use of this original account.

For when this account became transposed out of the situation and circumstances of its original setting in Jesus' public activity into that of the early Church, it had to be altered considerably. Both the rationale as well as the basis for such alteration is, of course, given in the fact that the Church was not interested in preserving a merely historical account of the original details of this mission. Rather, it was remembered and passed on as a paradigmatic event, a model for the life of the Church. This is how the gospel editors understood it. Thus it was only natural that they should lessen the emphasis upon the geographical and temporal specificity of the original account, so that its scope became completely indefinite—or embraced the entire world (of 72 nations) as in Luke 10. By the same token, the requirements of the Church's situation demanded that the original informal, hospitality-basis for the care of the Church's apostles be regularized and put on a solid, continuing basis—i.e., a salary basis—to be in effect as long as the Church would endure. But then his shift opened up

[1] See above, p. 52 n.1.

numerous possibilities for abuse, misunderstanding, and controversy that were not there before, and so the editors included what each felt to be the proper safeguards. Precisely in these redactional alterations do the individual attitudes of each editor become visible.

3. *The attitudes of the gospel editors toward this issue.*

We are now ready to answer the second main question of this chapter: what can we discern about the gospel editors' own attitude toward this regulation?

A. MATTHEW

Most commentators agree that Matthew has interpolated the saying in 10.8b: 'You received without pay, give without pay.' This little phrase, with its concern over possible mercenary motivations among the apostles, moves entirely within the sphere of salary thinking, and thus seems quite out-of-place within the outlook and presuppositions of the original account. Its location at the very head of the words regarding support, indeed, transforms their whole meaning, or rather, distorts it, by interposing thoughts of money into a context of hospitality.

In fact, it is not clear just what this addition of Matthew means —in the context. What does it do to the entire account? Perhaps an answer to this question can be found from a very interesting use of the same saying in a passage in the *Pseudo-Clementine Homilies*.[1] The apostle Peter is giving advice to a certain congregation which is about to appoint a pastor. He comes to the delicate question of the prospective bishop's support.

My brothers, there are things you yourselves should decide what it is right to do without waiting to be told by others. How is [your pastor-to-be] Zacchaeus going to buy the necessary food for himself if he devotes himself fully to spiritual labor among all of you? Even though he, too, has a belly, he will not have time to provide for it. Is it not therefore reasonable that you take some forethought for his life and not

[1] This is a writing from the milieu of early Syriac Christianity, dating roughly from the early third century; see J. Quasten, *Patrologia* I 6of.

wait until he has to ask you? That would be begging and he would prefer to die of hunger than submit to that. But then you yourselves would have to submit to God's punishment because you did not remember [how it is written], 'For the workman is worthy of his wages'. Now let none of you reply *'the Word which was freely given is going to be sold!'*[1] God forbid! When someone takes support who has the means for a living, it is he who sells the Word. But whoever accepts support because he does not have the means for a living, as even the Lord took food at meals and lived among friends (He who alone possesses all things), such a man does not sin. (*Hom.* III 71, my trans.)

Note the way these two sayings play off against one another. I suggest that this is a crystal clear illustration of the effect of Matthew's interpolation in the original account. It means giving the spiritual leader *anything* by way of financial assistance is to turn the Word of God into something to be bought and sold. As we saw from the Jewish parallels cited above,[2] this is the standard Pharisaic viewpoint. And it is most interesting to see that Peter does not deny this viewpoint outright. Rather, he makes a remarkable compromise based upon a distinction among bishops. A bishop who is independently wealthy sins if he demands (or accepts) support. Conversely, the people sin if they do not provide a poor bishop with his needs. This is precisely Paul's own solution, only stated in reverse. Where Paul weighed the relative wealth of congregations, Peter's advice is geared to the relative wealth of bishops. These might even be the two sides of one and same policy.

However that may be, we can see that the general effect of Matthew's interpolation was to constrict the original open-endedness in hospitality. The result is a fully new account, wherein the Lord ordains that minimal financial assistance be given the Church's apostles. As for other editorial changes, however, none are clearly visible. As the examination above showed, the rest seems to be a largely intact account containing very early tradition, which in turn probably rests upon certain events that occurred in the public activity of Jesus.

[1] Greek *oukoun ho dorean paraschetheis logos poleitai?*
[2] See above, pp. 54f.

B. LUKE

Luke's editorial alterations of the original account are far more complex than Matthew's. In the first place, the most obvious problem is why Luke repeated the story twice, in such different forms. As we saw from our discussion of Luke 9.1–5, Luke seems to be following the outline-structure of Mark's account, at the same time rejecting Mark's drastic alterations in favor of Q's material. The motivation behind this complex stance vis-à-vis Mark cannot, in my opinion, be explained with the evidence we now have.[1] The rationale for Luke's second account, the sending of the Seventy-two, is much easier to perceive, as many commentators agree. Luke was not very interested in the mission of the Twelve, seeing it purely in historical terms (i.e., as a past event having no further significance), and so he repeated the story in the form of another mission that more adequately spoke as a paradigm for the mission of the Church in the world. In repeating the account, he carefully worked over it.[2]

Many aspects of Luke's editorial revision of this account have been pointed out in the discussion above. For example, we concluded that Luke had recast the section on staying in houses so as to make room for a command that the apostles give up insisting on kosher foods wherever they went. We noticed other revisions which seemed intended to make this account communicate more clearly to audiences not familiar with Palestinian Jewish apocalyptic ideas.

As far as those changes which reveal Luke's own attitude toward the particular matter of support for apostles are concerned, however, we must now face a very peculiar fact. Surprisingly enough, Luke has Jesus later on in the gospel repudiate this

[1]At least, not within the assumptions of the Two-Document Hypothesis; but see next note.

[2]As noted on p. 66 n. 2, in contrast to the Two-Document Hypothesis, the phenomena in Luke 9 and 10 are easily explained on the Griesbach hypothesis. Luke excerpted Matthew's account making a brief account concerning the sending of the Twelve, and then used Matthew's account fully, extensively revising it, for the much more important mission of the Seventy-Two. This hypothesis also clears up the mysteries of Luke 9's account. It is not dependent upon Mark at all. The formal similarity to Mark 6 is due to *Mark's utilization of Luke 9*—with the revisions he introduced to bring the story into line with *his* concerns.

G

whole notion. We saw how, by prefacing the section on non-provision for the journey with the saying about sheep in the midst of wolves, Luke shows that he readily understood the saying about not taking any provisions for the journey as signifying that the brethren would see to all the various needs of the apostles. But then during the Last Supper, Luke has Jesus explicitly rescind this earlier instruction.

He said to them, 'When I sent you out without purse or haversack or sandals,[1] were you short of anything?' 'No,' they said. He said to them, 'But now if you have a purse, take it; if you have a haversack, do the same; if you have no sword, sell your cloak and buy one.'[2]

Thus 'Luke can distinguish between those commands of the Lord which were meant only for the contemporary situation [and those meant to be permanently in effect]. . . . The directions concerning equipment given when the apostles are sent out, . . . in Luke 22.35–37 are explicitly annulled for the period to follow', i.e., Luke's own period.[3] Although the new instructions do not say it in so many words, it is clear that Luke intends Jesus to imply that, henceforth, little or no support would be forthcoming for apostles. Each one had better have his own purse—with his own money in it!

If this is Luke's intention, then he has clearly gone beyond Matthew who only limits severely the original extent of support. Luke apparently wanted to abolish the practice altogether. Is there any confirmation in the rest of Luke's material that this really was his intention?

There is indeed. Luke explicitly returns to this subject in Acts, in Paul's farewell oration to the Ephesian elders at Miletus.[4] In a scene vividly recalling (and therefore perhaps modelled upon) the aged Samuel's parting speech to the people of Israel,[5] Paul

[1] Luke absentmindedly has Jesus refer back to instructions he gave, not to the Twelve, but to the Seventy-Two (cp. 9.3//10.4).
[2] Luke 22.35f. *JB*.
[3] H. Conzelmann *Theology* 13; cp. 187 note.
[4] Conzelmann seems to have overlooked the significance of this passage for his interpretation of Luke 10.3f., and 22.35ff.
[5] 1 Sam. 12, especially the reference to money, v.3; Conzelmann *Die Apostelgeschichte* (1963) 119.

takes up the matter of financial support and roundly declares that he never wanted *nor received* financial assistance from anyone.

I have never asked[1] anyone for money or clothes; you know for yourselves that the work I did earned enough to meet my needs and those of my companions. I did this to show you that this is how we must exert ourselves to support the weak, remembering the words of the Lord Jesus, who himself said, 'There is more happiness in giving than in receiving.'[2]

If the author of Acts knew anything of Paul's financial relations with the Philippian congregation, he chose to ignore it. He even brings forth a new saying of the Lord[3] to repudiate a second time the notion of congregations supporting apostles.

As H.-J. Degenhardt observes, the misrepresentation of Paul's real viewpoint and activity is considerable.[4] Paul is here put forward as the staunch advocate of glorious financial independence. I think Degenhardt is correct in suggesting, however, that Luke is not really insisting that the apostles of the Church must henceforth support themselves as had Paul. Rather, it is more likely that Paul is simply being portrayed here in vivid hues as the general ideal they should emulate.[5] The saying of the Lord, in fact, points directly to this conclusion since it is not really antithetical[6] but

---

[1] *Epithymein*—'long for, lust after, desire (sexually)', Bauer *Lexicon* s.v. The *JB* translation is not quite appropriate.

[2] Acts 20.33–35 *JB*.

[3] The correct translation of this saying of the Lord is considerably disputed. For the translation here adopted, and with the necessary references to the pagan history-of-religions background, see H. Conzelmann loc. cit., above p. 72 n. 5 ; further E. Haenchen *Die Apostelgeschichte* (1959) 526f. Opposed is J. Jeremias, *Unknown Sayings of Jesus* (1957) 77–81.

[4] 'It is remarkable that Luke has not pointed out how extraordinary it was, as Paul himself does when, in 2 Cor. 11.7–12, he singles it out as his special boast over against his enemies, that he became a burden to no one in the community'; *Lukas-Evangelist der Armen. Besitz und Besitzverzicht in den lukanischen Schriften* (1965) 175. Degenhardt rightly goes on to point out that Paul knows of a command of the Lord that apostles should be supported. For a discussion of the probability that the speech in Acts is entirely the work of Luke, see Haenchen, op. cit. above (n. 3), 524.

[5] Degenhardt, op. cit. 175.

[6] Against Jeremias, op. cit. above (n. 3).

comparative.[1] Luke's basic position is therefore something like advocacy of rigorous 'self-control' (Degenhardt), a position which, after all, comes out in practice rather close to Matthew's.[2]

C. MARK

We proposed an hypothetical rationale for Mark's revision of his account.[3] One significant feature of Mark's edition is that he seems to have singled out precisely the instructions regarding support to preserve most fully, while truncating or letting go nearly everything else. What about the changes he introduced regarding the equipment for the journey?[4] They are rather difficult to explain. Perhaps these so-called Markan permissions regarding staff and sandals mean that Mark took these instructions literally (i.e., as actual prohibitions) and, considering it wrong that the Church's apostles (or other leaders, see below) should look like penniless beggars, altered the instructions accordingly. It is quite possible that the original saying had confused many in this way.[5]

[1] Degenhardt, op. cit., 175.

[2] It is difficult to put aside the suspicion that this speech of Paul's is actually based directly on 1 Cor. 9. The curious reference to 'the weak' —completely unmotivated in this context—and especially Paul's claim that he has 'never' accepted support from anyone (precisely the one-sided impressed one gets from reading 1 Cor. 9), all are very peculiar reappearing here.

[3] See above, pp. 63ff.   [4] See above, p. 50.

[5] Taylor's observation that Mark made the exceptions since 'traveling barefoot and without a staff was strange to Western readers', may be quite correct. His continuation, 'the more rigid prohibitions of Matt. and Luke are doubtless more original' (*Mark* 304) is also partly correct, the reference to the 'rigidity' of the 'prohibitions' showing that Taylor has not rightly understood the intention of the passage as a whole. The possibility that Mark's version is the result of a mistranslation has been ruled out by M. Black; 'No example could make it plainer that Mark is not here simply translating or mistranslating; he is stating quite definitely that the staff was to be an exception. Perhaps the ultimate source of the contradiction may have been in the confusion in Aramaic of the words for "neither" and "except" or "but" and "neither". But it is likewise possible that Mark is here giving a purely Greek version of the saying, influenced, it may be, by the staff and sandals of the wandering Sophist. At any rate, what we have in Mark is not literal translation nor ignorant mistranslation, but probably considered interpretation, the work, not of a translator but of a Greek writer' (*Aramaic Approach to the Gospels*[3] 216).

Regardless of this alteration, however, it is still true that the saying means all shall be supplied apostles on arrival: tunics, food, lodging, money, etc. (Mark 6.8), as originally intended in the Q instructions. What is new is that Mark understands these instructions from Jesus to apply to the Church, viz., the Church is fully responsible for the support of its leaders. Whether Mark is actually thinking of apostles, however, is another question; we shall consider it in the next and final section. But it is clear that Mark stands out in sharp contrast to the other two Synoptic editors and Paul in this regard, and that demands an explanation. Perhaps by bringing all our results together, we may see how each illuminates the purposes and motivations of the others.

CHAPTER FOUR

Paul and the Editors of the Synoptic Gospels

It is remarkable how closely the problems revealed in the Church by a form-critical analysis of the Synoptic mission instructions correspond with the situation we see directly in Paul's letters concerning the same issue. On the one side, all of Paul's anger at those who abused this apostolic prerogative, his caution and even abstinence, can be perfectly seen mirrored in Matthew's drastic curtailment of this account's original scope and Luke's decisive repudiation of it altogether. On the other side, Paul does know of the legitimacy of this regulation *as a command from the Lord*.[1] Here also he joins with the Synoptic editors who, in spite of their modifications, nevertheless have preserved this command of the Lord as a guideline for the Church's life—at least in the case of Matthew and Mark. Thus Paul is a marvelously direct illumination upon our necessarily hypothetical references to the *Sitz im Leben* of the Synoptic accounts in their present form.

We asked earlier whether Paul's reaction was atypical. Now we know that it was not. On the other hand, it is worth noting that although Paul could be violently aroused by those who in his eyes abused this regulation, and who could frequently set it aside, was apparently not moved to give up the regulation as such. One might think he would like to; he certainly hated those who misused it enough to be inclined to abolish *their* use of it. But Paul does not react against the regulation itself. When he is citing the various reasons justifying his possession and potential use of this regulation in 1 Cor. 9, he does so straightforwardly and with a touch of emphasizing the obvious—not at all allowing the strong negative feelings we know he had about this authority to overflow in such a way that he moves to curtail the contents of the actual regulation itself.

In any case, it is clear that the Church was quite early forced to protect itself from the vagueness and open-endedness of this

---

[1] By this we mean specifically that it was among the traditions Paul received, which came to him from the Jerusalem or the Antioch community (or both), and their collections of memories and sayings of Jesus.

particular saying of the Lord. Indeed, a critical, even suspicious, note soon crept in, as we can see from this passage in Didaché about what to do when visited by an apostle.

Now you should welcome anyone who comes your way and teaches you all we have been saying. But if the teacher proves himself a renegade and by teaching otherwise contradicts all this, pay no attention to him. But if his teaching furthers the Lord's righteousness and knowledge, welcome him as the Lord.
Now about apostles and prophets: act in line with the gospel precept. Welcome every apostle on arriving, as if he were the Lord. But he must not stay beyond one day. [!] In case of necessity, however, the next day, too. If he stays three days, he is a false prophet. On departing, an apostle must not accept anything save sufficient food to carry him to his next lodging. If he asks for money, he is a false prophet.[1]

This passage is most instructive, for it tallies well with the outlook of Matthew, Luke and Paul: apostles were a problem (financially) for the Church. But the continuation in Didaché is equally illuminating. After quite literally throwing a bone to wandering apostles, it has this to say about another group of Church leaders, *who are obviously displacing the apostles.*

Every genuine prophet who wants to settle with you 'has a right to his support' [Greek: 'food' i.e., Matt. 10.10]. Similarly, a genuine teacher, just like a 'workman, has a right to his support'. Hence take all the first fruits of vintage and harvest, and of cattle and sheep, and give these first fruits to the prophets, *for they are your high priests*. If you have no prophet, give them to the poor. If you make bread, take the first fruits and give in accordance with the precept. Similarly, when you open a jar of wine or oil, take the first fruits and give them to the prophets. Indeed, of money, clothes, and of all your possessions [!] take such first fruits as you think right, and give in accordance with the precept.[2]

The Church is clearly shown here—at least in Syria—in a remarkable mid-metamorphosis. The older office of apostles is still, vestigially, revered and represented, but a newer office complete with a new image—the resident priest—is rapidly moving into the vacuum in the center of the Church's leadership.

---

[1] Did. 11.1–6 ed. C. Richardson.
[2] Did. 13 ed. C. Richardson, italics added.

Most significant for our purposes, however, is the revealing way in which the workman saying no longer is used about apostles but about resident spiritual leaders. Precisely the same shift is visible in one of the pseudo-Pauline letters, 1 Tim. 5.17: 'Let the elders who rule well be considered worthy of double honor, especially those who labor in preaching and teaching; for the Scripture says, "You shall not muzzle an ox when it is treading out grain", and "the laborer deserves his wages".' It clearly seems as if the Synoptic mission account came, perhaps around the turn of the century, to refer to *the resident bishop/elder*.

This may be an explanation for the peculiar aspects of Mark's version. Perhaps Mark has omitted all references to proclaiming the Kingdom of God because he does not want to resurrect the old association between this story and apostles. By the same token, he has no restrictions on the support provision, just as in Did. 13, precisely because he is not thinking of apostles at all but resident clergy, i.e., priests. Whatever the actual rationale may have been, the well-known fact is that by the turn of the century bishops were being supported and the earlier stage of opposition and resistance to this regulation disappeared entirely, once the apostles died away and new offices rose to take their place.[1]

Now we are ready to consider the very complex problem, where did Paul come by the metaphors he uses in arguing the validity of this regulation, and, in particular, what was the exact wording of the saying of the Lord he refers to in 1 Cor. 9.14? Did Paul know of anything resembling what we now have preserved in one of the Synoptic gospels? The answer is a definite yes.

To begin with, the image of the 'workman', found in the Q account, is the same basic metaphor in Paul's argument in Chapter 9.[2] That is, the workman saying *specifically* may well have been

[1] In this case, Mark would represent either a very early sign of the trend in this direction, or simply reflect the state of things (perhaps at Rome) shortly after the turn of the century. By mid-century, even the Montanists were paying salaries to their prophets, or, at least so Eusebius claims, who then smugly reproaches them for greed by quoting Matt. 10.9 against them. But then the Church and money have always been in tension, cp. *Apost. Const.* II 4, 25: the bishop should 'not be muzzled' while he is treading out the grain, but on the other hand, he is 'not supposed to eat it all up' either! *ANF* VII 409.

[2] Cp. Hahn, *Mission* 40, for the interesting suggestion as to the origin of the term 'worker'. He suggests that it is a missionary image drawn from the saying concerning the 'workers and the harvest', which is related in turn to the image of 'fishers of men'.

the basis of Paul's series of proofs in 1 Cor. 9.7–11, for they all illuminate different aspects of this saying. Thus, most commentators give this workman saying, as the actual saying of Jesus presupposed by the command of the Lord to which Paul refers in 1 Cor. 9. 14.

But here we return to the old question discussed at some length above, *which version of it?*[1] Matthew's or Luke's? Many overlook this problem entirely,[2] and those who don't tend to favor Luke's version as the one Paul knew.[3] The fact is, however, when Paul actually specifies what his authority consists in, he seems to be referring precisely to the Matthean version. He says that he has 'the authority [to be provided with something to] eat and drink' (9.4). Furthermore, this specific idea of 'food' appears again in the priest-Levite analogy, which is the actual point at which Paul introduces the command of the Lord in that peculiarly subordinating manner.[4] The whole point of that analogy is that the priests and Levites were entitled to get their *food* from the Temple's sacrifices. Putting this 'food' emphasis together with the reliance upon the 'workman' image throughout the rest of his argument, it is difficult to conclude otherwise than that Matthew's version of the saying, 'the workman is worthy of his food', is the saying Paul is assuming in 1 Cor. 9.14. *If* Paul is presupposing any saying now known from the Synoptic material[5] and *if* it is the workman saying as most think, then it would have to be Matthew's not Luke's version. This means that an independent line of argument is available to support the relative originality of the Matthean version over against Luke, insofar as Paul is a witness to a very early stage of this particular saying.[6]

[1] See above, p. 60.

[2] For instance, W. D. Davies *Paul and Rabbinic Judaism*[2] (1962) 140; Robertson-Plummer 187; J. Weiss 239; Bultmann *Theology* I 62; von Campenhausen *Begründung* 25 n.52.

[3] E.g, Allo 219; Moffatt 120.

[4] See above p. 16f. B. Gerhardsson can split off 9.14 from 9.13 only by ignoring the opening conjunction, 'and thus also', in v. 14; see *Memory* 317f.

[5] But see Allo 219.

[6] Héring is one of the few who refers 1 Cor. 9.14 to Matt. 10.10 'or . . . the whole group of recommendations in Matt. 10.8–14', but, as usual, without any explanation; see p. 73. The range of points of contact between traditions peculiar to Matthew and sayings of the Lord in Paul's possession is a most interesting phenomenon. See e.g., C. H.

Finally, one other characteristic of Paul's use of this command of the Lord must be noted. As J. Weiss observed, Paul merely refers to the saying of Jesus, he does not actually quote it. And this means that 'Paul therefore assumes that the wording is familiar to the Corinthians'.[1] What Weiss is calling to our attention is a certain allusiveness in the way Paul uses this command of the Lord. Indeed, we should gauge carefully the full extent of this allusion, for, as we have just noted, Paul *seems to be alluding to it all the way through the rest of his argument, besides at the very end where he refers to it directly.* The strongly homiletical, not to say rhetorical, character of his argument now becomes even more obvious. To the Corinthians, already quite aware of this saying and its general application in the life of the Church (scil., to ordain support for apostles), Paul's whole argument would have seemed as nothing more striking than an artistic elaboration on the two aspects of this proverb: workman and food. The concluding, abrupt switch to the priest-Levite analogy in v. 13 would then have been no more than special Pauline grace-note for added emphasis, brought in—with all of its rich connotations—at the point of association with 'food'. In short, Paul's allusiveness or indirectness in the way he uses sayings of the Lord stands out most clearly, at least in this case, precisely when he expressly cites one.

Dodd, 'Matthew and Paul' (1947) in idem *New Testament Studies* (1953) 53–66; further J. P. Brown, 'Synoptic Parallels in the Epistles and Form-History', *NTS* 10 (1963/64) 27–48.

As far as this particular case goes, there may be one more echo of Matthew's account in Paul's words. Later, in writing 2 Cor. 10–13, Paul remarks sarcastically that he had 'preached the Gospel free of charge' *dorean . . . euengelisamen* (2 Cor. 11.7). It may of course be just a coincidence, but is it possible that we have here Matthew's *dorean dote* (Matt. 10.8)?

[1] J. Weiss 239; cp. Gerhardsson *Memory* 318.

PART II

The Lord's Command Concerning Divorce

'As for those of you who are already married, I command—not I but the Lord—the wife not to separate from her husband . . . and the husband not to divorce his wife'. (1 Cor. 7.10f.)

In Part I, we discovered that Paul could oppose and disregard a widely-held church regulation because of the abuses keeping to it could cause. The fact that this regulation was in part based upon an explicit command of the Lord seemed to make no difference whatever.

We tried to discern some of the reasons why Paul took this course over against the command of the Lord and the regulation founded upon it, and in the process, disclosed the fact that a rather sizeable proportion of the leadership contemporaneous with him, including the editors of the Gospels of Matthew and Luke, felt the same way Paul did and had adopted the same or a similar position vis-a-vis this command of the Lord.

Now let us turn to a second case where Paul explicitly refers to a command of the Lord in order to guide the life of the Church. Let us hope that things are not so complicated this time! Indeed, we may well expect matters to be simpler, to judge from the usual commentaries' discussions of Paul's reference to the Lord's prohibition of divorce in 1 Cor. 7.10f. According to them, everything is quite straightforward and above-board: in the course of a series of inter-related decisions concerning marriage, Paul at one point inserts a command of the Lord to the effect that the Corinthians should not seek divorces, and then hurries on to other problems.

Unfortunately, however, the simplicity and brevity of Paul's use of this command of the Lord is quite deceptive. If anything, this case of Paul's use of a command of the Lord is even more complex and enigmatic than the last one. For example, what is Paul doing, having just emphatically urged every member of the Corinthian church to get married and in addition, not deny, except only for brief periods of time spent in prayer, any of the

82 THE COMMAND CONCERNING DIVORCE

sexual relations appropriate to marriage—so as not to give Satan a chance to tempt anyone to fornication, what is Paul doing here in v. 10 permitting a woman who has just gotten a divorce to remain separated indefinitely? Or again, if we pause to look carefully at what Paul says in the midst of quoting this command of the Lord:

> To the married I give charge, not I but the Lord, that the wife should not separate from her husband (*but if she does, let her remain single or else be reconciled to her husband*)—and that the husband should not divorce his wife. (1 Cor. 7.10f. *RSV* italics added)

a startling fact appears: Paul—in the midst of quoting a command of the Lord—applies it in such a way as flatly to contradict it! The Lord's command is: no divorce. But Paul's ruling is: let the woman divorce and remain single. There is no explanation whatever, and it is all so brief one cannot help having the uncanny feeling that one has not read the text aright. Surely something is taking place beneath the surface of the text which accounts for this strange manner of using the Lord's prohibition of divorce! Indeed, there is, but, as with the case we just finished discussing, we must proceed cautiously or the explanation will surely escape us.

CHAPTER ONE

Paul's Instructions on Marriage

As the outline of 1 Corinthians shows, the whole second half of the letter is made up of a series of separate discussions in which Paul takes up, one after the other, specific problems confronting the Corinthians. Thus he begins here in 7.1ff. with various questions pertaining to marriage, then at 8.1ff. he turns to the problem of eating meat offered to idols, at 12.1ff. to the subject of spiritual gifts, and at 16.1ff. to the contribution for the Jerusalem church.

Our concern is with his discussion of marriage and its related problems in Chapter 7. After a brief statement of the basic question of whether marriage is permissible at all (7.1–7), he then makes several subsidiary judgments concerning second marriages (7.8f.), divorce (7.10f.), and marriages with unbelievers (7.12–16). After these, he rises to a larger consideration of the ultimately unessential place of marriage—and all other merely human institutions, such as the slave/free distinction—in a world soon to be annihilated (7.17–24). He then picks up the question whether it is preferable not to be married. By this time, however, he has gone beyond the section relevant to this study, so we shall take leave of his discussion at that point. Let us begin, then, with Paul's opening remarks on marriage, and work toward the passage where he turns to the command of the Lord regarding divorce.

1. *Marriage is recommended for all* (1 Cor. 7.1–7)

In v. 1, two problems have attracted the attention of commentators: the source of the phrase, 'it is best for a man not to touch a woman', and what is meant by 'touch a woman'. Regarding the first problem, it is generally held that Paul is quoting from the letter sent by the Corinthians; i.e., this phrase is theirs, not his. Paul quotes it in order to specify what he is about to discuss among the many questions they raised in their letter.[1]

[1] So, e.g., J. Jeremias, 'Zur Gedankenführung in den paulinischen Briefen', *Studia Paulina in honorem J. de Zwaan* (1953) 151; Allo 153;

As to the second problem, namely, what 'touch a woman' means, debate centers around the question whether it means having sexual relations or whether it means no more than simply being married. Those who hold to the latter,[1] however, must ignore considerable philological evidence to the contrary, i.e., that this was a commonly used euphemism for sexual intercourse.[2] The argument is not completely academic, for the specificity of meaning is actually quite relevant in view of the fact that both Paul and the Corinthians favored marriages within which no sexual contact took place (see below).

The most important thing to note about the way Paul begins this discussion of marriage, however, is the fact that Paul *agrees* with this statement, this quote from the Corinthians' letter. This aspect of v.1 is well brought out by Moffatt's translation: 'It is indeed "an excellent thing for a man to have no intercourse with a woman".'[3] In short, Paul opens his section on marriage with a curt expression of his personal opposition to all sexual relations. As he says, several verses later, 'I wish everyone were like I am'— i.e., *celibate*.

'With the ascetics, Paul recognizes the value of celibacy for the sake of service for the Lord (7.32–35); but he has to remind them that celibacy is a gift and not a general requirement.'[4] Apparently some of the Corinthians, if we ponder the sentence quoted from their letter, were trying to assure the purity and spirituality of their congregation by advocating a ban on all sexual intercourse. As we saw, Paul is sympathetic to their aspirations. However, freedom from the desire for and the act of sexual intercourse was the ideal, and not everyone could attain to it. Not

---

Robertson-Plummer 130; J. J. von Allmen *Pauline Teaching on Marriage* (1963) 13, 56; Ph.-H. Menoud, 'Mariage et célibat selon Saint Paul', *RevTheolPhil* 3. ser. 1 (1951) 27 n.1; H. von Campenhausen, *Begründung* 20 n.37.

[1] E.g., Allo 153f.; J. B. Lightfoot 221; Robertson-Plummer 132.

[2] It occurs in the LXX, Josephus as well as pagan literature; see Bauer *Lexicon* s.v. *hapto* 2 a 2. So also Lietzmann-Kümmel 29; E. Kähler, *Die Frau in den paulinischen Briefen* (1960) 204 n.7. For further bibliographical references, see Hurd 158–63.

[3] Moffatt 75; cp. H. H. Rex, 'An Attempt to Understand 1 Cor. 7', *RefTheolRev* 14 (1955) 42; Allo 154; further von Campenhausen, 'Die Askese im Urchristentum', in idem *Tradition und Leben* (1960) 141ff.

[4] Menoud 'Mariage' 27.

everyone is free from this desire and hence able to avoid seeking occasions to fulfill it. In fact, as earlier passages in 1 Corinthians vividly show, serious moral lapses seem to have been found among the church members. Consequently any blanket advocacy of abstinence was nothing more than an invitation to disaster.[1] Because of the concrete realities of the actual membership of the Corinthian congregation, therefore, in 7.2ff. Paul erects a physical barrier—spelled out with extraordinary explicitness—against any further depredations of the all-too-obvious power of Satan in their midst. Since the majority do not possess the Spirit's gift of continence, marriage shall be as widely used as possible in order to prevent any occasion for fornication to occur (cp. 1 Cor. 6.15ff.).

Not only that, but, continues Paul, you shall not exercise any restraints over your sexual activity within the marriage!

The husband must give to his wife what she has the right to expect, and so too the wife to the husband. The wife has no rights over her own body; it is the husband who has them. In the same way, the husband has no rights over his body; the wife has them. (1 Cor. 7.3f. *JB*)

The incredible, indeed repulsively external, character of Paul's requirement, the mechanical sexuality envisioned for these marriages, is almost emetic in its conception.[2]

As strange as it may seem, some have found within these two verses' insistence upon the 'mutuality' of the sexual activity allowed, nay required, by Paul grounds for thinking that his attitude toward marriage must have been essentially a favorable

---

[1] It is completely impossible to achieve the proper perspective on Paul's attitude in this whole issue unless one notices that he has already begun the discussion of sexuality *prior* to Chapter 7—namely in 6.9ff. with its opening warning against immorality. In 6.12ff. he goes on to make a fundamental distinction between sins committed against the body, such as fornication, and all other bodily actions, such as eating. The latter is unimportant, for God is soon to destroy both stomachs and foods (6.13). But fornication *excludes from the Kingdom of God* (6.9). It is against the background of this distinction that Paul launches into his advice regarding marriage.

[2] Thus G. Delling *Paulus' Stellung zu Frau und Ehe* (1931) considerably underestimates the depth of Paul's intention to safeguard the Corinthians from sexual sin; see p. 75.

one.[1] Such, however, is far from the case. For Paul marriage, and in particular the sexual activity of marriage, is no more than 'a necessary evil due to the weakness of the flesh. Utterly out of the question is a high estimation of marriage such as we find, e.g., with the Stoic Musonius'.[2] Paul's ideal is stated clearly enough all through Chapter 7; marriage, therefore, is no more than a concession he must make in order to prevent worse evils from breaking out in their midst!'[3]

Having ordained marriage as the general rule—rather a polemical conception of marriage as a temporary weapon against the Devil—Paul then grants a qualification:

Do not withhold sexual intercourse from one another, unless you agree to do so for a time in order to devote yourselves to prayer. Then come together again. You must not let Satan tempt you through incontinence. (1 Cor. 7.5 Moffatt)

Paul here picks up a common belief found all through the ancient world, and indeed it is common in many parts of the world today, that sexual intercourse inhibits and pollutes one's relation with the pure sphere of the Divine.[4] Paul obviously agrees with this idea;

[1] This seems especially true among Roman Catholic interpreters, see e.g., Allo 155f.; Héring 51; Menoud 'Mariage' 22. It must be admitted, however, that these commentators hold their view relying heavily on an assumption of the Pauline authorship of Ephesians 5. But see also among the Protestants, Robertson-Plummer 132f. J. N. Sevenster *Paul and Seneca* (1961) also holds that Paul has a basically favorable view of marriage, but Sevenster has not only assumed the Pauline authorship of Ephesians (without any explanation), he also has inexplicably omitted any reference to 1 Cor. 7; see 198f. E. Kähler also holds that Paul's view is essentially positive, but her remarks tend to romanticize the Apostle, e.g., Paul 'sees the wife as a *person*'; *Frau* 23. On the whole subject, see especially W. Schrage, 'Die Stellung zur Welt bei Paulus, Epiktet und in der Apokalyptik', *ZThK* 61 (1964) 125–154. W.-G. Kümmel, 'Verlobung und Heirat bei Paulus (1 Kor. 7.36–38),' *Neutestamentliche Studien für Rudolf Bultmann* (*ZNW* Beih. 21, 1954) 275–295, includes a valuable survey of recent scholarship.

[2] Lietzmann-Kümmel 29; cp. Moffatt 76f.

[3] This is not the place to attempt an inquiry as to the origins of Paul's outlook. See however W. Schrage and W.-G. Kümmel, opp. cit. above n.1, and further, J. Leipoldt, *Griechische Philosophie und frühchristliche Askese* (1961) 33f.

[4] Cp. 2 Esdras 6.32; Test. Naph. 8.8; for references to later Christian and pagan literature, see Delling *Stellung* 72, 74 n.126; Lietzmann-Kümmel 30. On Qumran, see below, pp. 115ff.

it is *why* 'it is best not to touch a woman'. But even so, Paul will not allow anyone to attempt any ascetic endurance records, for prayer or any other high goal. His eyes are fixed on the power of the Adversary.

Finally, Paul says:

This is a suggestion, not a rule: I should like everyone to be like me, but everybody has his own particular gift from God, one with a gift for one thing and another with a gift for the opposite. (1 Cor. 7.6f. *JB*)

There is considerable disagreement as to the previous point of reference intended by the word 'this', at the beginning. Or, in other words, what is the 'suggestion' or 'concession' (*sungnome*) mentioned in v.6? Some think it refers to what he has just said in v.5, and they may be right. One can see why Paul might say this in order not to encourage anyone to attempt ascetic vigils beyond their 'continence-threshhold'.[1]

However, many commentators believe that what Paul is referring to is his advice that all should marry. The chief argument here is that the verse should be taken with the point that *follows* it. A new line of argument has recently been introduced by D. Daube. He suggests that the distinction in v.6 between 'concession' and 'command' is a conscious use on the part of Paul of a well-known legal distinction in Jewish jurisprudence when a course of action is allowed or conceded because of inability or unwillingness to follow the path of true righteousness.[2] Such an interpretation of Paul's words, of course, fits the context perfectly and may well be precisely what Paul intended, namely, concerning the situation as a whole and in view of the unfortunate need of the majority for marriage, in view of this Paul wants to make it clear that he is not giving a command but only a concession that they

[1] So Héring 52; von Allmen *Teaching* 58 n.17; H. H. Rex 'Attempt' 42.

[2] 'The rabbinic antithesis is *reshuth* over against *miṣwah* or *ḥobhah*.' Thus, when Paul says, 'I say this by way of concession not command,' Paul is using 'quite technical language of the nature of this ruling'; D. Daube, 'Concessions to Sinfulness in Jewish Law', *JJSt* 10 (1959) 1–13. Among other examples, Daube cites the case that Israel was *conceded* the institution of kingship over Samuel's most strenuous protest (see 1 Sam. 8). See further W. Bacher, *Die exegetische Terminologie der jüdischen Traditionsliteratur* I (1899) 58, 181ff.

H

may go ahead and marry.[1] But he could wish all were free from this unfortunate and perilous condition as he himself was (7.7).

2. *Widows and widowers* (1 Cor. 7.8f.)

Having set sexual sin apart from all other sin involving the body in 6.12ff., and then, in 7.2–7, having instituted the basic line of defense for the majority, namely, through a concession that they may marry, Paul now turns to special problems. The first one has to do with whether those whose spouses have died may remarry.

To the unmarried [widowers] and to widows I say this: it is a good thing if they stay as I am myself; but if they cannot control themselves, they should marry. Better be married than burn. (1 Cor. 7.8f. *NEB*)

Why does Paul permit second marriages where death has ended the prior marriage, whereas he will not allow a second marriage if divorce terminated it? There is no further discussion of this issue in his letters. Perhaps the following suggestion might be considered: Paul allows second marriage after death has terminated the first since there is no possibility of reconciliation with the separated partner, and there is after divorce (see below). In this sense, then, remarriage would actually be no more than a new form of the first marriage. But we shall return to this question later, after we have understood the issues more thoroughly.[2]

In the older commentaries, 'to burn' was taken to refer to the Last Judgment. Those were stern days, and so Paul's sentence was finished out, 'better to marry than to burn *in Hell*'.[3] It is now generally recognized, however, that this was not what Paul was

---

[1] So Moffatt 76; von Campenhausen *Begründung* 21 n.38; J. Weiss 175; von Allmen *Teaching* 13f., 56ff. For further bibliographical references, see Hurd 161f., Allo 158–161. To be sure, confusion as to Paul's meaning extends back as far as there are commentators. For example, Tatian (Clem. Alex. *Strom.* III 12.81.1f.) and Tertullian (*ad Uxorem* 1.3) believed that in the very way Paul had conceded marriage he *opposed* it! See further H. Chadwick art. 'enkrateia', *RAC* V 343–365.
[2] See below, pp. 134f.
[3] Such is, at any rate, the traditional Reformation exegesis. It involves the quaint assumption that the single partner will automatically rush into fornication, thereby meriting the torments of Hell. We might consider this view of marriage a prophylactic conception, over against Paul's older emetic view.

thinking of, but rather the idea of burning up with lust; e.g., 'better to marry than be aflame with passion' (*RSV*).[1]

3. Divorce; the command of the Lord (1 Cor. 7.10f.)

Paul then turns to a second special problem, and immediately refers to a command of the Lord dealing with it which settles the matter without any further discussion. The command of the Lord:

the wife should not separate from her husband . . . the husband should not divorce his wife (*RSV*)

is phrased in typical fashion according to the different status of men and women under Jewish law. Only the man could initiate proceedings in order to dismiss his wife; the woman could not do this. Hence, he could 'divorce' her, but she could not 'divorce' him. All a woman could do was to 'go away' or 'separate' from him; i.e., abandon her husband.[2] In short, both phrases of this command add up to simple, strict prohibition of divorce.

Between the two clauses, however, there is a parenthesis:

but if she does separate, let her remain unmarried or be reconciled to her husband. (*RSV*)

Actually, the first four words in the sentence are ambiguous in the Greek.[3] They can be translated, 'but if she should separate' (future)—which is the way the *RSV* editors have taken it—or 'but if she has separated' (past). Both are equally possible.[4]

[1] So Moffatt 77f.; Allo 163; Robertson-Plummer 138. See further F. Lang, *TWNT* VI 949 s.v. *puróo*.

[2] D. Daube, *The New Testament and Rabbinic Judaism* (1956) 362. The same differentiation in legal terminology is also to be found in contemporary Greek and Roman law; Lietzmann-Kümmel 31. See further Boaz Cohen, *Jewish and Roman Law* (1966) I, 377–408: 'Divorce in Jewish and Roman Law.' [3] *Ean de kai choristhe.*

[4] Lietzmann-Kümmel point out that to take it as future would be more typical where *ean* is followed by the Subjunctive. Thus, for example, many of the official translations have taken it in this way, see *KJV, NEB, JB;* so also Hurd 66. Lietzmann-Kümmel decide against this, however, 'because then Paul does not permit an exception to the command of the Lord, but only rules in the case of an already existing (unwitting?) violation'; 31. What Lietzmann-Kümmel do not seem to notice is that Paul 'permits an exception to the command of the Lord' in *either* case.

It is widely noted that Paul has in a curious fashion interrupted the very pronouncement of this command in order to pass immediately to an application of the first section of it, i.e., the part which applied to women. This is, of course, an obvious indication that Paul is not speaking theoretically any longer, but is dealing with an actual situation at Corinth. Whether from the letter, or from its bearers or from 'Chloe's people' (1 Cor. 1.11), Paul found out about a potential case of divorce, which was being instigated by the wife, and briefly directs his attention to it.[1]

So much is clear. But what was the problem? That is, is there any indication why the woman wanted a divorce? The usual view is that this woman wanted a divorce in order to live afterward in sexual continence. She wanted a divorce for ascetic reasons. 'Some wives,' conjectured Moffatt, 'of an ultra-spiritual temper, may have gone or wished to go further than to suspend marital relations (vss. 3–4). . . . The feminist party in the local church evidently claimed freedom to desert or divorce a husband.'[2]

To be sure, there is an a priori plausibility about this solution, but it faces certain difficulties. For one thing, it puts Paul in the curious position of permitting a *divorce* despite what he has just said a moment before about married couples not separating from each other for long, even for ascetic devotions (v. 5). That is, this solution causes Paul to appear to have forgotten what he said as soon as he uttered it. Not only that, it also causes him to go on to warn this 'ultra-spiritual feminist' that she may not marry someone else—a rather inexplicable gesture in view of her supposed renunciation of sex.[3]

On the other hand, Paul has just made provision for an ascetic

[1] Perhaps the best solution to the time-question of the opening phrase has been given by Allo, following J. Weiss (178): '*ean* is properly speaking the particle of the most general eventually, but the *kai* (–'even', 'indeed') would indicate an action already occurred or known'; 163. The divorce was about to happen when the letter bearers left Corinth to come to Paul. Thus it could have become a completed act by the time they had returned with Paul's answer, and so he writes as if it were.

[2] Moffatt 78. Other holders of the 'feminist ascetic' line are Robertson-Plummer 140; Allo 164; von Allmen *Pauline Teaching* 55 n.7. See further Hurd 167 n.1.

[3] Von Allmen vaguely senses the inconsistencies his approach betrays him into, 'in any case they are not to make of their present widowhood [sic] a pretext for thinking themselves available for any other husband', *Pauline Teaching* 55; cp. Moffatt 79.

renunciation of marital relations within the marriage bond. Why does he not seek to apply that to the present case? What purpose, in other words, would a *divorce* serve, especially since he does not allow another marriage afterward?[1]

But the most obvious objection is quite simple. If Paul really was concerned to keep this ascetically-minded woman from divorcing her husband in order to live alone, then why is it that he grants her the very divorce she wants right in the middle of citing the command of the Lord? To what purpose did he cite the Lord's command? Small wonder J. Weiss considered v.11a an interpolation![2]

In view of the difficulties this feminist-ascetic solution causes for our interpretation of the text, perhaps we should look elsewhere for an explanation. One thing is evident. Paul draws the line against marriage with someone else. That is to say, it is clear that one of the things this word of the Lord means to Paul is that *it forbids additional marriages after divorce.* A single life after divorce, or reconciliation with the original spouse; these are the only options open to the woman.

There is another early Christian writing in which this same view is found. In this case, divorce is not motivated by a desire for ascetic abstinence, but rather by the question what a husband should do if his wife is committing adultery.

'What then, sir, is the husband to do if his wife continue in [adultery]?' And he [the Shepherd] said, 'The husband should divorce her and remain by himself. But if he divorces her and marries another, he also commits adultery.' And I said to him, 'What if the woman who is divorced should repent, and wish to return to her husband: shall she not be taken back by her husband?' And he said to me 'Assuredly'.[3]

---

[1]As Hurd aptly observes, if Corinthian couples were already 'willing to practice intramarital asceticism, then divorce would seem to serve no useful function'; 167.

[2] J. Weiss 178f. Apart from the older commentators like Weiss, it is remarkable how few have noticed this anomaly. Among recent commentators, I have found only one: H. H. Rex, 'a surprisingly lax view of divorce', 'Attempt' 44. Most are still convinced that 'St. Paul, like our Lord, forbids divorce absolutely'; Robertson-Plummer 140; cp. H. von Campenhausen 'Askese' 141 n.140; *Begründung* 21.

[3] Hermas, *The Shepherd*, Mand. 4.1.6 ed. K. Lake.

This quotation from *The Shepherd* reveals that a sharp line is drawn against all second marriages, but that no such rigid opposition stood in the way of divorce per se, if it were followed either by remaining unmarried, or by reconciliation with the original spouse.[1]

Looking back at what Paul says in the parenthesis (1 Cor. 7.11a), perhaps it would be fruitful to assume that what the woman wanted was precisely what Paul denies to her—*another marriage*. Perhaps she wanted a divorce in order to marry someone else . . . what we might call 'normal' divorce, arising from such things as ungovernable hostility between the partners, or abandonment, or the inception of madness, and the like.[2]

Whatever the cause may have been, the fact remains that Paul *permits the divorce if it has taken place*: 'let her remain unmarried'. Nor does he give the slightest indication of realizing that he may be in conflict with the command of the Lord. On the contrary, the

[1] As a writing coming from the milieu of the Roman church, in the early second century, we must obviously allow for the fact that the author has imbibed Paul's own view in the advice he here sets forth. To be sure, it can as little be doubted that this viewpoint is informed by the Synoptic instructions regarding divorce. All of this is to the good, however, in providing us with an early reflection of how the Church— at Rome in any case—understood these regulations. Indeed, we shall have occasion to refer to his passage more than once to help us step over gaps in the canonical texts; see below.

[2] Against this interpretation, see J. Weiss 179; Allo 164; Delling *Stellung* 74f. It is important to remember that in contemporary Jewish law, as well as divorce in a marriage of *usus* in Roman law (which would probably be the case here), it was quite permissible for a divorced couple to reunite by common consent, even after the bill of divorce had been formally served, provided, of course, that the cause of divorce had not been some criminal act (e.g., on the Jewish side, adultery; n.b., the interesting contrast here with the Roman situation in Hermas' *Shepherd*!); see Moore *Judaism* II 122; H. F. Jolowicz, *Historical Introduction to the Study of Roman Law* (1952) 245f. Difficult to decide, of course, is the actual legal context being presupposed by Paul as that of the Corinthian church members. For an example of Jews living in the city of Alexandria not performing their civil and private tasks according to Jewish legal procedures but according to Hellenistic law and using the Hellenistic courts, see V. A. Tcherikover, *Corpus Papyrorum Judaicarum* (Tcherikover and Fuks edd.) I (1957) 33f. (example of divorce 34). That the kind of divorce Paul is thinking of here is one arising out of hostility between the partners seems directly suggested by his use of the term 'be reconciled' to refer to their reunion.

very mode of introducing it, 'I command, yet not I but the Lord', seems to suggest that Paul here desires to bring his most authoritative tradition to bear on an issue concerning which he will brook no opposition. We shall come back to this question after an examination of the Synoptic material concerning divorce, for we must somehow explain the fact that *Paul's application is in flat contradiction to the command of the Lord, which is a strict prohibition of divorce.*[1]

4. Marriages with unbelievers (1 Cor. 7.12–16)

In the first sentence of this section we come upon this peculiar statement: 'I say, not the Lord. . . .' What the meaning of Paul's obvious desire to indicate some sort of breach between what he has just given, as a command of the Lord, and what he is about to say in his own name, will be more fruitfully considered after it is understood what Paul says:

To the rest I say, not the Lord, that if any brother has a wife who is an unbeliever, and she consents to live with him, he should not divorce her. If any woman has a husband who is an unbeliever and he consents to live with her, she should not divorce him. For the unbelieving husband is consecrated through his wife, and the unbelieving wife is consecrated through her husband. Otherwise, your children would be unclean, but as it is they are holy. But if the unbelieving partner desires to separate, let it be so; in such cases the brother or sister is not bound. For God has called us to peace. Wife, how do you know whether you will save your husband? Husband, how do you know whether you will save your wife? (1 Cor. 7.12–16 *RSV*)

First, some of the terms require clarification. There is general agreement that the introductory phrase, *Tois de loipois*, 'But concerning the others . . .' is Paul's customary way of referring to non-believers (cp. 1 Thess. 4.13; 5.6). 'The others,' of course, are the non-believers who are the mates of the Christians in the congregation. Paul is now about to talk about 'them'.[2] This problem has come up apparently because there were several

---

[1] See below, pp. 132f.
[2] So Robertson-Plummer 141; Allo 165; Lightfoot *Notes* 225. 'To the rest' (*RSV*) is incorrect. But see P. Dulau, 'The Pauline Privilege', *CBQ* 13 (1951) 140–152.

'mixed' marriages in the Corinthian congregation, i.e., cases where the Gospel had appealed to only one member of a married couple, and when Paul had written in an earlier letter, 'Do not associate with immoral men' (1 Cor. 5.9), some wondered if Paul was telling them to divorce their unbelieving partners. So now Paul takes up the question of 'them', and assures the Corinthians that they should not seek divorces in such situations.[1]

A second major problem is how to translate the opening phrase in v.16. The common negative or doubtful translation, e.g., 'how do you know whether?' (*RSV*)[2] is incorrect. Rather, as J. B. Lightfoot, and before him most Catholic exegetes, understood it, the phrase expresses confident anticipation; e.g., 'Think of it: as a wife you may be your husband's salvation!' (*NEB*).[3] This positive ending, if correct (and the philological evidence is virtually

---

[1] See on this especially Hurd 157, 222ff., 238. On the other hand Paul is certainly not suggesting that the Corinthians may form such mixed marriages in the future; cp. Allo 165; Héring 53. That Paul is speaking unequivocally of divorce, the pair of terms *aphienai* and *chorizesthai* show. According to D. Daube, Paul's terminology is shifting around in these verses. 'With reference to a marriage where only one party is a believer, Paul uses the transitive *aphienai* both of the dissolution of the marriage by the husband and of its dissolution by the wife. The latter application of *aphienai* is justified since the procedure he has in mind is a non-Jewish one, Roman or Greek. Again, a little further on (v. 15) he uses *chorizesthai* of the dissolution of the marriage by an unbelieving partner, husband or wife. No special justification is needed here, the verb being a proper term for divorce'; *New Testament* 363; cp. Robertson-Plummer 141. On *chorizesthai* as a term for divorce in Roman law, see B. Cohen *Jewish and Roman Law* I 394 n.83. Most understand Paul to be speaking here of divorce; but see Dulau op. cit. above p.93, further T. P. Considine, 'The Pauline Privilege (Further examination of 1 Cor. 7.12–17),' *AusCathRec* 40 (1963) 107–119.

[2] Greek *ti gar oidas ei*? cp. Lietzmann-Kümmel 31; Allo 169.

[3] Cp. LXX 2 Sam. 12.22; Esther 4.14; Jon. 3.9; Joel 2.14. See most recently, J. Jeremias, 'Die missionarische Aufgabe der Mischehe (1 Kor. 7.16)', *Festschr. Bultmann* (1954) 255–260, who has discovered other examples of a positive connotation of this phrase from, besides the LXX, Epictetus, and *Joseph and Asenath*, also the early Greek fathers' exegesis of this passage (see 259). See further C. Burchard, 'Ei nach einem Ausdruck des Wissens oder Nichtwissens Joh. 9.25; Acts 19.2; 1 Kor. 1.16; 7.16', *ZNW* 52 (1961) 73–82; von Campenhausen *Begründung* 22 n.42. It seems to have always been the traditional Catholic exegesis; see, e.g., Dulau and Considine (referred to in previous note) and Héring. An exception however is Allo 169.

conclusive), simplifies the general thrust of the passage considerably. For one thing, it shows that Paul's thought is precisely
the same as that in the only other reference in the New Testament
to the proper Christian conduct in mixed marriages, namely,
1 Peter 3.1f. More important, it makes the ending of this section
consistent with the point Paul makes at the outset, so that his
advice throughout is: don't seek a divorce, try for peace!

What is the reason Paul gives for this recommendation? This
brings us to the difficult passage in v.14.

For the unbelieving husband is consecrated through his wife, and the
unbelieving wife is consecrated through her husband. Otherwise, your
children would be unclean, but as it is, they are holy. (*RSV*)

As Lietzmann-Kümmel say,

the conception upon which the argument is based is not stated. It may
be that just as the children become holy in some mysterious way
without their own assistance through physical descent from a Christian
man or woman, so also the heathen marriage partner is made holy
through sexual intercourse with the Christian partner. How the latter
is to be understood must perhaps be conceived according to analogy
from 6.15f. For this whole idea, compare Bab. Tal. Yebamoth 78a.[1]

Whatever the reasoning may have been, one thing is clear: Paul
wants to emphasize the value of remaining in such marriages, a
fact Menoud rightly singles out against all too-one-sided exposi-
tions of Paul's antipathy toward marriage.[2]

This brings up the final question, concerning which there is

---

[1] Lietzmann-Kümmel 31. On this passage in recent discussion, see
the bibliography in Lietzmann-Kümmel 176f. See further G. Delling,
'Nun aber sind sie heilig: Gott und die Götter', *Festschr. E. Fascher*
(1958) 84–93; G. Oesterle, 'Privilège paulinien', *Dictionnaire de droit
canonique*, fasc. 37s (1958) 229–280; G. Walther, 'Uebergreifende
Heiligkeit und Kindertaufe im NT', *EvangTheol* 25 (1965) 668–674;
J. M. Ford, ' "Hast thou tithed thy meal?" and "Is thy child koscher?"
(1 Cor. x 27ff. and 1 Cor. vii 14)', *JThSt* 17 (1966) 71–79. Not least
among the puzzling aspects of this passage is why, if the suggestion of
Lietzmann-Kümmel be correct, the sanctifying effect of sexual intercourse doesn't also purify the *porne* (6.15) instead of the other way
around?

[2] 'Marriage' 27 n.1, 29f.

considerable disagreenent: the scope of the *privilegium paulinum*, the traditional Catholic term for the exception Paul is here understood to make to the command of the Lord given in v.10f. On this ancient view: Paul permits both divorce and remarriage in the cases of such mixed marriages. A typical statement of the classical justification is given by Allo as follows:

' "He is not bound" . . . that is to say, "take your freedom" [this is a reference to a phrase in 1 Cor. 7.21: "if you have the chance of being free (from slavery), accept it" *JB*]; . . . Since the text says "take your freedom", is one permitted to contract another marriage? The Church has interpreted it thus, and it is this which the Canon lawyers term the "Pauline privilege". From the time of the Fathers—Chrysostom, Ambrose—this conclusion has been drawn from "he is not bound", an expression which furnishes a sufficient basis for this interpretation in the sense of *complete* freedom.'[1]

Against this view, however, Robertson-Plummer insist that 'all that "he is not bound" clearly means is that [the Christian man or woman] need not feel so bound by Christ's prohibition of divorce as to be afraid to depart when the heathen partner insists on separation'.[2] This is quite correct. Thus, when von Allmen believes 'it must be admitted that the freed Christian partner (v.15) could find his peace again by forming another couple',[3] he is placing a specific interpretation upon the term 'peace' which the Pauline usage hardly justifies. As a matter of fact, although it is not generally recognized, the statement, 'but God called you in peace', may well be adversative, and therefore should stand as a preface to the next, positive thought instead of the way it is usually translated. Paul would then be saying, 'If the unbelieving spouse wants a divorce, let him have it; you don't have to endure such things.[4] But *you* were called by God in peace (i.e., no divorces

[1] Allo 168f. italics added.
[2] Robertson-Plummer 143. So also W. Foerster *TDNT* II 416 s.v. *eirene*.
[3] *Pauline Teaching* 49; cp. Héring 54.
[4] *Ou dedoulotai ho adelphos . . . en tois toioutois.* Paul is not speaking here of being 'bound' to the spouse in marriage; cp. 'in such a case the brother or sister is not bound' *RSV*; 'tied' *JB*. When he means this, scil. being 'bound' in marriage, he uses another word: *dedesthai* (1 Cor. 7.39; cp. Rom. 7.1). Nor should this be translated so as to imply being 'bound' to the command of the Lord, as, e.g.,Robertson-Plummer (just quoted above). The command of the Lord did not actually forbid divorce (see below).

should be initiated by *you*, cp. v.12f.); who knows—maybe you will be the cause of his (or her) salvation!'[1]

In any case, to judge from what Paul says explicitly, nothing more is permitted the Christian than accepting the unbelieving partner's wish for divorce. Nothing direct is said about re-marriage.[2] The old Catholic exegesis rests on nothing more than the rationale inherent within divorce as such, viz., to make it possible for a man or a woman to get married to someone else. This can be seen, for example, from the formula required in the Jewish bill of divorce: 'Lo, thou art free to marry any man'.[3] The Church quite naturally assumed that since Paul permitted divorce, the *privilegium paulinum* included remarriage as well. The possibility that Paul was thinking of divorce *not* followed by remarriage seems never to have been much discussed.[4]

What evidence is there that this is indeed what Paul had in mind? Several things point in this direction. For one, it seems unlikely that he would permit here something he forbade in v.10f. Here, as there, divorce is permitted if unavoidable. But, although that is allowed, subsequent remarriage was not in the preceeding case. Now, insofar as the Christian partner, as a Christian, must be obedient to the command of the Lord, it is difficult to see how a second marriage is permitted by Paul in this case. Furthermore, there is a similarity between 'let her remain unmarried *or be reconciled*' (v.11a) with the general hopeful outlook in v.16 that not divorce but conversion occur.

Thus, our conclusion is that the *privilegium paulinum* does not extend to a second marriage on the part of the divorced Christian partner. As far as that goes, it is not even an 'exception' (*privilegium*) to begin with. This idea seems to be the result of the mistaken impression that Paul here made a personal ruling which conflicted with the command of the Lord cited in 7.10f. But, as we have already seen, either Paul already made an exception there,

---

[1] See however J. B. Lightfoot 226f.; further Jeremias 'Missionarische Aufgabe' 259.

[2] So also Robertson-Plummer 143; von Campenhausen 'Askese' 141, and idem *Begründung* 22; von Allmen *Teaching* 59.

[3] Mish. Git. 9.3 ed Danby. See further Daube *New Testament* 362–365; Jolowicz *Roman Law* 245.

[4] See Dulau 'Privilege' 140f.; further J. J. O'Rourke, 'The Scriptural Background of [CIC] can. 1120', *The Jurist* 15 (1955) 132–137; *Dictionnaire de droit canonique* s.v.

or, as is more like it, this command of the Lord never really prohibited divorce in the first place!

In fact, Paul seems to be faithfully following here the guidelines laid down in the preceeding case (v.11a). There as here, divorce is allowed (reluctantly). Remarriage, on the other hand, is not. Rather, in both cases, eventual reconciliation is held out as the alternative.

If it be true that Paul's application of the command of the Lord is precisely the same in both of these cases, then it is all the more strange that Paul begins *this* section by saying: 'As for "the others", *I* say—not the Lord—that if any brother has a wife, etc.' Indeed, this has been one of the strongest arguing points in the traditional Catholic exegesis: Paul is about to make a ruling in his own name, viz., to make an exception on a special case. What is the explanation of this?

P. Allo takes this introductory phrase to be a warning; 'for such a case, Paul avows that he does not have a precise command of the Lord to hand down'.[1] Thus Allo understands this phrase to mean what Paul later repeats much more explicitly about another question; 'Now concerning the unmarried, *I have no command of the Lord, but I give my opinion as one who by the Lord's mercy is trustworthy*' (1 Cor. 7.25 *RSV*). This means that it was the legally novel character of the problem which brought out this explicit demurrer on the part of Paul. The command of the Lord cited in 7.10f. apparently did not apply, as far as Paul was concerned, in the case before him in 7.12–16! The fact that he went ahead and gave a ruling *precisely in line with it*[2] must not be allowed to prevent our noticing that, to Paul, these were two very different problems. It is clear, for instance, what one crucial difference between the two cases must have been: the first dealt with the issue of divorce between members in the community, the latter with divorce in marriages which crossed the community line— perhaps where this very line was the source of conflict. Thus whereas the first divorce problem was settled without comment, Paul apparently felt that the domain of the Lord's jurisdiction *in respect to law for the community* did not extend fully into the latter

---

[1] Allo 165.

[2] So also B. Rigaux, 'Réflexion sur l'historicité de Jésus dans le message paulinien', *Analecta Biblica* 18 (1963) 270; B. Gerhardsson *Memory and Manuscript* (1961) 312–314.

case.[1] That this is indeed what happened is shown most vividly by the very presence of the argument in v.14. Even though Paul actually is relying upon the command of the Lord for guidance, nevertheless he seeks to justify his position independently by bringing in a totally new line of argument and found his decision upon that.[2]

This indication of a specific domain or jurisdiction within which commands of the Lord applied as community regulations is significant. But even more significant is Paul's apparent unwillingness overtly to stretch the applicability of a saying of the Lord—draw its consequences openly into the new (legal) context. This peculiar 'minimalism' of Paul's regarding the actual use of commands of the Lord, even while he carries the intent of the former over into the new (but legally related) context, is worthy of the most careful consideration.

With v.17, 'Nevertheless, let each one . . . etc.'[3] Paul indicates how all of the foregoing[4] is to be considered, viz., as an exception to his fundamental 'rule in all the churches'. In general, let all such eleventh-hour (1 Cor. 7.29, 31) changes, adjustments, and tampering with external circumstances, be held to a strict minimum.[5] And with this verse, we pass out of the context pertinent to our inquiry.

[1] See Gerhardsson Memory 313.

[2] The *lego ego* in 7.12 should not be taken as if Paul were not intending to speak authoritatively in what follows; cp. L. Cerfaux, 'La tradition selon saint Paul', *Recueil Lucien Cerfaux* I (1954) 259; Gerhardsson 313f.; misleading is von Campenhausen *Begründung* 22.

[3] For the correct translation of *Ei me* see Blass-Debrunner-Funk *Grammar* sections 376, 448 (8).

[4] Against Robertson-Plummer 144; Lietzmann-Kümmel 32; Allo 171; Héring 55. 'Nevertheless' refers not only to v.15f., but also to v.11a—i.e., to divorce—and probably even to v.2ff., i.e., to Paul's concession that all may marry. On this, see J. Jeremias, 'Missionarische Aufgabe' 259 n.14. One can hardly agree with Jeremias that v.5 is also in view; that is hardly a matter of altering one's *klesis*.

[5] See H.-J. Schoeps *Paul* (1959) 102f., 198f., 264.

Features of Paul's Use of This Command of the Lord

Having analyzed the context within which Paul appeals to the Lord's prohibition of divorce and observing the peculiar way in which he seems to apply it to a situation in the Corinthian community, and having noticed how Paul uses this same command in a second case while claiming not to, we are ready for the following general observations.

In the first place, as before Paul again says nothing as to his source for this command of the Lord. That is, he does not mention anything in the nature of a collection of such sayings.[1] Furthermore, it is not at all clear whether the actual saying Paul here refers to can be recovered. This will form one of the main goals in the next chapter, where we shall examine the Synoptic material on divorce.

Second, the authoritativeness of this prohibition is manifest. Thus, commands of the Lord *were* used to guide the life of the early Church. Indeed, we clearly saw Paul employ the Lord's command as a precedent—in his own name, to be sure!—in a new and special case. One could not find a plainer illustration and confirmation of this type of use of sayings of Jesus; a concrete application in this particular kind of *Sitz im Leben der Korinthergemeinde*.[2]

Third, it is most interesting to observe Paul's scrupulous concern with the difference between halakoth of the Lord and his own, his conservatism as to 'expanding' existing sayings of the Lord to fit new situations. Both of these points are vividly exemplified again at 1 Cor. 7.25: 'Now concerning the unmarried,

---

[1] Lietzmann-Kümmel 31; cp. W. D. Davies, *The Setting of the Sermon on the Mount* (1964) 353.

[2] This is perhaps the appropriate place to acknowledge my great debt to the discussion of this whole subject, in many ways the starting-point for the present study, by R. Bultmann in his epoch-making *History of the Synoptic Tradition* (ET 1963); see especially 130–150.

I have no command of the Lord, but I give my opinion as one who by the Lord's mercy is trustworthy' (*RSV*). As Moffatt observes,

The explicit care with which Paul here [in 1 Cor. 7.12] and in [1 Cor. 7] verse 25 distinguishes between what is his ruling . . . and a definite saying of the Lord (v. 10) is a significant indication that, even although as a prophet he had divine revelations, he did not cast them into the form of what Jesus had once said, in order to invest them with authority.[1]

Nothing we have said so far throws any light on our major outstanding question: how to account for the startling clash between the command of the Lord cited by Paul, and the application he derives from it (in 7.11a). In this regard, however, one last feature of Paul's use of this command of the Lord should be mentioned. Once again, just as in the case of 1 Cor. 9.14, Paul just *refers* to the saying of the Lord in question; he does not actually quote it. Is it possible that the clash is due to this fact, that Paul is not quoting the saying itself but only giving an extract in his own words? Is it possible that this contradiction arises because Paul has not referred to the essential part of the saying he is actually using? But why would he do that? In order to discover the answers to these questions, it is necessary to consider the sayings on divorce in the Synoptic gospels.

---

[1] Moffatt 80; cp. W. D. Davies, *Setting* 397. Irenaeus, the only early Father to comment on Paul's statement in 1 Cor. 7.25, never dreamed that Paul was admitting that he *didn't have* a pertinent saying of the Lord—and this perhaps ought to be a warning to us, against our interpretation of it. To Irenaeus, Paul was merely saying that he didn't intend to levy a regulation upon the Corinthians in the delicate area of continence, out of a pastoral feeling for their spiritual and moral weakness! See *adv. Haer.* IV 15.2.

CHAPTER THREE

The Sayings on Divorce in the Synoptic Gospels

1. *The account of Jesus' debate with the Pharisees regarding divorce* (Matt. 19.3–9//Mark 10.2–12)

Before we can arrive at a decision as to whether the Synoptic material represents any kind of common or unified tradition regarding divorce, and use this to compare to the tradition reflected in Paul's command of the Lord, it will be necessary to answer the question as to the relative originality of these two accounts. In the process of solving this problem, we shall try to discover each editor's motivations for entering the changes and additions that they do into their source-material. Perhaps along this route we shall find the key to the puzzling way Paul is handling the command of the Lord in 1 Cor. 7.10f.

A.   THE ORIGINAL ORDER OF THE STORY[1]

The major problem is apparent to anyone who compares the two accounts in a synopsis of the gospels: the stages of the dispute, although largely the same in content, are arranged in different order in the two gospels (see the chart below). Complicating matters is the fact that, despite the general belief that Matthew is faithfully following Mark here (there not being a Q account of this debate), nevertheless Matthew's version seems more original than Mark's. This impression is conceded even by some of the Two-Document Hypothesis' most renowned practitioners, e.g., Rudolf Bultmann and B. H. Streeter. The former considers 'the artificiality of the composition' in Mark to be obvious,[2] concluding that it 'was given its present form in the written tradition.'[3] By this, Bultmann apparently means that its present confused order is a result of Mark's own editorial work.[4]

---

[1]As for the way the term 'original' is intended, see above, p. 41 n. 1.
[2] Bultmann 47.   [3] Ibid. 48.
[4] It is actually rather difficult to decide what Bultmann means by this vague remark; see below, p. 122 n.2.

COMPARISON OF THE ACCOUNTS OF JESUS' DEBATE WITH THE
PHARISEES ON DIVORCE

Matthew 19.3–9	Mark 10.2–12
v. 3 Pharisees ask whether divorce may be granted for many reasons.	v. 2 Pharisees ask whether divorce is permissible (at all).
vv. 4–6 Jesus quotes Gen. 1 and 2, asserts that divorce is against the original law of creation.	v. 3 Jesus asks counter-question, what did Moses command?
v. 7 Pharisees challenge Jesus; why then did Moses command Israel to get bills of divorce?	v. 4 Pharisees reply; Moses permitted us to get deeds of divorce and to divorce.
v. 8 Jesus retorts that Moses conceded divorce to Israel because of its sinfulness.	v. 5 Jesus retorts that Moses wrote the law because of Israel's sinfulness.
	vv. 6–9 Jesus quotes Gen. 1 and 2, asserts that divorce is against the original law of creation.
v. 9 Jesus explains first answer: whoever divorces his wife (except in cases of adultery) and marries another commits adultery.	vv. 10–12 Jesus (later) in a house explains his answer privately to his disciples: any man who divorces and marries again commits adultery; any woman who divorces and marries again commits adultery.

What is wrong with Mark's version? To begin with, says Bultmann, as a Controversy-story it is completely mixed up in structure; 'the awkwardness of the construction shows its artificiality. Jesus replies with the [expected] counter-question in v.3 . . . [but it] is in no sense a counter-argument. The formulation of v.4 is completely impossible'.[1] Streeter is equally unequivocal:

Matthew's section on Divorce (Matt. 19.3–12) is both more naturally told and more closely related to Jewish usage than the parallel in Mark. . . . The reference to the law of divorce in Deuteronomy comes more appropriately, as in Matthew, as *their* reply to Him, than, as in Mark, as our Lord's original answer. And . . . Matthew's arrangement makes His final rejoinder, that this was merely permissive, more effective.[2]

Bultmann's assessment represents an advance over Streeter's, in that it is well-based on form-critical grounds. According to his

[1] Bultmann 27.
[2] *The Four Gospels*[2] (1930) 259.

I

approach, this account belongs to a (non-literary) genre he describes by the term Controversy-Dialogues.[1] Unfortunately, however, he is almost alone in attempting to investigate the material in this way. Much more typical is the reaction of a B. W. Bacon, for example, who simply points to the two so-called Matthean insertions, 'for any cause' (19.3), and 'except for unchastity' (19.9), and observes that they have changed Jesus' original statement on divorce 'from a prophetic principle to a bit of eecclesiastical legislation'.[2] Utterly oblivious is he of the major question as to whether Matthew is even dependent upon Mark's version at all. No so V. Taylor, who tries to defend Mark's version in the following rather lame fashion: 'Jesus asks what Moses had commanded. If the original question was hostile, [Jesus'] *counterquestion might have seemed to be playing into their hands*,[3] but the sequel proved otherwise'.[4] Indifference to the form-critical problems generally leads to utterly far-fetched speculation, as, e.g., this strange explanation from W. D. Davies.

Matthew refuses to follow Mark in making Jesus introduce the reference to Moses but prefers to let the Pharisees first do so . . . [since Matthew has a certain] anxiety not to place Jesus in direct antithesis to Moses . . . whereas the Markan Christ has no such scruples.[5]

[1] Bultmann 39–54; cp. 27. See further, M. Albertz *Die synoptischen Streitgespräche* (1921). It is curious that Albertz does not see anything amiss in Mark's formal arrangement (see 39ff.). This is no doubt a result of the fact that Albertz' treatment lacks scientific breadth. Whereas Bultmann arrived at a delineation of this form though some efforts at a comparative analysis of rabbinic and pagan as well as Christian literature (see *History of the Synoptic Tradition* 39–46), Albertz has constructed his categories on the basis of the New Testament literature alone, which is hardly adequate.

[2] *Beginnings of Gospel Story* (1909) 137. So also Klostermann *Matt.* 155; R. Hummel *Die Auseinandersetzung zwischen Kirche und Judentum im Matthäusevangelium* (1966) 50; G. Strecker *Der Weg der Gerechtigkeit*[2] (1966) 131; Taylor *Mark* 417; Bultmann 132; Beare 190f.; and frequently.

[3] That is, because it advanced their position, not Jesus'.

[4] *Mark* 417 italics added.

[5] *The Setting of the Sermon on the Mount* (1965) 105f. Among other things, Davies' explanation also mars a clear distinction being made in Matthew's version between Moses the original giver of the Torah and Moses as *Torah shebiktav*: the law itself.

E. Klostermann thinks he has found 'the strongest proof for the priority of Mark' in the little summarizing repetition in Matt. 19.8: 'but from the beginning it was not so', admittedly a Matthean stylistic characteristic.[1] Others point to the longer quotation of Gen. 2.24 in Matt. 19.5, as compared to Mark 10.7, as another typical indication of Matthew's expansion of Mark.[2]

Against all such piece-meal analyses and atomistic scrutinies of details in the two accounts, it must be emphasized that no adequate discussion will be possible until the form-characteristics are carefully taken into account. Once this is done, however, it is difficult to evade the impression that Mark's account has been thoroughly re-arranged—as Bultmann originally maintained.[3]

So far, the best form-critical analysis to have appeared is that of Lohmeyer-Schmauch, which we shall here quote in full.

Mark's composition is carried out in three parts; he begins with Moses' legislation concerning divorce, primarily in order to set it aside, then sets forth the fundamental Law of Creation which makes marriage insoluble, and in his supplement for the disciples he adds two prohibitions for husband and wife, that if divorced they may not marry again. *This composition is determined throughout by interest in the reader for whom the Mosaic divorce-practice is unimportant. Hence it is set aside at the outset before the positive command follows. Then an explanation is given to the disciples which appears to interpret this fundamental law for them, as the future missionaries to the Gentiles.*
For the audience of Matthew, on the other hand, the marriage and

[1] Lagrange lists thirteen occurrences of this Matthean summarizing *inclusio* (lxxxi); see further B. C. Butler *The Originality of St. Matthew* (1951) 150.

[2] So, e.g., Daube *New Testament* 78 f., 83. But K. Stendahl, *The School of St. Matthew²* (1968) 60, shows that completely different factors could have produced Matthew's longer reading, so that it would be independent of Mark.

[3] Difficult perhaps, but not impossible (see further below). That Mark is not obviously enough mutilated to provide a convincing case on form-critical grounds alone is shown above all by M. Albertz who finds nothing wrong with the Markan version, see *Die Botschaft des Neuen Testaments* I¹ (1947) 65f.; also idem *Die synoptischen Streitgespräche* 39f. But on this see above, p. 104 n.1; in addition, it must be noted that even an Albertz cannot refrain from seeing that 'the first exchange (Mark 10.2–4) [serves] . . . to establish the pertinent regulation *which answers the question*'; *Botschaft* 68. One might think Albertz would consider this a peculiar way for the story to go.

divorce regulations of Moses are completely familiar. *Thus there is no need to describe what Moses had commanded* and what, therefore, would be the consequence if one divorced one's wife.

Instead, it is possible to begin immediately by citing the decision according to the law of Genesis. The Mosaic regulation then appears next as an objection to this decision, and this is quite properly placed in the mouth of the antagonists. Moses is then authoritatively set aside, and it is possible in a conclusion to state definitively that any new marriage by a divorced man is adultery. *It is a Controversy-dialogue which lies before us, following the plan: Question/Answer, Objection/ Refutation, Conclusion.*[1]

Few have described the didactic organization of Mark's version of this story more accurately than this. The whole account is arranged so that Jesus' final comment, no longer a retort to the Pharisees as in Matthew, is a positive regulation laid down for the wider Church—and the obvious Greco-Roman legal basis of the *dual-divorce* terminology is a dead give away at this point[2]— appropriately given only to the disciples in a house (a favorite scene-shift gimmick of Mark's). The basic motivation for this rearrangement is quite correctly stated by Lohmeyer-Schmauch also: it is the Christian readers and hearers of his gospel that are in Mark's view. Their chief concern is only on the Lord's teaching on divorce; hence it is set apart and emphasized. This focusing of Mark's interest on the concluding saying is significant for another reason, however, and so we shall go further into this in a moment.

It must be admitted, however, that a discussion of the form-critical issues will not close the question all by itself. For example, a small number of critics, following the lead of Bultmann,[3] while not exactly denying the secondary character of the account in Mark, take the very fact of Matthew's better formal arrangement as an indication of *his* secondary character! Thus R. Hummel speaks of Matthew's tendency to turn Mark's didactic or other material into Controversy-dialogues.[4]

[1] Lohmeyer-Schmauch 281 italics added.
[2] See above, p. 89, and below, p. 133.
[3] See especially Bultmann 51.
[4] *Auseinandersetzung* 50f. Interestingly enough, all that Hummel offers by way of evidence is a reference to a page corresponding to p. 27 (note 1) of the English translation of Bultmann's *History of the Synoptic*

The same inconclusiveness plagues other criteria, as well. For example, E. Klostermann explains Matthew's different, legally-improved, version on the basis of his 'Judaizing' concerns.[1] Strangely enough, it is precisely this 'Jewishness' which has convinced many others, such as Streeter and Lagrange,[2] that Matthew's account is the more primitive.

In short, it is evident how inconclusive the discussion presently is as to originality, even after the form-critical assessments are carried through. The difficulty of the problems involved is well-indicated by the fact that C. G. Montefiore can devote almost twenty pages of closely-packed argument to this passage and still not reach any final decision one way or the other.[3] Much of this inconclusiveness, however, is directly caused by certain wide-spread mistaken ideas concerning the role and proper interpretation of the final saying in the account. Therefore, our next task shall be to consider it more carefully.

B. THE CONCLUDING SAYING ON DIVORCE-REMARRIAGE (Matt. 19.9//Mark 10.11f.)

Although there is considerable agreement that Matthew's version of the story seems more original than Mark's, or, in the case of Bultmann and Hummel, formally more free of confusion, curiously enough most scholars consider *Mark's* final saying about

---

Tradition. This must be a mistake, however, for Bultmann doesn't discuss this phenomenon there, but on (ET) p. 51. If we look there, the curious fact that emerges is that Bultmann's first example of this 'tendency' is the pericope dealing with the 'Great Commandment' (Matt. 22.23–33//Mark 12.18–27//Luke 20.27–40), a well-known case of the so-called 'Q-Mark overlap' (see above, p. 63). Yet Bultmann would argue that *both* Matthew and Luke *independently of each other* turned Mark's 'pure, scholastic dialogue, which ends with the questioner being praised', into a Controversy-dialogue! It is difficult to overcome the suspicion that this position about Matthew's ability to turn obviously late and secondary material *into primitive, authentic-sounding* tradition is no more than a hypothesis conjured up to explain—*away*—difficult and embarrassing phenomena which arise for the Two-Document Hypothesis, such as is the case with this Divorce debate account.

[1] *Matt.* 155.
[2] Streeter, see above, p. 103; Lagrange 366.
[3] Montefiore I 225–236; II 257–266. The various textual problems in the two accounts are not significant; see on this Taylor *Mark* 416–421.

divorce-remarriage to be more original than Matthew's. How is this possible? The paradox is neatly solved by arguing that this saying was orginally independent of the story and first added to it by Mark, in which he was followed by Matthew. The following reasons have been advanced to support this argument: (a) Mark's editorial change of scene into the house plus the motif of having the disciples ask Jesus further about his public teaching is his way of combining otherwise unrelated material.[1] (b) The version of this saying differs sharply in Matthew and Mark; Matthew speaks only of the man's activity (as would be expected under Jewish law), while Mark makes provision for both man and woman, using the active form of the verb 'to divorce' in both cases (typical only of Roman and Greek law). The difference between the two versions suggests that the saying had a circulation of its own.[2] (c) It is apparently independently attested in Q, as represented by Matt. 5.32//Luke 16.18.[3] (d) Most important, in Mark's account it is neither integral to the rest of the story nor required by it. As B. W. Bacon says, Mark 10.10f. 'takes no account . . . of vv. 2–9 but merely condemns all divorce with remarriage as adultery.'[4] W. L. Knox adds, 'Mark introduces 10.10ff. as a private explanation given to the disciples "in the house" after the discussion of divorce with the Pharisees, although there is no need for such an explanation';[5] because, as Lohmeyer-Schmauch point out, 'nothing . . . in the preceding discussion is mysterious or difficult'.[6] For these and other reasons, then, it is generally considered that this saying was originally an independent logion.[7]

However much this saying may appear extraneous and un-motivated in the Markan account, in Matthew's it is part of Jesus'

[1] Bultmann 67, 330, 332.

[2] Taylor *Mark* 421; W. L. Knox *Sources* II 22; Daube *New Testament* 365ff.; J. B. Lightfoot *The Apostolic Fathers* (1888) II 350; Jolowicz *Roman Law* 245; cp. Wettstein *Nov. Test.* I 602f. Further bibliography in Taylor *Mark* 420. The same legal power as presupposed by the saying in Mark is also presupposed by Paul's form of the divorce-prohibition (1 Cor. 7.10a-11b) according to Daube *New Testament* 365; see further above, p. 89 n.2.

[3] Bultmann 132; Beare 181; Strecker *Weg* 17, 132.

[4] Bacon 139.

[5] *Sources* II 22.

[6] Lohmeyer-Schmauch 282.

[7] See further Klostermann *Mark* 97. Further bibliographical references on Matt. 5.32//19.9 in Strecker *Weg* 130n.1.

answer to the *Pharisees*. That is to say, it is an integral aspect of the Controversy-dialogue as a whole.[1] Now insofar as it is correct to consider Mark's scene-shift into the 'house' and the prompting of Jesus for further explanations by the disciples as artificial editorial devices of Mark himself, insofar as these may be *removed* from Mark's present account as secondary details, the result is that in Mark also Jesus would be portrayed as giving this final answer to the Pharisees. Furthermore, it is also widely granted that the present wording of this saying in Mark is a result of editorial revision.[2] This leaves only one argument, based on the supposed existence of a Q version of this saying, still supporting the contention that this was an originally independent logion added onto this account. Now, although we hope to show that it is by no means necessary to posit a place for this saying in Q, nevertheless it may well have been the case that this saying in fact did have an independent circulation *as an abstract of this story as a whole* (including the final saying). Our task, therefore, must be to demonstrate the necessity of this saying to the rest of this account, thereby proving that this is its original setting and that the conclusive evidence for this is precisely the essential phrase—by no means a 'Matthean insertion'—'except for fornication'.

C. THE SO-CALLED MATTHEAN INSERTIONS: 'FOR ANY CAUSE' AND 'EXCEPT FOR FORNICATION'[3]

As already mentioned, the occurrence of these two phrases in Matt. 19.3 and 19.9 are widely taken to be manifest evidence of Matthean editorial additions serving to prove conclusively that Matthew interpolated Mark's account. However, this proof, like a snow-bank sheltered from the rays of the sun, may loom imposingly in the darkness, but rapidly melts away if ever exposed to the sun's relentless scrutiny. Indeed, it may well be that what is providing the cover in this case is a much larger structure, the

---

[1] See statement of Lohmeyer-Schmauch above, pp. 105f.

[2] See above, p. 108 n.2.

[3] For some strange reason, these clauses and their 'original' meaning, especially the latter clause, exercise a perennial attraction for budding Catholic biblical scholars, as a glance through the back issues of *Biblica* will show. Every year, a whole new crop of proposals and suggestions appears, and there is always quite a lively debate. It must be said, however, that it is marked in general by far-fetched and uninformed opinions. See, e.g., H. Zimmerman '*me epi porneia* (Matt. 19.9)—ein

Two-Document Hypothesis, which sinks its foundations into passages other than this one, we may be sure. Nevertheless, despite the tension caused for the Two-Document Hypothesis (and this will not be the only place this particular kind of tension has manifested itself)[1] we must insist upon the right to inquire not

---

literarisches Problem. Zur Komposition von Matt. 19.3–12', *Catholica* 16 (1962) 293–299; B. Byron, 'The Meaning of "Except it be for fornication",' *AusCathRec* 40 (1963) 90–95; J. J. O'Rourke, 'A Note on an Exception: Matt. 5.32 (19.9) and 1 Cor. 7.12 Compared', *Heyth Jour* 5 (1964) 299–302; A. M. Dubarle, 'Mariage et divorce dans l'Évangile', *Orient-Syrien* 9 (1964) 61–73; answered by J. Dauvillier, 'L'indissolubilité du mariage dans la nouvelle Loi', *Orient-Syrien* 9 (1964) 265–289; A. Mahoney, 'A New Look at the Divorce Clauses in Matt. 5.32 and 19.9', *CBQ* 30 (1968) 29–38; J.-C. Margot, 'L'indissolubilité du mariage selon le Nouveau Testament', *RevThéolPhil* 17 (1967) 391–403. See for the same misguided exegesis also among the Protestants, a typical example, H. G. Coiner, 'Those "Divorce and Remarriage" Passages (Matt. 5.32; 19.9; 1 Cor. 7.10–16), with Brief Reference to the Mark and Luke Passages', *Concordia Theological Monthly* 39 (1968) 367–384. A very common error on both sides is the claim that divorce as such was 'absolutely forbidden'. This, of course, would have special pertinence on the Catholic side; e.g., H. J. Richards, 'Christ on Divorce', *Scripture* 11 (1959) 22–32; H. Baltensweiler, 'Die Ehebruchsklauseln bei Matthäus: zu Matt. 5.32; 19.9'), *TheolZeit* 15 (1959) 340–356; M. Zerwick, 'De matrimonio et divortio in Evangelio', *VerbDom* 38 (1960) 193–212. This might also be the place to mention J. Bonsirven's suggestion that 'except for fornication' actually refers to marriage within the forbidden degrees, and must be connected to the Acts 15 decree so that Matthew permits divorce and remarriage among Gentiles accidentally married within the forbidden degrees, hence it is a later insertion into Jesus' original absolute prohibition of divorce— this view still has considerable support; e.g., in the articles mentioned above, see those by Dauvillier, Zerwick, Richards, and Baltensweiler. Easily the best recent articles are those by B. Vawter, 'The Divorce Clauses in Matt. 5.32', *CBQ* 16 (1954) 155–67 containing a very lucid account of recent scholarship (weighted toward Catholic contributions), and by M. R. Lehmann, 'Gen. 2.24 as the Basis for Divorce in Halakah and N.T.' ZAltWiss 72 (1960) 263–267 on which see the quote below on p. 128 n.1.

[1]As mentioned before (see p. 66 n.2), it is not the purpose of the writer to offer this study as a critique of the Two-Document Hypothesis. On the contrary, it is a study of the way the sayings of the Lord were handled in the early Church, and, as such, moves fully within the framework of the Two-Document Hypothesis. That the two passages from the Synoptic gospels taken under study in fact offer grounds for doubting the validity of this hypothesis may well be the case, but this is purely coincidental to the central thrust of our investigation.

only after possible interpolations on the part of Matthew, but also after possible *omissions* on the part of Mark. To illustrate, let us ask, with regard to the first phrase, what the Pharisees' question actually means in Matthew's version, and what their question— without this phrase—means in Mark's.

It is generally agreed that the Pharisees' question in Matthew: 'Is it against the Law for a man to divorce his wife *on any pretext whatever?*' (*JB*), comes directly out of the current Pharisaic controversy over the 'grounds of divorce [which was one of the issues] actually debated at the time between the schools of Hillel and Shammai'.[1] The phrase gives precisely the view of the School of Hillel, who taught that a man could divorce his wife for all sorts of reasons—even burning the food!²

What have the Pharisees asked according to Mark's version, i.e., minus this phrase? There Jesus is asked, 'Is it against the Law for a man to divorce his wife?' (*JB*). Now, in view of their knowledge of Deut. 24.1, wherein Moses explicitly lays down the legal grounds for divorce, as well as establishing the procedure for getting divorced, and even more in view of Mishnah tractate Gittin (Divorces)—a whole compendium of regulations concerning divorce procedures—the earlier history of which must have included (as we can see in it) precisely the debates of Hillel and Shammai of Jesus' time, this is a very strange question for these Pharisees to ask. In view of the overwhelming evidence that *nothing whatever in the Law suggests that divorce is illegal*, any commentator who proposes to defend the primitive historical character of Mark's version of the Pharisees question, that it is more original than Matthew's, has no alternative, it seems to me, but to search for ulterior and sinister motives on the part of the Pharisees for putting such an obviously phony question to Jesus.

¹ Streeter *Four Gospels* 259; cp. Billerbeck I 312–321; Moore *Judaism* II 121–126; R. H. Charles *The Teaching of the New Testament on Divorce* (1921) 85ff; Taylor *Mark* 417; Lagrange 366; Montefiore I 229–231; Cp. further Josephus who said it was the Jewish (read Pharisaic) custom to get a divorce 'for any reason whatsoever' *kath' hasdepotoun aitias*; *JA* 4.253. This is of course generally the situation today in modern Western society. Divorce may be granted for a 'variety of reasons': desertion, physical and mental cruelty, infidelity, insanity, impotency, conviction of a felony, bigamy, nonsupport, and so on. It is, to be sure, uncommon for all of these to be found in any one collection of regional statutes.

² Mish. Git. 9.10.

No doubt such deep analysis will attract some who are unable or unwilling to familiarize themselves with sufficient Jewish juris-prudence to make a historically reliable judgment on the matter. The fact is, Mark's version of the question is inconceivable in a Palestinian Pharisaic milieu. This is, of course, simply another way of saying that this is not where it arose. On the other hand, if we simply transpose the whole story in Mark into the setting of the early Hellenistic Church, everything immediately fits perfectly. For it is well known that in that milieu, divorce as such was in fact discouraged as much as possible. Thus Mark's question: 'Shall there be divorce (at all)?' makes perfect sense; and Jesus' answer is, appropriately enough, 'No'. As Lohmeyer-Schmauch argue, this is quite simply the Church's question to itself.[1]

Having begun with quite different statements of the Pharisees' question, the two accounts continue in divergent directions. Matthew sets forth an account of a legal debate between Jesus and his learned opponents. Mark develops the same theme although the legal precision is missing entirely from the debate,[2] and Jesus ends up merely rejecting the Pharisees' view-point out-of-hand. The two conclusions of the debate contrast equally sharply. Matthew's version gives as a part of the speech to the Pharisees a concluding statement to the effect that more than one marriage is adulterous, and that therefore divorce is excluded—except divorce where there has already been adultery. Mark's version concludes with a special instruction to the disciples, in another location ('in the house'), consisting of two strict prohibitions of divorce and remarriage on the grounds that they are adulterous, and carrying no qualification of any kind.

It is almost the universal scholarly consensus that Mark's version is the more 'stringent', and therefore more early. Bacon's comment is typical: Matthew has changed 'a prophetic principle into a bit of ecclesiastical legislation'.[3] This consensus, however, is based on four errors: the rejection of the so-called 'Matthean insertions' as secondary to the original account, the consequent misunderstanding of Jesus' answer in Matthew's version as a whole, considering Mark's final answer to have a more 'radical character' (Bultmann) than Matthew's, and inattention to the

[1] See above, pp. 105f.
[2] See further below, pp. 127f.
[3] *Beginnings* 137; see above, p. 104 n.2.

possibility that in contrast to Matthew's, Mark's final saying is incomplete.

To begin with, Matthew's clause *is not an exception but a necessary aspect of Jesus' answer given in vv.* 4–6. This point was made already fifty years ago by Paul Billerbeck:[1] remarriage is completely ruled out in vv. 4–6 because it breaks the marital union envisioned for man in the Age of Creation. Thus, in the clause in v.9 'Jesus recognizes only fornication as grounds for divorce, since through it the marital union has already been actually destroyed.'[2]

In the second place, Jesus' final answer is not a 'prohibition of divorce' (Davies et al.) as such, anyway—as if Jesus were setting forth laws. On the contrary, Matthew describes an occasion when Jesus was challenged on the question of divorce by some Pharisees (representing, naturally enough, Hillel's view) and he cuts them down with a very sharp legal argument. Nothing of the Church is present here. Indeed, the first requirement must be to leave Mark's version and its preoccupations completely aside for a moment and consider Jesus' final statement according to the situation portrayed *in Matthew.* But since this is apparently such an unorthodox approach to this passage, perhaps we should dwell briefly on what is wrong with the usual interpretation of Matthew's final saying. Let us in fact ask the question whether 'except for fornication' is an 'exceptive clause' (Beare) in the sense of providing a loop-hole in Jesus' prohibition of divorce and remarriage? Is it really the case that 'the original rigorism [of Mark] has been relaxed?'[3]

Those who do consider 'except for fornication' a loop-hole in Jesus' prohibition of divorce take the position that Jesus thereby allows a second marriage in these special cases of prior marital infidelity. But the text does not actually seem to support this conclusion. Has Jesus actually permitted divorce *and remarriage*? Is it not true, instead, that the exceptive clause is no more than a side-clarification inserted to allow for the prior act of adultery, accompanying the basic answer that divorce with remarriage is adultery?

---

[1]And several times since by others; e.g. M. R. Lehmann, op. cit. above p. 110, and, of course, in the commentary on Matthew in the Meyer series, by E. Lohmeyer, rev. W. Schmauch (see below).

[2] Billerbeck I 312.

[3] Strecker *Weg* 132.

It is simply one part of a logically consistent, two-part deduction based upon the particular definition of marriage enunciated in Matt. 19.4–6. Lohmeyer-Schmauch bring this point out well.

The much referred-to clause 'except for fornication', which is also found in Matt. 5.32, is frequently understood as a limitation of the absolute prohibition of divorce. But that is an error, for if marriage means the 'becoming-one-flesh of man and wife', then the wife's fornication has already destroyed the marriage before the husband separates from her.[1]

It is essential to observe how polemically-formulated Jesus' answer is. Far from being a 'bit of ecclesiastical legislation' (Bacon) —even though we shall have to ask in a moment how Matthew may have understood and used this story—Jesus' final statement is formulated solely as a cutting rebuttal to the Pharisees' first question: 'The intention of the Creator is strict monogamy, a single sexual union for each man and woman; your constant divorcing and remarrying is brazen effrontery before God. There should be *no* divorce, unless the marital union is already destroyed *de facto*; then let it be destroyed *de jure* as well.' What these Pharisees get from Jesus is essentially a stern denunciation of their sexual vagrancy, holding up against their legitimized lust a view of marriage in which divorce does have its necessary place, but solely as the unavoidable legal consequence of failure at a deeper level of marital kinship.

In view of this, it is both unnecessary and hardly likely that Jesus allowed for second marriages under certain circumstances. For the exceptive clause is not an exception to the strict repudiation of single sexual union as the Law of Creation. All Jesus allows is the obvious (from the point of view of Jewish law) right that a husband not be required to live with an unfaithful wife, but may send her away. She through her own lust has broken with the Law of Creation. In this sense, Jesus does make an exception to the general rejection of divorce. But there is no compelling indication that the husband is then free to contract another marriage.

If it is generally known what the source of the Pharisees' question in Matthew's version was, and if we have succeeded in

[1] Lohmeyer-Schmauch 282.

clarifying what Jesus' concluding reply was, still remaining is the whole central part of the debate: Jesus' main answer and the Pharisees' sarcastic response to it. So, if the most serious problems of clarification are now behind us, perhaps the way is clear to proceed more easily to the important questions concerning the basic contentions Jesus makes in his answer. Above all, let us seek to discover the origin of the strange view that more than one marriage is adultery, regardless of whether there has been a legal divorce or not.

D. THE ASSUMPTIONS AND HORIZON OF JESUS' ANSWER (Matt. 19.3–9)

Thus far, we have been primarily concerned with establishing the integrity of the Matthean version of this Controversy-dialogue. Before we can give an answer as to its relation to the version in Mark as well as the other traces of this story in Matt. 5.32 and Luke 16.18, and with that, certain observations as to the history of the development of this account, it is necessary to ascertain more precisely what Jesus meant that constant divorce and remarriage was a crime against the Creator.

The answer to this question does not seem to lie far away. Indeed, it is now customary to observe that Matthew's two so-called insertions in vv. 3 and 9 stem from and fit this account perfectly into the Pharisaic debate then (scil., the first quarter-century of our era) taking place between the two rival parties, the Houses of Hillel and Shammai, and that if the Pharisees ask Jesus Hillel's question, Jesus gives Shammai's answer.[1]

The difficulty in this view is that Shammai obviously stood for divorce and remarriage, merely opposing Hillel in limiting the grounds for divorce to one cause: adultery. But Jesus, if our interpretation be correct, really rejects all remarriage and *consequently* all divorce, except when necessitated by adultery. Thus when the Pharisees in Matthew's version ask Jesus about divorce in such a way that it is clear they are holding the position of Hillel's ruling, the answer Jesus gives them is apparently not that of Shammai at all—*but Qumran.*

[1] The similarity with Shammai's answer is especially noticeable at Matt. 5.32, 'except on the ground of fornication' *parektos logou porneias*; Moore *Judaism* II 124 n.4 'verbatim'. See further below, p. 126 n.2.

For instance, we read in the Damascus Document, now conclusively known to have been circulated at Khirbet Qumran,[1] a
description of three 'nets of Belial' (IV.14) which have caught the
house of Israel, i.e., three sinful things which have been made to
'appear to them [presumably by the Pharisees] as three kinds of
righteousness' (IV.16f.). These are 'fornication (*zenuth*)',
'Mammon', and 'conveying uncleanness to the Sanctuary', i.e.,
the Temple in Jerusalem (IV.17f.).[2] Concerning 'fornication',
the account goes on to specify that two kinds of fornication are
involved. The second kind is marrying within the forbidden
degrees (V.8–11) and does not concern us. As for the first kind,
however, this is what the text says:

[Israel is] caught in two kinds of fornication: (first) to take two women
(as wives) in their (masc.) lifetimes although the foundation of creation
is male and female He created them.[3]

We know that the Essenes included some married members, at
least among those 'living in camps (villages?)'.[4] Furthermore,
evidence is accumulating that marriage was also a part of the life
of some of those living at the sect's Center at Khirbet Qumran as
well.[5] The point of CD 4.20f. seems then to have one possible
explanation: it is a prohibition of more than one marriage, whether

[1] Numerous fragments of the Damascus Document (representing
the A recension found in the Cairo Geniza) have been recovered from
Caves IV, V, and VI, including previously missing portions of the
beginning and end of that recension as well as several pages missing
from the middle of the A recension found in Cairo; see J. T. Milik *Ten
Years of Discovery in the Wilderness of Judaea* (1959) 38, 151f. This
means that the already well-known parallel between Jesus' answer in
Matt. 19.3–9 and CD 4.20f., especially with respect to the use of Gen.
1.27 over against Deut. 24.1, may now be placed in the *Essene* milieu.
Naturally, the mere presence of these fragments in the Essene library
says nothing as to their having been central Essene policy, or typical of
the majority viewpoint. But the many copies found, and the numerous
fragments discovered, do show that it was popular to some degree.
[2] Translations from ed. C. Rabin *The Zadokite Documents*[3] (1958)
16.
[3] CD 4.20f. ed. Rabin; cp. Gen. 1.27.
[4] Cp. Josephus *BJ* 2.160f.; see F. M. Cross *The Ancient Library of
Qumran*[2] (1961) 97; further H. Ringgren *The Faith of Qumran* (1961)
238.
[5] Ringgren *Faith* 140.

in the form of polygamy or in the form of remarriage following divorce.[1]

What is so important about this passage, however, is not just that it is identical with Jesus' answer in its repudiation of multiple marriages. Even more significant is that it arrives at this position by arguing in an identical fashion from 'the order of creation' against, if not Moses (which is not really in view here), what must have been the current, normative oral interpretation of Moses (the *Torah shebe-'al pe*). For this is precisely the procedure Jesus follows against his Pharisaic interlocutors, and just in this is revealed the unmistakable apocalyptic signature: the expectation of the imminent return of the Time of Creation, the primordial age of perfection soon to manifest itself through God's direct intervention. Indeed, the time is felt to be so close at hand as to provide a basis for opposition to the polluted legal traditions of men.[2] Whatever may have been the basis of Shammai's view, this particular point of similarity between the Damascus Document and Jesus' appeal to the age of Creation establishes the thoroughly apocalyptic horizon of Jesus' answer.

This realization is the basic clue needed to explain why more than one marriage—under any conditions—is considered fornication. In the apocalyptic sense of opposition to and superiority over the present, evil age, against which is placed the glittering, dream-vision of the dawn of a perfect Creation, from this opposition stems the apocalyptic social and religious critique. Thus it is that both the Essenes as well as Jesus take as their standard the single pair of Adam and Eve for all human marriages acceptable to God. What about the various laws of divorce, then? Only one conclusion is available to the apocalyptic: 'Moses gave them to you because of your sinfulness!' The desire for more than one wife—despite the clear testimony of scripture—in the present Age is for no other reason than that men have given themselves over to shameless lust. It is totally immaterial that they adopt various pretenses to cloak their fornication through 'laws' which 'allow' such activity. There is to be one marriage per couple; the laws of divorce are

---

[1] So D. Daube *New Testament* 85; A. Dupont-Sommer *The Essene Writings from Qumran* (1962) 129 n.1. C. Rabin's reading at 13.17 (*Zadokite* 66) is incorrect; the text speaks of community discipline, not divorce.

[2] Cross *Library* 76 n.35a; Albertz *Botschaft* 39ff.

sham laws invented by men. Any second marriage after a divorce is—adultery against the *original and still married first wife*. 'Whom God hath joined let no man put asunder.'

It is customary to interpret Jesus' answer as implying a high and lofty regard for the place of marriage in God's plan of creation. This may be true, but it is important to observe the fact that anything in the way of an idealization of the married estate, or of a profound appreciation of sexual union, on the part of Jesus is quite out of the question. For example, among the Essenes (who here as at so many other points appear in close kinship with Jesus' viewpoint) this strict emphasis upon single marriages was by no means due to a strong and positive evaluation of monogamous marriage. On the contrary, *marriage appears to have been an exception in a context of celibate asceticism.* The majority of the Essenes living at Qumran had no part in marriage.[1] Josephus describes this situation quite precisely in his report concerning one group of totally celibate Essenes and another, resembling the first group in every respect, which practiced single marriage for the sake of procreation alone.[2]

F. Cross's observation on this phenomenon is very helpful: 'This area of Essene life can best be understood, not by positing a sect of marrying Essenes alongside a celibate sect, but by recognizing an ambiguous attitude toward marriage integral to the structure of the Essene faith.'[3] Then, after arguing that it was primarily the Community's stance of total preparedness for the great Final Battle, so that all the rules of Holy War were in effect (in particular those of ritual purity), that provides the theological basis for their continence, Cross continues,

the Essene in his daily life thus girds himself to withstand the final trial, purifies himself to join the holy armies [of angels], anticipates the coming conditions in God's inbreaking kingdom. This is the situation which prompts counsels against marriage, at least for some.[4]

Cross does not give any reason as to what may have led those Essenes who did marry to do so. Was it a concession to the weaklings as with Paul? The very way in which Cross portrays the reasons for remaining celibate make it difficult to avoid the

---

[1] Cross 97–99; Ringgren *Faith* 139f., 237f.

[2] *BJ* 2.120f.//*JA* 18.21 and *BJ* 2.160f.   [3] *Library* 98.

[4] Ibid. 99. See further G. W. Buchanan, 'The Role of Purity in the Structure of the Essene Sect', *RevQum* 4 (1963) 397–406.

conclusion that anything less than celibacy would be tantamount
to ritual impurity and therefore unpreparedness to take part in the
great Final Battle —a generally unacceptable condition from the
sect's point of view. What may have been the reason? Josephus'
explanation is usually dismissed as a Stoicising distortion: those
who married he says, did so because 'if all decided the same thing
[scil., not to marry], the race [of the Jews] would quickly be cut off.
. . . For they believed progeny to be the most important . . . part
of life.'[1]

As a matter of fact, Josephus explanation may not be so wide
of the truth. From a much older writing exhibiting the same kind
of 'priestly apocalyticism' (Cross) as that of the Dead Sea sect,
there is a passage denouncing divorce, this time linked up with
the other verse in Jesus' argument from Genesis, namely, Gen.
2.24: 'therefore a man leaves his father and his mother and cleaves
to his wife, and they become one flesh.' The significant aspect of
this passage from Malachi 2.13–16, however, is that together with
the rejection of divorce goes an emphasis upon single marriage
for the sole purpose of godly children:

And here is something else you do: you cover the altar of Yahweh with
tears, with weeping and wailing, because he now refuses to consider the
offering or accept it from your hands. And you ask, 'Why?' It is
because Yahweh stands as a witness between you and the wife of your
youth, the wife with whom you have broken faith, even though she was
your partner[2] and wife by your covenant. Did he not create a single
being[3] with flesh[4] and breath of life? For what is this single being
destined? God-given offspring. Be careful of your own life, therefore,
and do not break faith with the wife of your youth. *For I hate divorce,
says Yahweh the God of Israel.*[5]

[1] *BJ* 2.16of. (no parallel in *JA*); cp. *c.Ap.* 2.199.
[2] Gen. 2.18.
[3] Gen. 2.24 'the two shall become one flesh'. It is possible that what
this phrase actually means, in view of the mention of child-bearing, is
actually Gen. 1.27: 'God created man in his own image, . . . male and
female he created them . . . and said, "Be fruitful and multiply".'
(*RSV*) Interesting are the speculations of Daube that what is intended
here is a reference to an androgynous Adam/Eve composite being; see
Daube *New Testament* 71–86, and idem 'Evangelisten und Rabbinen,'
ZNW 48 (1957) 119–126; further P. Winter 'Genesis 1.27 and Jesus'
Saying on Divorce', *ZAW* 70, (1958), 26of.
[4] Text obscure. For a different reading cp. Brown-Driver-Briggs
Lexicon s.v. *she'ar.*
[5] Mal. 2.13–16 *JB*, italics added.

K

This quote from Malachi[1] adds considerable weight to the trust-worthiness of Josephus' explanation of the marrying-Essenes' motivation, although his formulation omits any reference, as usual, to the apocalyptic ideology. If so, then a clear conflict emerges in the Essene attitude toward marriage, producing the ambiguity Cross mentioned.

On the one side was the desire for ritual purity because of the great Crisis into which all things soon would come. On the other side, there may have been a desire to prepare for the long term requirements of their position as the Elect, soon to inherit the whole Creation purified of defilement and wickedness, with all of the responsibilities and privileges pertaining. It would be a difficult decision to make, which side to give preference.

One thing is clear, however. The emphasis upon continence was only a temporary one. We do not find any thorough-going ascetic dualism of body *vs.* soul here. But equally clear is the complete lack of any romantic idealization of marital bliss: 'two eternal souls/sweetly intertwin'd as one.' Jesus' answer, with the reference to Gen. 2.24, may well have had in mind the interpretation of that passage we found in Malachi 2.13–16, i.e., marriage for the purpose of raising godly children. But the insistence upon monogamy stems not from any philosophical insight as to where the true strength of a society resides (viz., the family), nor any developed theory of personality, but rather from a hatred of what is here viewed as uncontrolled lust. Thus any sexual unions beyond the first are all lumped together as adultery, divorce or no.[2]

---

[1] The LXX has a different text. O. Eissfeldt, *The Old Testament. An Introduction* (1965) 442, gives as a probable date for this writing as a whole the first half of the fifth century. For its priestly character, cp. its 'stress upon the value of strict fulfillment of cultic duties' (443), e.g., in its second section (Malachi 1.6–2.9) which reproaches the priests for offering inferior sacrifices. The last two sections (3.6–12 and 3.13–21) are apocalyptic warning and exhortation. The section warning against marriage with foreign women (2.11b–13a) brings this writing into close proximity with another document from the sphere of priestly apocalypticism, fragments of which have also been found at Qumran, the *Book of Jubilees*.

[2] If we have to some degree disclosed some of the assumptions and the horizon of Jesus' answer here in Matt. 19.3–9, it is not our purpose to try to relate them to the assumptions behind Jesus' answer in the account of the Sadducees' question concerning the resurrection (Matt. 22.23–33//Mark 12.18–27//Luke 20.27–40); however, see below, pp. 129f.

In any case, it should now be clear how Hillel's position looked against the horizon presupposed by Jesus' answer: as sheer disobedience to the Creator's original plan, and as hypocritically legalized caving in before the pressure of sexual passion. And that is the brunt of Jesus' initial reply.

Not about to suffer such condemnation in silence, the Pharisees sarcastically inquire of Jesus, that if this is the case, why are there laws about divorce in Scripture? Only they overreach themselves: 'Why then did Moses command us to get divorces?' Jesus' reply is an acid correction in their legal terminology: 'Moses did not *command* you, he *permitted* you to get divorces—because of our sinfulness!' In order to get the full impact of Jesus' retort, one must be familiar with the precise meanings of these two terms, and the implications behind Jesus' scathing correction of the Pharisees' wording. It involved a distinction, known to the legal terminology of the time, between ordinary laws given for the regulation of the people, and other laws or institutions which were given only because of Israel's inability or unwillingness to live in the path of true righteousness. Such were 'concessions to the sinfulness of the people', as D. Daube explains it. We encountered precisely the same use of these terms earlier, in our investigation of Paul's discussion of marriage (1 Cor. 7.6).[1] Regarding this passage, Daube says:

when Jesus parried the Pharisaic [query, why had Moses commanded men to get] bills of divorce, by maintaining that this was admitted because of the people's wickedness, he was using an established category; it was an argument which both his followers and his opponents would understand. Divorce (Jesus contended) runs counter to that complete union between man and wife which God designed when first creating the world. It was sanctioned for a vicious society by Moses, who could only interpose certain safeguards [against unchecked immorality]. But the final community will do without it, in accordance with the original divine plan'.[2]

This significant conflict in the legal terminology has become lost completely in Mark's version. There in Jesus' first reply, he

[1] See above, pp. 87f.
[2] D. Daube 'Concessions to Sinfulness in Jewish Law', *JJSt* 10 (1959) 10. Cp. Ptolemy *ad Flor.* 4.1–9. On not making laws the majority cannot (or will not) obey, see Daube 8f., and Davies *Setting of the Sermon on the Mount* 394 n.1.

is made to ask, 'What did Moses *command* you to do?' Then,
obviously totally ignorant of the nuances he is destroying, Mark
reverses the tables and gives the Pharisees the chance to correct
Jesus' mistaken terminology when he has them say, 'Moses
permitted us to get bills of divorce. . . .' This shift probably
explains the next alteration in Jesus' second answer (v.5), 'because
of your sinfulness Moses *wrote* this command for you'. All this
serves to demonstrate vividly what Lohmeyer-Schmauch point
out, that Mark has little interest in the Law of Moses, and less
understanding of it.

E. THE ORIGINALITY OF MATT. 19.3–9

Now that we have had opportunity to gain a fairly clear
conception of both the central thrust as well as the general horizon
of Jesus' reply to the Pharisees, and, in the course of the discussion,
having noticed many dissimilarities between the account of
Matthew and that of Mark, we should finally be sufficiently
informed to arrive at a decision as to the question of the relation of
these two versions to one another. We therefore adopt the position
of Lohmeyer-Schmauch that Matthew and Mark are literarily
independent of each other at this point, i.e., Matthew is not
dependent upon Mark's version of the story.[1] Furthermore, we
agree also with B. H. Streeter that Matthew's version is more
original and represents earlier tradition, a possibility that Bultmann
also admits, but doubtfully.[2] In our view, we have tried to demon-

[1] Lohmeyer-Schmauch 280; against this view see Taylor *Mark* 415;
Beare 190; Klostermann *Matt.* 155; Strecker *Weg* 130; Daube *New
Testament* 78, 83f.; who is followed by H. Zimmerman, '*mē epi porneia*
(Matt. 19.9)—ein literarisches Problem. Zur Komposition von Matt.
19.3–12', *Catholica* 16 (1962) 293–299. Montefiore, see p. 107 above,
leaves it open.

[2] Streeter *Four Gospels* 259 postulates a 'Mark-"M" overlap' which
serves, as with two other cases he mentions, to explain why Matthew's
account 'appears to be in some ways more original than Mark's.'
Bultmann remarks concerning Streeter's opinion, 'Streeter . . . draws
the conclusion that Matthew must have had access to a parallel tradition
for this passage. That is undoubtedly possible, but to my mind not
certain'. He then goes on to give as a 'trace' of the Markan version in
Matthew the use of the contrasting terms 'command-concede' (Matthew)
and 'command-write' (Mark). In referring to this, however, Bultmann
seems unaware of the possible original legal significance of these terms,

strate that Matthew's version is more early in the sense that it
stands closer to the oral tradition since its formal character is
beautifully intact, recondite Palestinian legal terminology appears
accurately used, the apocalyptic tenor is vividly present, and there
are no ecclesiastically-motivated alterations in the account itself.
As for Mark's version, on the other hand, we adopt the position
of Bultmann, that Mark 10.2–12 was 'given [its] present form in
the written tradition';[1] i.e., by the editor. The general problem as
to which gospel is dependent upon which will of course not be
decided by this one case alone, but the fact is—and our investigation emphatically confirms this—it is widely agreed that in the
question as to which of the two preserves more faithfully the
original story, the evidence has persuaded a consensus to favor
Matthew.[2]

We may go further. If Matthew's account is the more early,
is it also historically reliable as well? The reader will no doubt
have observed that, all along, we have been arguing on the basis of
an implicit assumption of the relative historical accuracy of this
account in Matthew. It was this assumption which led us to
press for the points of possible contact specifically among Jesus'
contemporaries (Hillel, Shammai, Qumran), while neglecting to
look for other, later figures and religious trends contemporaneous

---

and therefore omits any consideration of Mark's apparent *misuse* of
them, which reveals his secondariness compared with Matthew. Not
only this, despite his emphatic assertion of the obvious 'artificiality' of
the Markan version of this story on form-critical grounds, Bultmann
still somehow thinks Matthew is dependent upon Mark's version (see
27 n.1 and 132).

[1] Bultmann 48.

[2] This is of course all the more noteworthy in light of the fact that
this same consensus also holds to the priority of Mark, and Matthew's
literary dependence upon Mark. In some ways, the problem is especially acute in this passage, as there is no Lukan parallel to solve the
problem of the obvious lateness of Mark's account *via* an appeal to Q,
such as we had in the first part of our study. Thus really sophisticated
studies are pushed to the wall to explain this peculiar phenomenon,
and, e.g., Streeter must concoct yet another 'parallel source'—a task he
of course found quite easy, almost a favorite pastime (e.g., 'L', 'proto-
Luke', 'M', 'Q'). While on the other hand, Bultmann opts for the
quite implausible solution that Matthew has reshaped the material in
Mark to reflect more accurately early Palestinian conditions. See
further next note.

with the early Church, or even with Matthew specifically. In doing this, however, we have not been unaware of the justifiable objection that all such points of contact we traced vis-à-vis Jesus' milieu could simply be due to Matthew's careful and learned editing of some story he received in the tradition. This is, in a way, a problem similar to Bultmann's contention regarding Matthew's alleged 'form-creating' activity, whereby Matthew reworks the material so that it *looks early*.[1]

With the evidence at our disposal, it is difficult to meet such an objection. Two things may be said, however. There is the general argument from the trustworthiness of Matthew's writing as a whole, i.e., the degree to which he *ordinarily* alters his source material. To be sure, we cannot at this point enter upon a dis-cussion of such a difficult issue, but, nevertheless, it is one way of answering the objection mentioned above, at least in part.

Its weakness, however, is that it is no more than a general rule, and therefore is vulnerable to the criticism that, whatever may be true for Matthew's habitual use of source-material, in this particular case, he has reworked the material. At this point, one must simply ask the basic methodological question first formulated and brilliantly utilized by the Tübingen School, are there any signs of editorial or ecclesiastical *Tendenz* in the structure of the account, or its chief figures, or the points of view expressed? The best answer so far available to this question is: it seems to be

---

[1]Although we will try to take this objection seriously and seek to show how we would answer it using our interpretation of the evidence, it may well be that the difficulty in answering it with any conclusiveness is not so much because of the paucity of the evidence or the inappro-priateness of our interpretation, but because it is meaningless as an hypothesis. This is not the place to launch into a full-scale critique of such a viewpoint, but it must certainly be noted that that is a strange hypothesis indeed which can show how certain accounts in the gospels are *early* because they more faithfully preserve characteristics of the oral form of the account, while other accounts may be adjudged as *late* because they have been made to look early through editorial revisions towards better oral form-characteristics! That is, precisely because they look early is a sign of their lateness. This surely stands the truth on its head. Needless to say, furthermore, it would be virtually impossible to conceive of *any* case which could disprove such an hypo-thesis. But this simply means that it is meaningless, for an hypothesis must be able to be falsified in order for it to assert anything. This is precisely what this hypothesis does not allow, it would seem.

minimal—confined mainly to taking Jesus' answer to be a binding regulation on the Church (see below next section). But as for the rest, I do not see any compelling evidence that this is not a fairly accurate account of an actual debate Jesus had, or at least a beautifully formulated précis of Jesus' actual opinion over against the School of Hillel, whether expressed on one single occasion or not.

2. *The gospel editors' use of this account*

A. MATTHEW

Although Matthew seems to have left the story intact, he clearly considers it important as a 'saying of the Lord'. This is shown in the first place by his appending a little explanatory dialogue between Jesus and the disciples (19.10–12). Following Jesus' 'prohibition of divorce (i.e., remarriage)'—for that is clearly how *Matthew* understands it—the disciples are made to say, 'If that is how things are between husband and wife, it is advisable not to marry!' (*JB*).

A handful of commentators have pointed out the remarkable awkwardness of the disciples' reaction here. For example, W. D. Davies says:

The reaction of the disciples to the proclamation in 19.9 reflects no credit on them: they virtually make the attractiveness of marriage contingent upon the possibility of divorce, and that on easy terms. . . . It might be expected that Jesus would have reacted violently against such an attitude as the disciples here display, castigating their low appreciation of the marriage state. But this we do not find.[1]

The explanation is that Matthew sought to build a bridge over into the next saying concerning 'eunuchs for the Kingdom of Heaven', and this unfortunate and artificial response of the disciples is it. Nevertheless, it is noteworthy that the disciples' reaction—which Matthew apparently intended to sound something like: 'Your view of marriage is most rigorous! No doubt few are capable of it.'—is turned down. That is, Jesus is portrayed as holding the

---

[1] That is to say, we do not find it despite the fact that Jesus has just finished 'castigating' the Pharisees for propounding exactly the same view; *Setting* 393. Cp. Lohmeyer-Schmauch 282; G. D. Kilpatrick *Origins* 83.

general position (taking 19.3–12 as a whole) that celibacy is a gift for some ('not all can receive it'),[1] while for everyone else, marriage must be once-for-all. It is a position corresponding precisely with Paul's.

In the second place, Matthew reckoned the account important enough to fashion an extract of it for use in his series of anthitheses in the Sermon on the Mount. The weird formulation there (5.32) —entirely from the woman's point-of-view—is probably best explained that Matthew, as Bultmann says of Mark (see below), 'wanted a ruling not only for the man but for the woman, too'. It is by no means necessary to postulate an existence for this saying in Q.[2]

Finally, it is important to observe the care with which Matthew preserves both sides of Jesus' position concerning divorce. Both the rejection of remarriage as well as the demand for divorce in cases of infidelity were equally important for him, and, we may no doubt add, for Jesus as well. Under Jewish law, for example, adultery was punishable not by divorce exactly but by stoning. That is to say, adultery required drastic action—in any case, certainly not permitting the marriage simply to continue.[3] Paul's reaction to the case of fornication in Corinth was not at all extreme (1 Cor. 5.1ff.); there, as E. Käsemann rightly says, Paul demanded capital punishment since the man had committed a capital

[1] For further discussion of this difficult passage, see J. Blinzler, 'Eisin eunouchoi Zur Auslegung von Matt. 19.12', ZNW 48 (1957) 254–270; Q. Quesnell, ' "Made Themselves Eunuchs for the Kingdom of Heaven" (Matt. 19.12),' CBQ 30 (1968) 335–358; and especially C. Daniel, 'Esséniens et Eunuques (Matthieu 19.10–12)', RevQum 6 (1968) 353–390, who argues that it refers to voluntary celibacy (=eunuch) for the sake of the Kingdom of God. On the place of celibacy in the Qumran sect, see further above, pp. 118f.

[2] For Matthew being responsible for 5.32, see Bultmann 148; Klostermann Matt. 46; W. L. Knox Sources II 99. The similarity with Shammai's position in the crucial phrase in Matt 5.32 is no accident. We have already noted that Jesus' position did resemble Shammai's view, in part. No doubt we must reckon with Matthew's familiarity with this debate as well, coming out here in the precisely accurate use of the legal terms involved (for Shammai's inverted reading of Deut. 24.1, see the references given above, p. 111 n.1.

[3] Moore Judaism II 125. Whether stoning was actually still carried out in this period, see H. Mantel, Studies in the History of the Sanhedrin (1961) 307ff.

offense.[1] This point is necessary to emphasize, for it has direct bearing upon how we are to assess Mark's version's concluding saying.

B. MARK

Let us now consider Mark's version as a whole and the last saying in particular. To begin with, following Lohmeyer-Schmauch, we saw that Mark's whole account is a secondary re-arrangement of the account better attested in Matt. 19.3–9, and that this rearrangement was motivated by Mark's didactic concern to edify the Church. Secondly, the general result was that all the weight is thrown onto the conclusion of the story, which Mark has recast as a special instruction to the disciples forbidding all divorce and remarriage. We also noted that this instruction was expanded, no doubt for the reason Bultmann suggests: 'a legal ruling was wanted not only for the man, but for the woman too.'[2]

Here we come to the last two of the errors mentioned above: considering Mark's final answer to have a more 'radical character' (Bultmann) than Matthew's, and neglect of the possibility that Mark's final saying is incomplete.[3] In the first place, insofar as Mark 10.11f. simply brands all divorce and remarriage as adultery, it is certainly 'radical' as compared with contemporary Pharisaic law—if by radical one means it stands in sharp contrast against it. But Mark's final saying is certainly not any more radical, as we have learned by now, than Matthew's saying since the two are identical in respect of forbidding remarriage. On the other hand, leaving aside the matter of remarriage, we must ask what a strict prohibition of divorce would mean? Here we must address generations of biblical exegetes who glibly assert that Jesus 'prohibited divorce absolutely'.[4] Are we to suppose that in Mark's view marriage, once initiated, was to be maintained regardless of what each of the partners did? The *lack of finesse* of Mark's version of Jesus' concluding statement, the lack of legal precision indeed—when compared with Matt. 19.9 and 5.32—must be pointed out. Even Hermas, who has no great reputation these days

---

[1] 'Sätze heiligen Rechtes', in idem, *Exegetische Versuche und Besinnungen* II (1964) 72ff.

[2] Bultmann 132. On the Greco-Roman legal context presupposed by Mark's formulation, see above, p. 89 n.2.

[3] See above, pp. 112f.   [4] See above, p. 109 n.3.

for his intellectual acuity, knows better than Mark what to do when one of the partners ceases to be faithful.[1]

We suggest, however, that Mark's version *did not mean* that all marriages should be kept together regardless of the circumstances and at any cost. As we have seen from the way Hermas handles a case of infidelity, and the fact that Matthew's version actually contained a legal provision for such cases, and finally from the way Paul also corresponds to this general position (allowing divorce but not remarriage), the conclusion seems inevitable that some sort of silent burden of oral interpretation is being assumed by Mark's formulation, indeed, precisely the same sort we see operating in 1 Cor. 7.10f. This is a rejection of divorce and remarriage. Paul's formulation is even briefer, being simply a rejection of divorce alone. But the fact that he proceeds immediately to *grant* a divorce, makes it clear that his saying—wording to the contrary notwithstanding—meant something else.

Thus, using Paul's example as the crucial piece of evidence, we maintain that there was a tendency to use this account, as shown by Mark 10.11f, Matt. 5.32, Luke 16.18, and 1 Cor. 7.10f, *to abstract Jesus' polemical reply into a community regulation specifying a ban on divorce-remarriage whose essential purpose was just the*

[1] See above, p. 91. We refer of course to the fourth error mentioned above, namely, inattention to the possibility that Mark's final saying (as well as Luke 16.18) is incomplete. M. Lehmann puts it very well: 'There is nothing new or surprising in this discussion [in Matt. 19.3–9. It] may have been part of the widely and often held disputations between followers of Hillel and Shammai during the same period. We thus see that the saving clause 'except it be for fornication' cannot be a scribal interpolation. In fact, it is *the cardinal point* in the general legal discussion of the time. The account of the same episode in Mark 10.11, and a similar version in Luke 16.18, leave out the reservation for fornication. Although NT critics hold Mark to be the source of both Matthew and Luke, there can be no doubt that the fuller Matthews [sic] account renders the correct text. *The omission of the conditional clause in Mark and Luke must be called the scribal error, not the reverse, as has been held till now*'; 'Gen. 2.24 as the Basis for Divorce in Halakah and NT', *ZAW* 72 (1960) 266 italics added. Lehmann holds that Jesus' position was simply Shammai's, viz., remarriage is permitted in cases involving adultery. Although we cannot follow him in this, he does make the interesting observation that such a narrow scope for divorce also seems to have been the Essene position as well. As evidence, he cites the stress on Exodus 23.7 'keep far from every false thing' in 1QS V 15; cp. the Shammaite view expressed in bKethuboth 17a.

prohibition of remarriage, divorce being allowed under certain circumstances. Mark, with his enlarged conclusion, represents an interesting sort of middle term in this tendency, as also Matthew who has kept both the original account intact as well as a home-made abstract of it. Paul's formulation is of the briefest sort, yet it clearly falls within the general pattern. Luke also fits the same pattern, but this may not be so obvious. Let us see if we can retrace the well-nigh lost path this account took in his gospel.

C. LUKE (16.18)

It is customary to argue that Luke passed over this account in his source (Mark), apparently preferring to use only the independent logion from Q dealing with the same subject.[1] But was there such a saying in Q? It has already been demonstrated that the usual grounds for arguing that this saying has been added to the accounts in Matthew and Mark are erroneous; that it is intrinsic to this story, at least as preserved in Matthew (the most original form of it). Furthermore, as commonly held, Matt 5.32 is not from Q but Matthew himself. Now insofar as we know that Luke did in fact receive a version of this account, presumably Mark's, in his source(s), what is to prevent us from concluding that he simply took the final saying and omitted the rest?

The likelihood that this is what happened can be shown along two different lines of argument. For one thing, we do know that by the time Luke wrote, the tendency to abstract this account precisely in some form of its final saying was already taking place, and Luke could have done the same thing. That is, the final saying seems to have been a sort of detachable handle for the account, able to be referred to independently as a saying of the Lord, as at 1 Cor. 7.10, Matt. 5.32—and here.

In the second place, we can see from Luke's attitude toward marriage why he would have both rejected the larger account and yet preserved the final saying. Luke's feelings on the subject of marriage come clearly into view nowhere else more vividly than in the astonishing passage in 20.34–36.

[1] Indeed, it is usually asserted that Luke 16.18 preserves the closest approximation to the *ipsissima verba Iesu*; see F. Neirynck, 'Het evangelisch echtscheidingsverbod', *Collationes Brugenses et Gandarenses* 4 (1958) 25–46; further below p. 133.

Jesus said, 'The children of this world take wives and husbands, but those who are judged worthy of a place in the other world and in the resurrection from the dead *do not marry because they can no longer die for they are the same as angels.* (*JB* italics added).

Perhaps there are some who would be willing to argue that this represents a closer approximation of Jesus' words than the parallels in Matt. 22.30//Mark 12.25, but as a glance at a gospel synopsis shows, it is hard to doubt that this is Luke himself speaking here.   It fits well into his well-known, hard-line asceticism.[1] If this is right, then we can see how Luke would consider the story of Jesus' defense of monogamy repugnant and unworthy, not so much because its view was 'too Jewish' (W. L. Knox), but because it was too *physical*.   On the other hand, there might well have been a need, from Luke's point of view, for a strict regulation forbidding more than one marriage—to control the spiritual weaklings who could not remain celibate.

Puzzling is the way Luke has formulated this saying, however. It speaks about both men and women, but it is given only from the male point of view as Matt. 19.9. Why Luke would alter Mark's appropriate dual formulation, considering his Gentile readership, is difficult to explain.[2]

---

[1] See above, Luke's attitude toward the question of support for apostles as it finally comes out in Acts, pp. 72f. Cp. also the difference between Matt. 19.29//Mark 10.29 and Luke 18.29; or Matt. 22.5 and Luke 14.18ff., especially v.20. Further, J. Leipoldt *Griechische Philosophie und frühchristliche Askese* (1961) 35f. Remarkable is the case of Clement of Alexandria who, when confronted by the heretic Tatian and other radical ascetics using this word of the Lord in Luke 20.35f. to support their fierce opposition to marriage, argued that they had misinterpreted Jesus, basing his argument—apparently without realizing the differences involved—on the *parallel saying* in Matt. 22.30//Mark 12.25. See *Strom.* III 12.87.1. But we need not go that far back to find examples of this confusion; see Klostermann *Luke* 195. Much better is B. K. Diderichsen, 'Efterfølge og Ægteskab i Lukas-evangeliet', *Festskrift til J. Nørregaard* (1947) 33, H. von Campen-hausen's comment ('Askese', 138 n.127) notwithstanding.

[2] At least, in terms of the Two-Document Hypothesis—unless one has recourse to various unknown sources. But see below, p. 131 n.1.

D. CONCLUSIONS

In general, we propose that Matt. 19.3–9 contains a central, early account, probably resting on solid historical reminiscence of Jesus' actual views regarding the Hillelite teaching on divorce and remarriage. In this account, interestingly enough, Jesus' outlook is very closely related to the Essenes' similar repudiation of the Pharisaic laissez-faire policy regarding remarriage. In using this account, the gospel editors and apparently also the apostle Paul tended to fasten upon the final saying, which rejected all remarriage and required divorce under certain circumstances. In using the saying, however, the original formulation became distorted slightly so that it came to be just a prohibition of divorce and remarriage, or, in the case of Paul, no more than a prohibition of divorce. We therefore deduced that what such a summary abstract really meant was a blanket prohibition of remarriage, but that, as originally in the account as well as in two examples of the Church's regulating actual cases, divorce was in fact permitted under certain compelling circumstances. What seems to have emerged from our investigation, then, is a certain general pattern of usage of this account that seems quite consistent and which explains the main question left in our discussion of Paul's use of the command of the Lord concerning divorce.[1]

---

[1] It is worth noting that such pericopes as this are precisely those in which the Griesbach hypothesis shines at its best. The early, historically reliable, authentic ring of Matthew's version is due to its close proximity to the events recorded. Luke rejected Matthew's account as a whole, the possible reasons for which have been elaborated, but now we may add that the similarity with the male-emphasis in Matthew's account's final saying is readily explained. Luke was not dependent on Mark's dual version (in 10.11f.) at all. Also, we have seen that there is no need to invent a Q document to account for either Matt. 5.32 or Luke 16.18. Finally, Mark 10.2–12 also fits perfectly into the scheme. Desiring a teaching from the Lord prohibiting extra marriages, Mark more or less blindly reworked Matthew's entire account, emphasizing in clearer (i.e., Gentile) legal terms the teaching he was after at the end, now directed specifically to the disciples. For other examples of Griesbachian analysis, see, e.g., W. R. Farmer *Synoptic Problem* 255–257; and, in general, F. C. Baur *Das Markusevangelium nach seinem Ursprung und Charakter* (1851).

CHAPTER FOUR

Paul and the Editors of the Synoptic Gospels

Once again, it is remarkable how closely the way in which Paul cites and applies this command of the Lord corresponds with what we have discerned through a form-critical analysis of the pertinent Synoptic material. Although we have by no means cleared up all the problems involved, we have seen enough to have been able to trace at least the outlines of a development of a saying of the Lord from its origin, as a polemic remark of Jesus in the milieu of Palestinian Judaism, to its eventual transformation into a regulation concerning divorce and marriage in the early Church. In any case, there can be little doubt that the tradition Paul is relying on in 1 Cor. 7.10f. is precisely the same as that recorded in various forms in the Synoptic gospels.

This opens up an interesting question. Are we to suppose, then, that Paul may have been alluding to the *entire* account by means of its 'handle?' Two features of Paul's statements point in this direction. First, we have shown that Paul's manner of applying his command of the Lord fit perfectly within the general pattern of usage exhibited by the Synoptic editors. The tell-tale clue is the fact that Paul intends a prohibition of remarriage, with this rejection of divorce, which points unmistakably to the *main* contention in Jesus' answer in the body of the account.

Second, Paul's seeming awareness and use of the whole account is revealed by two other points in his wider discussion. He turns to the theme of 'two becoming one flesh' (Gen. 2.24)—an integral part of Jesus' position—at two crucial places; in 6.15f. where he refers to intercourse with the *porné* ('prostitute'?), and again in 7.12–16 where it seems to have been the basis of his argument urging Christians married to unbelievers not to seek a divorce. But there, interestingly enough, Paul derives from it the added point that the purpose for such marriages is *godly children*; just what is implied in Jesus' answer in Matt. 19.3–9! To be sure, the missionary context is not missing in Paul's additional hope that the unbelieving spouse will be converted.

If it be true that Paul is thinking of the entire account, however, then this is the time to emphasize—as in the previous case—how *allusively* it is being used. It is below the surface of his argument, *even when he refers to it directly*. Nothing briefer, misleading even!, can be imagined as a citation of the position of the Lord on this subject than what Paul gives in 1 Cor. 7.10f. Furthermore, that Paul can give such a quick, short-hand excerpt of it plus application without any discussion whatever is clear evidence that the Corinthians would completely understand what he was doing. These facts have important bearing on the problem of how to judge the extent of his use of sayings of the Lord traditions in general, a question we shall pursue more fully in the next section.

What can be said as to which of the Gospel traditions is closest to the Pauline formulation? There is hardly any agreement between the various discussions of this question. Some argue that Paul is dependent upon a semi-Q tradition made up of Mark 10.9+Luke 16.18,[1] or Matt. 19.6+Luke 16.18 (but not Matt. 5.32=19.9).[2] J. Moffatt thinks Paul is referring to the final summarizing verse in Mark (10.11f.),[3] but F. W. Beare (with C. R. Feilding) points out that there is 'no parallel' between Mark 10.11f. and 1 Cor. 7.10f. because the two are concerned with two very different problems.[4] He and V. Taylor opt instead for the body of the account rather than its summary, or Q.[5] The majority of critics simply wave in the general direction of all of the Synoptic material at once.[6] The reasons for the disagreement are valid. Paul presents the command of the Lord with respect to both sexes in equal terms (like Mark), but on the other hand he preserves authentic Jewish legal terminology (unlike Mark, but like Matthew and Luke). At the same time, his citation says nothing whatever about adultery, thus seeming to stem from the body of the account, and not its ending at all, despite its other similarities with that. Thus it might be a kind of summary of the whole. Yet just in this he resembles all of the gospel editors who tended to summar-

[1] Robertson-Plummer 140.
[2] Lietzmann-Kümmel 31.
[3] Moffatt 78.
[4] Beare 192.
[5] Taylor *Mark* 419.
[6] Lightfoot 225; Allo 163; Héring 53.

ize the account in terms of the final saying, whose parallelism Paul's command resembles (e.g. Mark). Indeed, in merely passing on the final saying alone, he seems to resemble only Luke who, in 16.18, does no more than that.

If we look in the wider context for other traces of kinship, the results are no more conclusive. In 1 Cor. 7.7, Paul warns against making the ideal of abstinence a rule for all, which is why in 7.1–6 he advocates marriage for the majority. This view is an exact duplicate of Matthew's own position, as we saw in the discussion of Matt. 19.10–12. But whether or not this similarity is due to Paul's familiarity with the traditions Matthew records in 19.10–12 does not appear. Much more likely is a general resemblance between Paul's outlook and that of the editor of Matthew.

At the same time, Paul leans in the direction of Luke's ascetism, for Paul also believed that marriage, together with all social and cultural institutions (which he gathers together in the significant pairs referred to in Gal. 3.28; 5.6; 6.15; 1 Cor. 7.18f.) is soon to be obliterated in the resurrection, and may best be so treated in the present (e.g., 1 Cor. 7.29–31).[1] Nevertheless, we look in vain for so extreme a statement as that in Luke 20.34ff.

In contrast to the previous example, therefore, the question as to which of the various Synoptic formulations seems presupposed by Paul's formulation must be left open. There seem to be points of contact in several different ways, but, in general, the evidence is insufficient for a clear-cut decision.

Finally the study of the Synoptic material and its affinities with the Essene teachings on marriage and divorce may have shed light on a question raised above concerning the grounds Paul had for distinguishing between remarriage after the death

---

[1] W.-G. Kümmel, 'Verlobung' 294 n. 74, and W. Schrage, 'Stellung' 130f., maintain that Paul's view is not a dualistic ascetism, apparently in the Platonic sense, since it is founded upon his apocalypticism. But it is difficult to see why Paul's view is any the less dualistic than Greek or Persian views just because it is not a static dualism of metaphysical realms of being. He certainly believes that the sexual difference will be done away with, *including the physical body as such* (1 Cor. 15.50), in the resurrection. Hence, it is a basically negative feature of 'this age'. Menoud rightly points out, Paul would never have dreamed of saying, as he did about circumcision, ' "marriage is nothing and celibacy is nothing" '; ('Mariage' 33). In view of his belief that celibacy was a gift of the Spirit, such a formulation would have been impossible.

of the first partner and remarriage following divorce. As we saw, Paul allowed the former (1 Cor. 7.8f.) but forbade the latter, and did so without any explanation in the context. Perhaps the crucial factor, as the Essene material suggests, is whether the one or the other may be considered a result of unbridled lust (=fornication). Thus, in the case of remarriage following the death of the original partner, another marriage would not be the result of the voluntary dismissal of the first partner, but he would simply represent a surrogate. Quite different, then, would be the active seeking of another mate *via* divorce. This could well be interpreted as the fruit of excessive lust. In fact, we might even say that remarriage following the death of the original partner is consistent with Paul's warning not to cause enforced continence upon one's mate.[1]

[1] In any case, such a distinction as Paul made was not admitted on all sides in the early Church. Rigorists such as Athenagoras held to the contrary that 'he who severs himself from his first wife, even if she is dead, is an adulterer in disguise'; *Leg. pro Christ.* 33. So also, at length, Tertullian, *de Exhortatione castatis.*

PART III

Results

Results

1. *Paul's intimate relation with the Synoptic tradition*

In these two, materially unrelated cases, it has been demonstrated how a saying of Jesus, which had passed into the tradition of the early Church, was used to regulate its life as a command of the Lord. Or, to be more precise, it was showed how the Church *tried* to use sayings of the Lord in its tradition, despite the fact that new developments in the Church frequently made this difficult. It was one of the major themes of this demonstration that if Paul and the editors of the Synoptic gospels are compared in this respect, that is, if the Synoptic editors' intentions, as to how the older traditional sayings of Jesus were to be interpreted and applied, are compared with Paul's actual interpretation and application at Corinth and elsewhere, they turn out to resemble each other almost perfectly. Even the degree of divergence and discrepancy is the amount we would expect. As far as these two cases are concerned, Paul stands squarely within the tradition that led to the Synoptic gospels, and is of one mind with the editors of those gospels, not only in the way he understands what Jesus (the Lord) was actually commanding in the sayings themselves but also in the way he prefigures the Synoptic editors' use of them.

For example, this was shown in the first case through Paul's accurate paraphrase of the Lord's command that there be an unrestricted scope in the support to which apostles were entitled (1 Cor. 9.14). As we saw, this was the intention in Jesus' original instruction.[1] On the other hand, we showed that Paul disregarded this command of the Lord most of the time, defending his course (and that of his associates) in such a way that we could see the problem was a financial one.[2] This corresponded to Matthew's *alteration* of the original (i.e., Q) account, in which—by interpolating a strict injunction that apostles were not to accept 'wages' (Matt. 10.8b)—he limited the original open-endedness of the saying,[3] and it corresponded also to Luke's complex alterations,

---

[1] See above, p. 67f.
[2] See above, pp. 30 f.
[3] See above, pp. 69f.

the eventual outcome of which was to recommend that apostles be given no support whatever.[1]

Furthermore, it seemed to be the case that Paul's whole series of arguments in 1 Cor. 9.4–14 was little more than a homiletical rehearsing of the two aspects of Matthew's (i.e., Q's) version of the workman-food saying in Jesus' instructions (Matt. 10.10 as opposed to Luke 10.7).[2] On the other hand, Paul stood together with Luke, over against Matthew, in discussing the question of support for apostles in a context dealing with the problem of unclean foods, while Luke introduces a few words of advice from 'Jesus' regarding unclean foods in a context dealing with support for apostles. A verbatim correspondence was even found to obtain between Luke 10.8 and 1 Cor. 10.27: 'eat whatever is set before you.'[3]

In the second case, Paul's self-contradictory manner of citing and applying the command of the Lord proved to be completely inexplicable on the basis of the evidence in his letters alone.[4] Yet, once we turned to a careful examination of the Synoptic accounts, one riddle after another cleared up, as crucial insights emerged, not only from a series of comparisons with the way the Synoptic editors handled the same saying,[5] but most importantly from a careful inquiry into what the central thrust of Jesus' original statements on remarriage had been,[6] as this was compared and contrasted with various groups in the contemporary Palestinian milieu.[7]

It turned out that Paul had, again correctly, interpreted Jesus' original saying to forbid remarriage but not divorce,[8] and that the clash between Paul's application (based on this interpretation) and the wording of the command he actually cites simply reflected current practice, as shown by the Synoptic editors' referring to Jesus' saying by means of a *rough approximation* of the final phrases in Jesus' answer.[9] In this case, Mark and Matthew

[1] See above, pp. 71ff.
[2] See above, pp. 78f.
[3] See above, pp. 46f.
[4] See above, pp. 92f., 101.
[5] See above, pp. 125–131.
[6] See above, pp. 115–122.
[7] Most intriguing in this respect was the close similarity in both cases to the Essene theory and praxis; see above, pp. 45, 67f., 115f.
[8] See above, pp. 117f., 132.
[9] See above, pp. 126, 128f., 129.

provided the crucial clues as to how the tradition was operating to produce something like Pauls' behavior.[1] In addition, Paul's over-all stance regarding the advisibility of (single) marriage for the majority, with celibacy being the higher way for the few, was shown to correspond precisely with the way Matthew took the Lord's advice—Mark and Luke being rather different at this point.[2] But again, Paul seemed in some ways to be closer to Luke than to Matthew or Mark, as far as sharing Luke's intensely ascetic outlook was concerned. Where Matthew (and possibly Mark) may have had some positive feelings concerning the place of marriage—probably reflecting Jesus' view here[3]—for Luke and Paul it was a concession to spiritual weakness in order to forestall irremediable sins.[4]

To repeat, Paul's concrete application of these traditional sayings of the Lord in the context of his churches fits almost perfectly into a general pattern of similar interpretation and application of the same sayings in the Church of his day, as typified by the three Synoptic editors.

2. *Paul's conservatism regarding the tradition itself*

When Paul argued his legitimate authority to require the Corinthians to support him, we should note that, despite his strong negative feelings toward those who abused this regulation, he showed no inclination to tamper with what we later learned from the Synoptic accounts was Jesus' original wide scope of support intended: the apostle was to receive anything he needed[5] —money, lodging, board, assistants, and so on. That is, he did not seek to abolish or curtail *it*. Instead, he and his associates simply made a practice of setting this regulation aside whenever they encountered circumstances where to have kept to it would have made them an hindrance to the Gospel.[6] But Paul does not react against the regulation itself.

In the second case, when Paul came to the problem of whether there should be divorce in marriages between Christians and unbelievers (1 Cor. 7.12–16), despite the fact that he has just cited a command of the Lord regarding divorce, Paul emphatically

[1] See above, pp. 126, 128f.
[2] See above, pp. 125f., 129f.
[3] See above, p. 125.
[4] See above, pp. 83ff., 87, 130, cp. 118f.
[5] See above, pp. 67f., 76
[6] See above, pp. 28–33.

announces that in the following case he, not the Lord, is giving the
ruling. We accounted for Paul's peculiar behavior by the fact
that two quite different kinds of divorce were in view, and that
Paul had moved from the Lord's command because *it did not apply
in the second case*.[1] But, in the light of a fresh examination of what
was in the oldest tradition as Jesus' saying on marriage and divorce,
it turned out that—demurrer notwithstanding—Paul was in fact
still relying on the saying of the Lord referred to just before, both
materially in the ostensibly independent line of argument (1 Cor.
7.14) he introduces to back up 'his' decision,[2] as well as formally
in the decision itself.[3]

The point of these observations is to highlight Paul's reserve
in the way he uses this type of tradition, his clear unwillingness to
'stretch' the word of the Lord so that it will henceforth be more
servicable. Indeed, Paul goes to some lengths in making it clear
to the Corinthians that he is not 'adding or subtracting' from the
Lord's command.[4] But Paul's conservatism regarding this type
of tradition does not seem in accord with the degree to which this
allegedly took place during the rise and development of the
Synoptic tradition, according to the view of many form-critics.
To hear them tell it, new sayings of the Lord were constantly being
created and *surreptitiously or accidentally* included with the older
authentic sayings, while the older sayings were being surreptitiously or accidentally discarded or modified to fit the needs of new
developments, and so on. Even less does it accord with the
freedom the gospel editors seem to display, where such inventing,
altering, rearranging, omitting, and combining took place on an
astonishingly massive scale, a fact which can be seen by anyone,
form-critic or otherwise, who has a synopsis.

It is not our intention to enter here into these difficult questions,
except to point out one characteristic of the current discussion and
relate this study's findings to it. Even as the Scandinavians are
assaulting the fortress of form-criticism from without, a 'palace
revolution' is quietly going on within. Just when K. Stendahl and
H. Riesenfeld and B. Gerhardsson have proved to their satisfaction
that there never was any such thing as the illiterate group of

[1] See above, pp. 98f.
[2] See above, p. 132.
[3] See above, p. 98.
[4] See Moffatt's comment here, quoted above, p. 101.

peasants which made up the 'creative community'[1] posited by the older form-critics to explain the divergences between the Synoptic accounts,[2] W. Marxsen, H. Conzelmann, and others involved in the recent redaction-criticism,[3] are slowly obviating the need to posit it at all by assigning more and more of the divergences to the creativity of the gospel editors. Thus, while the former are demonstrating the conservatism and rigidity of a highly literate and trained transmission-personnel, the latter are demonstrating the freedom and creativity of those who finally edited (or should we say, 'wrote'?) the gospels.[4] Not a little interest attaches to the

[1] See above, pp. xxviif.

[2] See further Bultmann *Theology* I 47f. Of course, this is the view still most prevalent among form-critics, see E. Käsemann, 'Sätze heiligen Rechtes im Neuen Testament', *Exegetische Versuche und Besinnungen* II 69–82; F. C. Grant, 'The Authenticity of Jesus' Sayings', in the Bultmann Festschr. of 1954, 137–143; E. E. Ellis, 'Luke XI 49–51: An Oracle of a Christian Prophet?' *Expository Times* 74 (1963) 157–58; D. E. Nineham, 'Eye-witness Testimony and the Gospel Tradition I', *JTS* 9 (1958) 13–25, continued, Part II *JTS* 9 (1958) 243–252, concluded Part III *JTS* 11 (1960) 253–264; A. Wilder, 'Form-history and the Oldest Tradition', *Neotestamentica et Patristica* (1962) 3–13; C. C. Cowling, 'The Involvement of the Community in the Apostolic Tradition', *Church Quarterly Review* (1963) 6–18; W. Trilling, 'Jesusüberlieferung und apostoliche Vollmacht', *Trier Theologische Zeitung* 71 (1962) 352–368; F. W. Beare, 'Sayings of the Risen Jesus', *Christian History and Interpretation* (1967) 161–181. For the opposite view, see e.g., F. Neugebauer, 'Geistsprüche und Jesuslogion. Erwägungen zur der von der formgeschichtlichen Betrachtungsweise R. Bultmanns angenommenen grundsätzlichen Möglichkeit einer Identität von prophetischen Geistsprüchen mit Logien des irdischen Jesus', *ZNW* 53 (1962) 218–228.

[3] W. Marxsen, *Der Evangelist Markus. Studien zur Redactionsgeschichte des Evangeliums*[2] (1959); ET J. Boyce et al. 1969. H. Conzelmann, *Die Mitte der Zeit*[2] (1957); ET G. Buswell, *The Theology of St. Luke* (1961).

[4] The recent developments in redaction-criticism not only assure us that we need not worry any longer about that creative community of illiterate Galilean peasants, which seemed so real in the early days of form-criticism, also fading away are the innumerable 'sources' bandied about so energetically during the hey-day of 19th century source-criticism, the time of men like Ewald, Wellhausen, and Holtzmann in Germany, Sanday, Burkitt and Streeter in England. Works such as that of Stendahl on Matthew, Marxsen on Mark, and Conzelmann on Luke, are drastically transforming the grounds of discussion. This can be seen, for example, in the following quite revolutionary remark of

outcome of these developments, especially how the two groups will
settle their differences. We only wish to indicate that this study
appears to confirm *both* views to some degree. Paul seems to have
treated the tradition very carefully, while the gospel editors
changed it around to suit their aims just as freely.

It is, to be sure, a matter of degree, however. Paul's intense
disgust at those apostles who insisted upon their right to be
supported in trying situations, and his own refusal to keep to it if
this hindered the Gospel, became the basis for his 'treating this
commandment as a permission' (Gerhardsson, Moffatt). But this
is already to take the first step, indeed the fateful step, toward
making revisions in the regulation itself. What is even more
significant, Paul explicitly placed his non-observance of this
regulation in the context of a great, over-arching missionary
strategy, according to which he claimed the freedom to keep or set
aside all sorts of contemporary religious distinctions for the sake
of the Gospel *including Christian ones such as the strong-weak
distinction and even obedience to the Lord's command regarding
support for apostles.*[1] We must not miss the significance of what
Paul reveals here. He has justified a specific innovation over
against a community regulation founded upon a command of the
Lord by means of appeal to a general, all-inclusive principle. But
this is to relativize the entire tradition of the sayings of the Lord.

Conzelmann: 'Although the use of new material [i.e., special sources]
by Luke cannot be disputed, nevertheless *the most important alterations*
[in Luke's passion narrative] *are the result of Luke's editorial work and
are the expression of his own views*'; *Theology of St. Luke* 200. This is an
astonishing declaration to those who remember the days when one
scurried about seeking to find traces of the special source which Luke
'followed' in his passion narrative, meticulously counting up lists of
'uncharacteristic terms', drawing parallels with the gospel of John,
1 Corinthians, and the like. It is probably not mere coincidence that,
along with the rise in willingness to give up relying upon innumerable
hypothetical 'sources' the current period is also experiencing a growing
criticism of the Q-hypothesis, which necessarily is to launch a
radical attack on Two-Document Hypothesis; see especially, W. R.
Farmer, *The Synoptic Tradition* (1964). Interestingly enough, if
current trends in redaction criticism continue, Farmer's (or rather
Griesbach's) hypothesis of the priority of Matthew seems destined to
coincide with a redaction-historical verdict of Matthew's relative
earliness, in the not-too-distant future.

[1] See above, pp. 33–36.

What Paul does with this command of the Lord could be done with others, at least in principle . . . for the sake of the Gospel's unhindered advance. This clear and straightforward declaration of Paul's is striking, and must be carefully considered in any investigation of the question how the sayings of the Lord—regardless of how they were transmitted—were actually *used* in the Gentile mission setting. Thus Paul seems to be a middle term, containing within himself a veneration for the earliest tradition of the words of the Lord, as well as a lively innovativeness in applying them to guide the missionary Church. Both positively and negatively, i.e., both in terms of preserving and using commands of the Lord for the guidance of the Church, as well as indicating severe stress and adopting new methods when these commands became unsuited to the needs of the missionary situation, in both ways Paul is a direct confirmation of the editorial motivations and concrete Church conditions which form-critical analysis of the Synoptic accounts posits as the explanation for the various phenomena exhibited by them in their relationships to each other and to the earlier tradition. In Paul, the earliest form of the command of the Lord is still intact—but the concrete innovation has already taken place, in the name of the Lord. Or, to put it still another way, one might well see how a Paul, were he to 're-publish' the teachings of the Lord in story form, using the popular genre of a pious biography of the founder of their religion,[1] would have been careful to omit the original saying about supporting apostles from it altogether as being too dangerous for the Church (or at least limiting its financial scope drastically), and expand the legal applicability of the saying about divorce so that it would be more relevant.[2]

[1] See the case for this in M. Hadas and M. Smith, *Heroes and Gods. Spiritual Biographies in Antiquity*, New York (1965). Their very suggestive argument is vitiated by the fact that they do not seek to bring in any of the debate on this issue that has already gone on for a long time. See, e.g., C. W. Votaw, 'The Gospels and Contemporary Biographies', *AmerJourTheol* (1915) repr. Facet Books (Fortress 1970); answered by K. L. Schmidt, 'Die Stellung der Evangelien in der allgemeinen Literaturgeschichte', in *EUCHARISTERION* [Festschr. Gunkel] (1923) 50–135. The viewpoints of both were later discussed in the exceptionally lucid review of the whole question by H. J. Cadbury, *The Making of Luke-Acts* (1961). For the older discussion, see above all, P. Wendland, *Die Urchristliche Literaturformen*[2],[3] (1912).

[2] In any case, it is simply untrue that the teachings of Jesus were formed into a sacred, fixed code, that was absolutely binding. This frequently-heard romantic notion appears also in Gerhardsson, for

3. *How much of the Synoptic tradition did Paul use?*

Although this question has not been a primary concern of this study certain results of the investigations undertaken above may shed new light on it. Two in particular are of importance: Paul's extensive allusiveness even when he says he is using a saying of the Lord, and the strong indications that he is intimately related to that complex of traditions now preserved in the Synoptic gospels.

To begin with, it has been frequently noted in the past that, in these two commands of the Lord, Paul does not directly quote the saying of the Lord but just 'produces a halakah based on such a saying'.[1] That is, he only alludes to the actual saying; he uses it indirectly. Now we must go further and point out that Paul's indirectness is a *major aspect* of his use of these two sayings of the Lord in both contexts. For example, we found grounds for suggesting that Paul is alluding to the workman/food saying *all through the context of* 1 *Cor.* 9.4–14.'[2] Even when he comes to the actual reference to the Lord's command he does not stop *alluding* to this saying.[3] As for the other case, we found traces of the original saying (as reconstructed from the Synoptic material)[4] lying beneath several points in Paul's argument. He derives the

---

example, when he says, 'Paul subjects himself to the tradition from the Lord, and regards what Jesus bound as being bound indeed'; *Memory* 320. Strangely enough, Gerhardsson is able to say this just after he admits that 'Paul classified Jesus' commandment [regarding support for apostles] as a permission . . . *not as an obligation*'; op. cit. 319. To be sure, Gerhardsson is fully alive to the gradations in degree of obligation among Paul's various types of authoritative pronouncements (see, e.g., 305ff.), but what he leaves as an anomaly in Paul, we have sought to put into its proper perspective, namely, that for Paul the demands of the Gospel transcended the authority of specific commands of the Lord. We might note, in this connection, a very perceptive treatment in the field of NT ethics of Paul's use of commands of the Lord, see W. Schrage, *Die konkreten Einzelgebote in der paulinischen Paränese* (1961); especially the section titled, 'Die Herrenworte als Norm christlichen Lebens' (238–249). In good Lutheran fashion, Schrage opens his discussion by considering the one case where Paul overruled an explicit command of the Lord.

[1] Gerhardsson, *Memory* 318.
[2] See above, p. 80.
[3] See above, p. 21.
[4] See above, pp. 31, 122ff.

proper application regardless of the distorted, short-hand excerpt he mentions as the Lord's command,[1] he uses the same original account again while claiming not to (1 Cor. 7.12–16),[2] and it also seems to be beneath the surface when he is discussing the *porne* (1 Cor. 6.15f.).[3] The rather surprising result may be formulated as follows: *it is precisely when one examines Paul's explicit use of the sayings of the Lord that one most clearly perceives how indirectly and allusively he depends upon them.*[4]

A further observation should be added. In neither case does Paul give any indication that his interpretation of the saying of the Lord is in any way controversial, and, in the second case, the fact that he can give an extraordinarily misleading paraphrase of the saying involved and, practically in mid-breath, apply it in contradictory fashion—all with no explanation whatever—these things plainly say that it is a situation filled with signs of mutual understanding and common reliance upon sayings that are well known, including their proper interpretation and application. Paul does not stop to explain because he does not need to. But this means, as far as the allusiveness we described above is concerned, that Paul's use of the command of the Lord everywhere in his remarks *would certainly not have been lost on the Corinthians*. They would have recognized the source of his views immediately.

In the second place, we have already discussed above how much Paul has in common, both with the oral tradition lying behind the Synoptic accounts as well as with the Synoptic editors' own points of view. We should speak here of Paul's intimate relation with this entire tradition, as indicated by these two examples (and a few others). But this raises a very interesting possibility: the great number of admittedly authentic sayings of the Lord contained in the Synoptic *gospels* suggests that the amount of Synoptic *tradition* current among the Pauline congregations and known to Paul could have been far higher than the number of times he openly refers to sayings of the Lord. Is this reflected in any way in his letter? How many sayings of the Lord does Paul actually use in his letters?

It is not necessary to repeat here the many familiar arguments which deal with the question of how many sayings of Jesus Paul knew of or used in his work. In general, those urging a high

[1] See above, pp. 127f., 133. [2] See above, pp. 97f.
[3] See above, p. 132. [4] See above, pp. 80, 133.

number have had recourse to two types of proof: one which
simply claimed that Paul *must* have desired to know and use such
traditions,[1] and another which pointed to the numerous parallels
between the ethical teachings in Paul's letters and sayings of Jesus
recorded in the canonical gospels.[2] The weaknesses of both
arguments have long since been exposed.[3] In more recent times,
a third line of argument has been advanced, to the effect that Paul's
use of technical tradition-transmission terminology in his letters
proves that he had a role in this process, which was to be understood to have taken place in much the same way as the later
rabbinic transmission-process was carried out.[4] This hypothesis
is still being considered.

On the other side, those contending that Paul had few sayings
of Jesus tend to advance two chief arguments. First, the very few
times Paul refers to such sayings is pointed out as manifest
evidence of the general number in his possession,[5] while on the
other hand, it is argued that, regardless of how many may have
been available to Paul, he was not interested in what Jesus taught
in any case. He was proclaiming faith *in* Jesus, not the faith *of*
Jesus.[6]

We have already discussed our appraisal of the solution to this
question which consists in an uncontrolled and haphazard gathering of parallels which are forthwith arbitrarily designated Pauline
allusions to the sayings of Jesus, and proposed our alternative to
it.[7] We are now prepared to ask a question of the other side.
When it is asserted that Paul rarely uses sayings of Jesus, what,
precisely, is meant by this? To judge from standard procedure,
what is meant is use, scil. use *explicitly*. Let us hear a typical
statement of Bultmann's on this once again.

That Paul considered it valuable to have a word of the Lord for the
purposes of discipline, i.e., community order, 1 Cor. 7.25 demonstrates.
All the clearer is it, then, when he otherwise cites (*zitiert*) none where
one might be expected, it is because he knows of none.[8]

The problem with this view becomes apparent immediately if
we ask, when did it become customary to refer to the sayings of

[1] See above, p. xxv.   [2] See above, p. xxii.
[3] See above, pp. xxiii, xxv. [4] See above, p. xxvi.
[5] See above, p. xxiv   [6] See above, pp. xviif., xxv.
[7] See above, pp. xxix–xxxiii.
[8] Bultmann, 'Die Bedeutung des geschichtlichen Jesus für die
Theologie des Paulus,' in idem *Glauben und Verstehen* I[3] (1958) 190.

Jesus explicitly, carefully, and, as it were, accurately? The answer to this is well-known. Although a Tertullian and an Irenaeus may have succeeded most of the time in keeping their citations explicit and unscrambled, the same thing cannot be said for Justin Martyr, or II Clement, or I Clement. In them, however, the degree of explicitness is clearly on the rise. But if we go back farther, to someone like Polycarp or Ignatius, or the other Apostolic Fathers, we can see much less explicit citation of traditional material (whether sayings of Jesus or of Paul or of the Old Testament). On the contrary, a general *allusiveness* covers over the dependence we know is there, thanks to our modern, critical editions.[1]

In other words, is it not *anachronistic* to assume that Paul has not referred to a saying of Jesus if he did not do so openly, carefully, and with quotation marks, as we do?

But we have demonstrated that Paul does not refer to the sayings of the Lord in this way. Perhaps the most revealing example is 1 Cor. 7.12–16, where Paul uses Jesus' saying to guide his decision *precisely in a context where he has expressly claimed he is not*! Now if that can happen, what are we to say about those long stretches of theological argument, advice, command, hymn, blessing, and exhortation, where Paul says nothing about his sources?

Therefore, if Paul was a part of the larger pattern of Synoptic tradition-transmission as Gerhardsson argues, and represents an early stage of its interpretation and application, as we have for these two sayings shown to be the case, and if it is precisely Paul's characteristic way to *cite* sayings of the Lord by doing so allusively, then the argument that Paul knew only a few sayings, because he only mentions a few openly, falls to the ground, and the numerous verbal correspondences between his text and those of the Synoptic gospels, as well as other more distantly related parallels in ethical exhortation, show that Paul actually used—*cited*—a considerable number of Jesus' teachings.

[1] Compare, for example, Paul's *allusive* quotations of the Old Testament; see E. E. Ellis *Paul's Use of the Old Testament* (1957). For a painstaking and comprehensive investigation of the way in which words of the Lord were used or referred to during the apostolic and post-apostolic period, see especially H. Koester, *Synoptische Ueberlieferung bei den apostolischen Vätern* (1957); further bibliography in Koester XI–XVI.

This automatically destroys the allied argument that Paul was not interested in sayings of Jesus, and also shows how anachronistic Schweitzer's question was.[1] Paul *was* 'sheltering himself' behind the authority of the Lord because his readers would generally have recognized Who was speaking in Paul's words.[2]

To be sure, we advocate no blanket endorsement of the fantasies of Arnold Resch. The warning that many of the parallels (where Paul does not say he is depending upon a word of the Lord) are to be accounted for as common Jewish tradition must still be rigorously heeded. But at least this much may be agreed upon: the alleged contrast between Pauline Christianity and that branch of the early Church which preserved the Palestinian Jesus-tradition that finally ended up in the Synoptic gospels[3] is a figment of the imagination. In fact, they were one and the same branch—for precisely in Paul's careful preservation of, and yet selective and discriminating obedience to, the Lord's commands, do we see prefigured the characteristic traits of the Hellenistic Christian gospel editors.

[1] Quoted above, p. xxiv.

[2] The refutation of the argument that Paul didn't know many words of the Lord because he didn't use any when he needed them the most, as, e.g., in his dispute over the importance of the Law (cp. Bultmann *Theology* I 189), is slightly more complicated. For one thing, Paul well knew (what we are beginning to find out) that Jesus never had radically overthrown the Torah at all (see Gal. 4.4; Rom. 15.8). As a result, all the sayings of Jesus on the Torah, or related to this issue, probably were in the possession of his opponents among the Jerusalem circle. *The reason Paul did not appeal to any sayings of Jesus in support of his stand on the Torah was because there weren't any.*

[3] See Bultmann's statement of this contrast, above, p. xxi.

Appendix

TABLE OF THE SYNOPTIC MISSION INSTRUCTIONS

(text from *RSV*)

MATTHEW	MARK	LUKE 9	LUKE 10
10.1 And he called to him his twelve disciples	6.7 And he called to him the twelve, and began to send them out two by two	9.1 And he called the twelve together	10.1 After this the Lord appointed seventy others and sent them on ahead of him two by two
and gave them authority over unclean spirits, to cast them out, and to heal every disease, and every infirmity. [vv. 2–4 names of twelve disciples]	and gave them authority over the unclean spirits.	and gave them power and authority over all demons	
		and to cure diseases.	into every town and place where he himself was about to come.
5 These twelve Jesus sent out, charging them, 'Go nowhere among the Gentiles, and enter no town of the Samaritans, 6 but go rather to the lost sheep of the house of Israel.			2 And he said to them, 'The harvest if plentiful but the laborers are few; pray, therefore the Lord

of the harvest to send laborers out into his harvest.

3 Go your way; behold I send you out as lambs in the midst of wolves.

2 And he sent them out to preach the kingdom of God

and to heal.

3 And he said to them 'Take nothing for your journey, no staff, nor bag, nor bread nor money

and do not have two tunics.

4 Carry no
purse, no bag,

no sandals;

and salute
no one on the road.

8 He charged them to take nothing for their journey except a staff; no bread, no bag, no money in their belts; but to wear sandals and not put on two tunics.

7 And
preach as you go, saying, 'The kingdom of heaven is at hand.'
8 Heal the sick, raise the dead, cleanse lepers, cast out demons.
You received without pay, give without pay.

9 Take no gold, nor silver, nor copper in your belts, 10 no bag for your journey, nor two tunics, nor sandals, nor a staff;

for the laborer deserves his food.

[Matt. cont'd]

11 And whatever town or village you enter, find out who is worthy in it and stay with him until you depart.

12 As you enter the house, salute it.

13 And if the house is worthy, let your peace come upon it; but if it is not worthy, let your peace return to you.

[Mark cont'd]

10 And he said to them, 'Where you enter a house,

stay there until you leave the place.

[Luke 9 cont'd]

4 And whatever house you enter,

stay there and from there depart.

[Luke 10 cont'd]

5 Whatever house you enter,

first say, 'Peace be to this house!'

6 And if a son of peace is there, your peace shall rest upon him; but if not, it shall return to you.

7 And remain in the same house eating and drinking what they provide, for the laborer deserves his wages; do not go from house to house.

8 Whenever you enter a town and they receive you, eat what is set before you.

9 Heal the sick in it and

14 And if any one

will not receive you or listen to your words,

shake off the dust from your feet as you leave that house or town.

15 Truly, I say to you, it shall be more tolerable on the day of judgment for the land of Sodom and Gomorrah than for that town.
16 Behold, I send you out as sheep in the midst of wolves; so be wise as serpents and innocent as doves.'

---

11 And if any place

will not receive you and they refuse to hear you, when you leave, shake off the dust that is on your feet

for a testimony against them.'

---

5 And wherever they

do not receive you.

when you leave that town, shake off the dust from your feet

as a testimony against them.'

---

say to them, 'The King-dom of God has come near to you'.
10 But whenever you enter a town and they do not receive you,

go into its streets and say,
11 'Even the dust of your town that clings to our feet

we wipe off against you;

nevertheless, know this, that the Kingdom of God has come near.'

12 I tell you, it shall be more tolerable on that day for Sodom than for that town.'

Bibliography

Aland, K., M. Black, B. M. Metzger, A. Wikgren, eds. *The Greek New Testament*. New York, London, Edinburgh, Amsterdam, 1966.

—— ed. *Synopsis quattuor evangeliorum. Locis parallelis evangeliorum apocryphorum et patrum adhibitis*. Stuttgart, 1964.

Albertz, M. *Die Botschaft des Neuen Testaments*. I, 1. Zurich, 1947.

—— *Die synoptische Streitgespräche. Ein Beitrag zur Formengeschichte des Urchristentums*. Berlin, 1921.

Allegro, J. M. 'Fragments of a Qumran Scroll of Eschatological Midrashim', *JBL* 77 (1958) 351–365.

Allmen, J. J. von. *Pauline Teaching on Marriage*, trans. The Faith Press. London, 1963.

Allo, E.-B. *Saint Paul. Première épître aux Corinthiens* (Études Bibliques). Paris, 1935.

Allon, G. *The History of the Jews in Palestine during the Period of the Mishnah and the Talmud* [Hebrew]; Tel Aviv, 1954.

Audet, J. P. *La Didaché: Instructions des apôtres* (Études Bibliques) Paris, 1958.

Bacon, B. W. *The Beginnings of Gospel Story*. New Haven, 1909.

Balcomb, R. E. 'The Written Sources of Paul's Knowledge of Jesus.' Unpubl. Diss. Boston University, 1951.

Ball, W. E. *St. Paul and the Roman Law*. Edinburgh, 1901.

Baltensweiler, H. 'Die Ehebruchsklauseln bei Matthäus: zu Matt. 5.32; 19.9,' *TheolZeit* 15 (1959) 340–356.

Barret, C. K. 'Cephas and Corinth (1 Cor. 1.12; 3.22; 9.5; 15.5),' *Festschrift für O. Michel*, 1–12. Köln, 1963.

—— 'Christianity at Corinth,' *BJRL* 46 (1963–64) 269–297.

—— 'Paul and the "Pillar Apostles",' *Studia Paulina in honorem J. de Zwaan*, 1–19. Haarlem, 1953.

—— 'Things Sacrificed to Idols,' *NTS* 11 (1964/65) 138–153.

Bauer, J. B. 'Uxores circumducere. 1 Kor. 9.5,' *BZ* NF 3 (1959) 94–102.

Bauer, W. *A Greek-English Lexicon of the New Testament and Other Early Chrisrian Literature*. Trans and ed.. W. F. Arndt, F. W. Gingrich. Cambridge, 1957.

Baur, F. C. *Kritische Untersuchungen über die kanonischen Evangelien, ihr Verhältniss zu einander, ihren Character und Ursprung.* Tübingen, 1847.

—— *Das Markusevangelium nach seinem Ursprung und Character.* Tübingen, 1851.

Beare, F. W. *A Commentary on the Epistle to the Philippians* (Black's New Testament Commentaries). London, 1959.

—— 'Sayings of the Risen Jesus', in *Christian History and Interpretation: Studies Presented to John Knox*, 161–181. W. R. Farmer, C. F. D. Moule, R. R. Niebuhr, eds. Cambridge, 1967.

—— *The Earliest Records of Jesus.* Nashville, 1962.

Belkin, S. *Philo and the Oral Law. The Philonic Interpretation of Biblical Law in Relation to the Palestinian Halakah.* Cambridge, Massachusetts, 1940.

Black, M. *An Aramaic Approach to the Gospels.*[3] Oxford, 1967.

Blackman, P. *Mishnahyoth.* 6 vols. London, 1953.

Blank, J. *Paulus und Jesus. Eine theologische Grundlegung* (Studium zum Alten und Neuen Testament 18). München, 1968.

Blass, F., A. Debrunner, *A Greek Grammar of the New Testament and Other Early Christian Literature.* Trans. and rev. R. W. Funk. Chicago, 1961.

Blinzler, J. 'Eisin eunouchoi. Zur Auslegung von Matt. 19.12', *ZNW* 28 (1957) 254–270.

Bonsirven, J. *Exégèse rabbinique et exégèse paulinienne.* Paris, 1939.

Bornkamm, G. 'The Letter to the Romans as Paul's Last Will and Testament', *Australian Biblical Review* 11 (1963) 2–14.

—— 'The Missionary Stance of Paul in 1 Cor. 9 and in Acts', *Studies in Luke-Acts. Essays Presented in Honor of Paul Schubert*, 194–207. L. Keck, J. L. Martyn, eds. New York, 1966.

Braun, H. *Spätjüdisch-häretischer und frühchristlicher Radikalismus. Jesus von Nazareth und die essenische Qumransekte.* Tübingen, 1957.

Brown, F., S. R. Driver, C. A. Briggs, eds. *A Hebrew and English Lexicon of the Old Testament.*[2] Oxford, 1957.

Brown, J. P., 'The Form of Q Known to Matthew', *NTS* 8 (1961/62) 27–42.

—— 'Mark as Witness to an Edited Form of Q', *JBL* 80 (1960) 29–44.

—— 'Synoptic Parallels in the Epistles and Form-history,' *NTS* 10 (1963/64) 27–48.

Brückner, M. 'Zum Thema Jesus und Paulus,' *ZNW* 7 (1906) 112–119.

Brun, L., A. Fridrichsen. *Paulus und die Urgemeinde*. Giessen, 1921.

Buchanan, G. W. 'The Role of Purity in the Structure of the Essene Sect,' *RevQum* 4 (1963) 397–406.

Bultmann, R. D. 'Die Bedeutung des geschichtlichen Jesus für die Theologie des Paulus,' in idem, *Glauben und Verstehen* I.[3] Tübingen, 1958. Originally published in *Theologische Blätter* 7 (1929) 137–151.

—— Art. *kauchema kauchaomai TDNT* III 645–653.

—— *The History of the Synoptic Tradition*. Trans. J. Marsh. New York, 1963.

—— *Theologie des Neuen Testaments*.[3] Tübingen, 1958.

—— *Theology of the New Testament*. Trans. K. Grobel. London, 1955.

Burchard, C. 'Ei nach einem Ausdruck des Wissens oder Nicht-wissens. John 9.25; Acts 19.2; 1 Kor. 1.16; 7.16,' *ZNW* 52 (1961) 73–82.

Butler, B. C. *The Originality of St. Matthew. A Critique of the Two-Document Hypothesis*. Cambridge, 1951.

Byron, B. 'The Meaning of "Except it be for fornication",' *Aus-CathRec* 40 (1963) 90–95.

Cadbury, H. J. *The Making of Luke-Acts*. London, 1961.

Campenhausen, H. von. 'Die Askese im Urchristentum', in idem, *Tradition und Leben. Kräfte der Kirchengeschichte*, 114–157. Tübingen, 1960.

—— *Die Begründung kirchlicher Entscheidungen beim Apostel Paulus* (Sitzungsber. der Heidelb. Akad. d. Wiss., Phil.-hist. Kl.). Heidelberg, 1957. Reprinted in idem, *Aus der Frühzeit des Christentums*, 30–80. Tübingen, 1963.

—— *Kirchliches Amt und geistliche Vollmacht in den ersten drei Jahrhunderten*[2] (Beitr. z. hist. Theol. 14) Tübingen, 1963.

Carrington, Ph. *The Primitive Christian Catechism*. Cambridge, 1940.

Cerfaux, L. *Recueil Lucien Cerfaux*. 2 vols. Gembloux, 1954. The following essays were consulted: 'La tradition selon saint Paul', I 253–264; 'Les deux points de départ de la tradition chrétienne', I 265–282.

Chadwick, H. ' "All Things to All Men" (1 Cor. 9.22),' *NTS* 1 (1954/55) 261–275.

—— Art. 'enkrateia' *RAC* V 343–365.

Charles, R. H. *The Teaching of the New Testament on Divorce,* Oxford, 1921.

Cohen, B. *Jewish and Roman Law. A Comparative Study.* 2 vols. New York, 1966.

Coiner, H. G. 'Those "Divorce and Remarriage" Passages (Matt. 5.32; 19.9; 1 Cor. 7.10–16), with Brief Reference to the Mark and Luke Passages,' *Concordia Theological Monthly* 39 (1968) 367–384.

Collins, J. J. 'Chiasmus, the "ABA" Pattern and the Text of Paul,' *Analecta Biblica* 18 (1963) 573–583.

Congar, Y. M.-J. 'Die Kasuistik des heiligen Paulus,' *Festgabe für F. X. Arnold,* 16, 41. Freiburg, 1958.

Considine, T. P. 'The Pauline Privilege (A Further Examination of 1 Cor. 7.12–17),' *AusCathRec* 40 (1963) 107–119.

Conzelmann, H. *Die Apostelgeschichte* (Handb. z. N.T. 7). Tübingen, 1963.

—— *The Theology of St. Luke.* Trans. G. Buswell. New York, 1960.

Corbett, P. E. *The Roman Law of Marriage.* Oxford, 1930.

Cowling, C. C. 'The Involvement of the Community in the Apostolic Tradition,' *Church Quarterly Review* (1963) 6–18.

Cross, F. M., Jr. *The Ancient Library of Qumran. A Comprehensive Survey of the Dead Sea Scrolls and the Community Which Owned Them.*[2] New York, 1961.

Cullmann, O. *The Early Church. Studies in Early Christian History and Theology.* Abr. ed. Trans. and ed. A. J. B. Higgins. Philadelphia, 1966. Consulted was, 'The Tradition' (1954).

Dalman, G. *Jesus-Jeschua. Studies in the Gospels.* Trans. P. P. Levertoff. New York, 1929.

Danby, H. *The Mishnah. Translated from the Hebrew with Introduction and Brief Explanatory Notes.* Oxford, 1964.

Daube, D. *Collaboration with Tyranny in Rabbinic Law.* Oxford, 1965.

—— 'Concessions to Sinfulness in Jewish Law,' *JJSt* 10 (1959) 1–13.

—— *The New Testament and Rabbinic Judaism.* London, 1956.

—— *Studies in Biblical Law.* Cambridge, 1947.

Daniel, C. 'Esseniens et Eunuques (Matthieu 19.10–12),' *RevQum* 6 (1968) 353–390.

Dauvillier, J. 'L'indissolubilité du mariage dans la nouvelle Loi,' *Orient-Syrien* 9 (1964) 265–289.

Davies, P. E. 'The Macedonian Scene of Paul's Journeys,' *BibArch* 26 (1963) 91–106.

Davies, W. D. *Paul and Rabbinic Judaism.*[2] London, 1962.

—— *The Setting of the Sermon on the Mount.* Cambridge, 1964.

—— *Torah in the Messianic Age* (*JBL* Monogr. Ser.) Philadelphia 1952.

Degenhardt, H.-J. *Lukas—Evangelist der Armen. Besitz und Besitzverzicht in den lukanischen Schriften. Eine traditions- und redactionsgeschichtliche Untersuchung.* Stuttgart, 1965.

Delling, G. 'Nun aber sind sie heilig: Gott und die Götter,' *Festschr. E. Fascher*, 84–93. Berlin, 1958.

—— *Paulus' Stellung zu Frau und Ehe* (Beitr. z. Wiss. vom A. u. N. T. 56). Stuttgart, 1931.

DeWette, W. M. L. *An Historico-Critical Introduction to the Canonical Books of the New Testament.* Trans. 5th German ed. 1848 by F. Frothingham. Boston, 1858.

Dibelius, M. *From Tradition to Gospel.* Trans. B. L. Woolf. New York, 1935.

Diderichsen, B. K. 'Efterfølge og Ægteskab i Lukasevangeliet,' *Festskrift til Jens Nørregaard*, 31–50. København, 1947.

—— *Den Markianske Skilsmisseperikope. Dens Genesis og Historiske Placering.* Gyldendal, 1962.

Didier, G. 'Le salaire du désintéressement,' *RecSciRel* 43 (1955) 228–251.

Dihle, A. Art 'Ethik' *RAC* Lief. 45, 646–695. Stuttgart, 1965.

Dodd, C. H. *'ENNOMOS CHRISTOU,' Studia Paulina in honorem J. de Zwaan*, 96–110. Haarlem, 1953.

—— *Gospel and Law. The Relation of Faith and Ethics in Early Christianity.* New York, 1951.

—— 'Matthew and Paul,' in idem, *New Testament Studies.* London, 1953.

—— 'The Primitive Catechism and the Sayings of Jesus,' *Studies in Memory of T. W. Manson*, ed. A. J. B. Higgins; 106–118. Manchester, 1959.

Dubarle, A. M. 'Mariage et divorce dans l'Évangile,' *Orient-Syrien* 9 (1964) 61–73.

Dulau, P. 'The Pauline Privilege,' *CBQ* 13 (1951) 140–152.

Dupont-Sommer, A. *The Essene Writings from Qumran.* Trans. G. Vermes. New York, 1962.

Easton, B. S. *The Gospel According to St. Luke. A Critical and Exegetical Commentary.* New York, 1926.

Eissfeldt, O. *The Old Testament. An Introduction including the Apocrypha and Pseudepigrapha, and also the Works of Similar Type from Qumran; The History of the Foundation of the Old Testament.* Trans. P. R. Ackroyd. New York, 1965.

Ellis, E. E. 'Luke XI 49–51: An Oracle of a Christian Prophet?' *Expository Times* 74 (1963) 157–158.

Fannon, P. 'Paul and Tradition in the Primitive Church,' *Scrip* 16 (1964) 47–56.

Farmer, W. R. *The Synoptic Problem.* New York, 1964.

Feine, P. *Der Apostel Paulus. Das Ringen um das geschichtliche Verständnis des Paulus.* Gütersloh, 1927.

—— J. Behm. *Introduction to the New Testament.* Rev. W. G. Kümmel. Trans. A. J. Mattill, Jr. Nashville, 1965.

Fitzmeyer, J. A. 'Qumran and the Interpolated Paragraph in 2 Cor. 6.14–7.1,' *CBQ* 23 (1961) 273–280.

Flusser, D. 'The Dead Sea Sect and Pre-Pauline Christianity,' *Scripta* 4 (1958) 215–266.

Ford, J. M. ' "Hast thou tithed thy meal?" and "Is thy child kosher?" (1 Cor. x 27ff. and 1 Cor. vii 14),' *JThSt* 17 (1966) 71–79.

Fridrichsen, A. D. *The Apostle and His Message.* (Upps. Univ. Årsskr.) Uppsala, 1947.

—— 'Jesus, St. John and St. Paul,' *The Root of the Vine. Essays in Biblical Theology.* New York, 1953.

Funk, F. X. *Die apostolischen Väter* (Sammlung ausgewählter kirchen- und dogmengesch. Quellenschriften 2 Rh. 1 H.) I. Teil. Neubearb. v. K. Bihlmeyer. Tübingen, 1924.

Furnish, V. P. 'The Jesus-Paul Debate: From Baur to Bultmann,' *BJRL* 47 (1964/65) 342–381.

Gärtner, B. *The Areopagus Speech and Natural Revelation* (Acta Sem. Neotest. Upsal. 21). Uppsala, 1955.

—— *The Temple and the Community in Qumran and the New Testament. A Comparative Study in the Temple Symbolism of the Qumran Texts and the New Testament* (Soc. for N.T. Stud. Monogr. Ser. 1). Cambridge, 1965.

Georgi, D. *Die Gegner des Paulus in 2. Korintherbrief. Studien zur religiösen Propaganda in der Spätantike* (Wiss. Monogr. z. A. u. N. T. 11). Neukirchen-Vluyn, 1964.

—— *Die Geschichte der Kollekte des Paulus für Jerusalem* (Theol. Forsch. Wiss. Beitr. z. kirchl.-evangel. Lehre 38). Hamburg-Bergstedt, 1965.

Gerhardsson, B. *Memory and Manuscript. Oral Tradition and Written Transmission in Rabbinic Judaism and Early Christianity* (Acta Sem. Neot. Upsal. 22). Lund, Copenhagen, 1961.

Glombitza, O. 'Der Dank des Apostels. Zum Verständnis von Phil. 4.10–20,' *NovTest* 7 (1964) 135–141.

Goldin, J. *The Fathers According to Rabbi Nathan* (Yale Judaica Series 10). New Haven, 1955.

—— *The Living Talmud. The Wisdom of the Fathers and Its Classical Commentaries*. New York, 1957.

Goodenough, E. R. *The Jurisprudence of the Jewish Courts in Egypt. Legal Administration by the Jews under the Early Roman Empire as Described by Philo Judaeus*. New Haven, 1929.

Grant, F. C. 'The Authenticity of Jesus' Sayings,' *ZNW* Beih. 21 (1954 [Bultmann Festschrift]) 137–143.

Guillaumont, A., H.-Ch. Puech, G. Quispel, W. Till, Y. A. al Masih. *The Gospel According to Thomas. Coptic Text Established and Translated*. Leiden, New York, 1959.

Hadas, M., M. Smith. *Heroes and Gods. Spiritual Biographies in Antiquity*. New York, 1965.

Haenchen, E. *Die Apostelgeschichte* (Krit.-exeg. Komm. u.d. N. T. 3). Göttingen, 1959.

Hahn, F. *Mission in the New Testament* (Studies in Bib. Theol. 47). Trans. F. Clarke. London, 1965.

Hanson, R. P. C. 'The Assessment of Motive in the Study of the Synoptic Gospels,' *Modern Churchman* 10 (1967) 255–269.

Harnack, A. von. *The Constitution and Law of the Church in the First Two Centuries* (Crown Theol. Lib. 31). Trans. F. L. Pogson, ed. H. D. A. Major. New York, 1910.

—— *The Mission and Expansion of Christianity in the First Three Centuries*. Trans. J. Moffatt. New York [Harper Torchb. ed.], 1961.

—— *Souces of the Apostolic Canons*. Trans. L. A. Wheatley. London, 1895.

Heitmüller, W. 'Zum Problem Paulus und Jesus,' *ZNW* 13 (1912) 320–337.

Herford, R. T. *The Ethics of the Talmud: Sayings of the Fathers Edited with Introduction, Translation and Commentary.* New York, 1962.

Héring, J. *La première épître de saint Paul aux Corinthiens* (Comm. du Nouv. Test. 7). Paris, Neuchâtel, 1949.

Hermesdorf, B. H. D. 'De apostel Paulus in lopende rekening met de gemeente te Filippi,' *Tijdschrift voor Theologie* 1 (1961) 252–256.

Holm-Nielsen, S. *Hodayot. The Psalms of Qumran.* Aarhus, 1960.

Holmes, B. T. 'Luke's Description of John Mark,' *JBL* 54 (1935) 63–72.

Hummel, R. *Die Auseinandersetzung zwischen Kirche und Judentum im Matthäusevangelium* (Beitr. z. evang. Theol. 33). München, 1966.

Hunter, A. M. *Paul and his Predecessors.*[2] London, 1961.

Hurd, J. C., Jr. *The Origin of 1 Corinthians.* London, 1965.

Isaksson, A. *Marriage and Ministry in the New Temple. A Study with Special Reference to Matt. 19.3–12 and 1 Cor. 11.3–16* (Acta Sem. Neot. Upsal. 24). Trans. N. Tomkinson. Lund, 1965.

Jellicoe, S. St. Luke and the Seventy-Two,' *NTS* 6 (1960) 319–321.

Jeremias, J. 'Chiasmus in den Paulusbriefen,' *ZNW* 49 (1958), 145–156.

—— 'Zur Gedankenführung in den paulinischen Briefen,' *Studia Paulina in honorem J. de Zwaan,* 146–154. Haarlem, 1953.

—— 'Die missionarische Aufgabe der Mischehe (1 Kor. 7.16),' *ZNW* Beih. 21 (1954 [Bultmann Festschrift]) 255–260.

—— *The Parables of Jesus.*[2] Trans. S. H. Hooke. New York, 1963.

—— *Unknown Sayings of Jesus.* Trans. R. H. Fuller. New York, 1957.

Jolowicz, H. F. *Historical Introduction to the Study of Roman Law.* Cambridge, 1952.

Kähler, E. *Die Frau in den paulinischen Briefen unter besonderer Berücksichtigung des Begriffs der Unterordnung.* Frankfurt a.M., 1960.

Käsemann, E. *Exegetische Versuche und Besinnungen* II. Göttingen 1964. The following essays were consulted: 'Sätze heiligen Rechtes im Neuen Testament,' II 69–82 (originally pub. in *NTS* 1 (1954/55) 248–260); 'Zum Thema der urchristlichen Apokalyptik,' II 105–130 (orig. pub. in *ZThK* 59 (1962) 257–284); and 'Eine paulinischen Variation des "Amor Fati",' II 223–239 (orig. pub. in *ZThK* 56 (1959) 138–154).

Kilpatrick, G. D. 'Galatians 1.18 *historesai Kephan*,' *New Testament Essays. Studies in Memory of Thomas Walter Manson*, 144–150. Manchester, 1959.

—— *The Origins of the Gospel According to St. Matthew.*[2] Oxford, 1950.

Klostermann, E. *Das Lukasevangelium*[2] (Handb. z. N.T. 5). Tübingen, 1929.

—— *Das Markusevangelium*[4] (Handb. z. N.T. 3). Tübingen, 1950.

—— *Das Matthäusevangelium*[2] (Handb. z. N.T. 4) Tübingen, 1927.

Knox, W. L. *St. Paul and the Church of Jerusalem.* Cambridge, 1925.

—— *The Sources of the Synoptic Gospels.* Ed. H. Chadwick. 2 vols. Cambridge, 1953.

Koester, H. '*GNOMAI DIAPHOROI*: The Origin and Nature of Diversification in the History of Early Christianity,' *HarvTheol Rev* 58 (1965) 279–318.

—— 'The Purpose of the Polemic of a Pauline Fragment (Phil. 3),' *NTS* 8 (1961/62) 317–332.

—— *Synoptische Ueberlieferung bei den apostolischen Vätern* (Texte u. Unters. z. Gesch. d. altchr. Lit. 65) Berlin, 1957.

Krauss, S. 'Die jüdischen Apostel,' *Jewish Quarterly Review* 17 (1905) 370–383.

Kümmel, W. G. *Heilsgeschehen und Geschichte. Gesammelte Aufsätze* 1933–1964. Marburg, 1965. The following essays were consulted: 'Jesus und Paulus,' 81–106 (pub. previously in *Kirchenblatt für die ref. Schweiz* 7–8 [1939]); 'Die "konsequente Eschatologie" Albert Schweitzers im Urteil der Zeitgenossen,' 328–339 (pub. previously in *De H. J. Holtzmann à Albert Schweitzer. Ehrfurcht vor dem Leben. Albert Schweitzer. Eine Freundesgabe zu seinem* 80. *Geburtstag* (1955); also in French, *RHPhR* 37 (1957) 58–70).

—— 'Verlobung und Heirat bei Paulus (1 Kor. 7.36–38),' *ZNW* Beih. 21 (1954 [Bultmann Festschrift]) 275–295.

Kugelman, R. '1 Cor. 7.36–38,' *CBQ* 10 (1948) 63–71.

Lagrange, M.-J. *Evangile selon Saint Matthieu*[7] (Études Bibliques) Paris, 1948.

Lang, F. Art. *puroo TWNT* VI 949f.

Lattey, C. 'How Do You Account for the Lack of Direct Quotations in the Epistles from Our Lord's Sayings?' *Scrip* 4 (1949) 22–24.

Lehmann, M. R. 'Gen. 2.24 as the Basis for Divorce in Halakah and New Testament,' *ZAW* 72 (1960) 263–267.

Leipoldt, J. *Die Frau in der antiken Welt and im Urchristentum.*[2] Leipzig, 1955.

—— *Griechische Philosophie und frühchristliche Askese* (Ber. u. d. Verhandl. der sächs. Akad. d. Wiss. zu Leip.; Phil.-hist. Kl. 106). Berlin, 1961.

Liddell, H. G., R. Scott. *A Greek-English Lexicon.* 9th ed. rev. and ed. H. S. Jones et al. Oxford, 1961.

Lietzmann, H. *An die Korinther I/II* (Handb. z. N.T. 9). 4 Aufl. von W. G. Kümmel. Tübingen, 1949.

Lightfoot, J. B. *Notes on the Epistles of St. Paul.* London, 1895.

Linssen, J. *Het Apostolaat volgens St. Paulus: een bijbels-theologische Studie van 1 Kor. IX.* Nijmegen, 1952.

Linton, O. *Das Problem der Urkirche in der neueren Forschung. Eine kritische Darstellung* (Upps. Univ. Årsskr., Teol. 2). Uppsala, 1932.

Lohman, T. 'Die verwendung autoritativer Ueberlieferungen im Urchristentum mit besonderer Berücksichtigung der nachpaulinischen Briefliteratur. Unpubl. Diss. Jena, 1952. Cp. *ThLZ* 79 (1954) 58ff.

Lohmeyer, E. *Das Evangelium des Matthäus.* (Krit.-exeg. Komm. u.d. N.T. 1). 3 Aufl. von W. Schmauch. Göttingen, 1962.

Lohse, E. *Die Texte aus Qumran.* München, 1964.

—— 'Ursprung und Prägung des christlichen Apostolats,' *Theologische Zeitschrift* 9 (1953) 259–275.

Loisy, A. *L'Évangile selon Luc.* Paris, 1924.

Maddox, R. J. 'The Son of Man and Judgment.' Unpubl. diss. Harvard Divinity School, 1963.

Mahoney, A. 'A New Look at the Divorce Clauses in Matt. 5.32 and 19.9,' *CBQ* 30 (1968) 29–38.

Mantel, H. *Studies in the History of the Sanhedrin* (Harvard Semitic Series 17). Cambridge, Mass., 1961.

Marcus, R. *Law in the Apocrypha* (Columbia Univ. Oriental St. 26) New York, 1927.

Margot, J.-C. 'L'indissolubilité du mariage selon le Nouveau Testament,' *RevThéolPhil* 17 (1967) 391–403.

Maurer, C. 'Grund und Grenze apostolischer Freiheit. Exegetische-kritische Studie zu 1 Kor. 9,' *Antwort. Festschrift Karl Barth zum siebzigsten Geburtstag*, 630–641. Zurich, 1956.

Marxsen, W. *Der Evangelist Markus. Studien zur Redactiongeschichte des Evangeliums.²* Göttingen, 1959.

Menoud, P.-H. 'Mariage et célibat selon Saint Paul,' *RevThéol Phil* 1 (1951) 21–34.

Metzger, B. M. 'Seventy or Seventy-two Disciples?' *NTS* 4 (1959) 299–306.

Michel, O. Art. *oikonomia TWNT* V 154f.

Milik, J. T. *Ten Years of Discovery in the Wilderness of Judaea* (Studies in Bib. Theol. 26). Trans. J. Strugnell. London, 1963.

Moe, O. *Paulus und die evangelische Geschichte.* Leipzig, 1912.

Moffatt, J. *The First Epistle of Paul to the Corinthians* (The Moffatt N.T. Comm.). New York, London, 1930.

Montefiore, C. G. *The Synoptic Gospels.* 2 vols. London, 1927.

Moore, G. F. *Judaism in the First Centuries of the Christian Era. The Age of the Tannaim.* 3 vols. Cambridge, Mass., 1962.

Morris, L. '*KAI HAPAX KAI DIS*,' *NovTest* 1 (1956) 205–208.

Mosbech, H. 'Apostolos in the New Testament,' *StTh* 2 (1949/50) 166–200.

Munck, J. *Paul and the Salvation of Mankind.* Trans. F. Clarke. Richmond, Va., 1959.

Neirynck, F. 'Het evangelisch echtscheidingsverbod,' *Collationes Brugenses et Gandarenses* 4 (1958) 25–46.

Neugebauer, F. 'Geistsprüche und Jesuslogion. Erwägungen zur der von der formgeschichtlichen Betrachtungsweise R. Bultmanns angenommenen grundsätzlichen Möglichkeit einer Identität von prophetischen Geistsprüchen mit Logien des irdischen Jesus.' *ZNW* 53 (1962) 218–228.

Nineham, D. E. 'Eye-witness Testimony and the Gospel Tradition,' Part I *JTS* 9 (1958) 13–25; Part II ibid., 243–252; Part III *JTS* 11 (1960) 253–264.

Norquist, N. L. 'The Transmission of the Ethical Tradition in the Synoptic Gospels and the Writings of Paul.' Unpubl. diss. Hartford Seminary Foundation, 1956.

Oesterle, G. 'Privilège paulinien,' *Dictionnaire de droit canonique* fasc. 37s. 1958), 229–280.

O'Hagan, A. 'Greet no one on the way' (Luke 10.4b), *Studii Biblici Franciscani Liber Annuus* 16 (1965/66) 69–84.

O'Rourke, J. J. 'A Note on an Exception. Matt. 5.32 (19.9) and 1 Cor. 7.12 Compared,' *Heythrop Journal* 5 (1964) 299–302.

—— 'The Scriptural Background for can. 1120,' *The Jurist*, 15 (1955) 132–137.

Oulton, J. E. L., H. Chadwick. *Alexandrian Christianity* (Libr. Christ. Class. 2). Philadelphia, 1954.

Petrie, S. ' "Q" is Only What You Make It,' *NovTest* 3 (1959) 28–33.

Quesnell, Q. ' "Made Themselves Eunuchs for the Kingdom of Heaven" (Matt. 19.12),' *CBQ* 30 (1968) 335–358.

Rabin, C. *Qumran Studies* (Scripta Judaica 2). Oxford, 1957.

—— *The Zadokite Documents.* Oxford, 1958.

Rahtjen, B. H. 'The Three Letters of Paul to the Philippians,' *NTS* 6 (1959/60) 167–173.

Resch, A. *Der Paulinismus und die Logia Jesu* (Texte u. Unters. N.F. 12) Berlin, 1904.

Rex, H. H. 'An Attempt to Understand 1 Cor. 7,' *RefTheolRev* 14 (1955) 41–51.

Richards, H. J. 'Christ on Divorce,' *Scrip* 11 (1959) 22–32.

Richardson, C. C., E. R. Fairweather, E. R. Hardy, M. H. Shepherd. *Early Christian Fathers* (Libr. Christ. Class. 1) Philadelphia, 1953.

Riesenfeld, H. *The Gospel Tradition.* Philadelphia, 1970.

Rigaux, B. 'Reflexions sur l'historicité de Jésus dans le message paulinien,' *Analecta Biblica* 18 (1963) 265–274.

Ringgren, H. *The Faith of Qumran. Theology of the Dead Sea Scrolls.* Trans. E. T. Sander. Philadelphia, 1963.

Robertson, A., A. Plummer. *A Critical and Exegetical Commentary on the First Epistle of St. Paul to the Corinthians* (Intern. Crit. Comm.). New York, 1911.

Roller, O. *Das Formular der paulinischen Briefe. Ein Beitrag zur Lehre vom antiken Briefe* (Beitr. z. Wiss. v. Alt. u. N.T. 58). Stuttgart, 1933.

N

Schlier, H. *Der Brief an die Galater*[12] (Krit.-exeg. Komm. u. d. N. T. 17). Göttingen, 1962.

Schmidt, K. L. 'Die Stellung der Evangelien in der allgemeinen Literaturgeschichte,' in *EUCHARISTERION Studien zur Religion und Literatur des Alten und Neuen Testaments. Hermann Gunkel zum 60. Geburtstag ... dargebracht,* 50–135. Hrsg. v. H. Schmidt. Göttingen, 1923.

Schmithals, W. *Die Gnosis in Korinth. Eine Untersuchung zu den Korintherbriefen.*[2] Göttingen, 1965.

—— 'Die Irrlehrer des Philipperbriefes,' *ZThK* 54 (1957) 297–341.

—— 'Paulus und die historische Jesus,' ZNW 53 (1962) 145–160.

Schoeps, H.-J. *Paul.* Trans. H. Knight. Philadelphia, 1959.

Schrage, W. *Die konkreten Einzelgebote in der paulinischen Paränese. Ein Beitrag zur neutestamentlichen Ethik.* Gütersloh, 1961.

—— 'Die Stellung zur Welt bei Paulus, Epiktet und in der Apokalyptik. Ein Beitrag zu 1 Kor. 7.29–31,' *ZThK* 61 (1964) 125–154.

Schweitzer, A. *Paul and His Interpreters.* Trans. W. Montgomery. London, 1912.

—— *The Mysticism of Paul the Apostle.* Trans. W. Montgomery. London, 1931.

Schweizer, E. *Church Order in the New Testament* (Studies in Bib. Theol. 32). Trans. F. Clarke. London, 1963.

Seeberg, A. *Die Beiden Wege und das Apostledekret.* Leipzig, 1906.

—— *Der Catechismus der Urchristenheit.* Leipzig, 1903.

—— *Christi Person und Werk nach der Lehre seiner Jünger.* Leipzig, 1910.

—— *Die Didache des Judentums und der Urchristenheit* Leipzig, 1908.

Selwyn, E. G. *The First Epistle of St. Peter.* London, 1955.

Sevenster, J. N. *Paul and Seneca* (Suppl. Nov. Test. 4). Leiden, 1961.

Stählin, G. Art. *egkope TDNT* III 855f.

Stanley, D. M. 'Pauline Allusions to the Sayings of Jesus,' *CBQ* 23 (1961) 26–39.

Stendahl, K. Art. 'Kirche II. Im Urchristentum,' *RGG* III[3] 1297–1304.

—— *The School of St. Matthew*[2] (Acta Sem. Neot. Upsal. 20). Philadelphia, 1968.

—— ed. *The Scrolls and the New Testament*. New York, 1957.

Strack, H. L. *Introduction to the Talmud and Midrash*. Trans. Jewish Pub. Soc. New York, 1963.

—— P. Billerbeck. *Kommentar zum Neuen Testament*. 6 Bde. München, 1922–63.

Strecker, G. *Der Weg der Gerechtigkeit. Untersuchung zur Theologie des Matthäus*[2] (Forsch. z. Rel. u. Lit. d. Alt. u. N. Test. 82). Göttingen, 1966.

Streeter, G. H. *The Four Gospels. A Study of Origins.*[2] London, 1930.

—— 'St. Mark's Knowledge and Use of Q,' *Studies in the Synoptic Gospels*, ed. Wm. Sanday. Oxford, 1911.

Suggs, M. J. 'Concerning the Date of Paul's Macedonian Ministry,' *Nov.Test.* 4 (1960) 60–68.

Taylor, V. *Behind the Third Gospel*. Oxford, 1926.

—— *The Formation of the Gospel Tradition.*[2] London, 1935.

—— *The Gospel According to St. Mark*. London, 1955.

Tcherikover, V. A., A. Fuks. *Corpus Papyrorum Judaicarum.* 3 vols. Cambridge, Mass., 1957–64.

—— *Hellenistic Civilization and the Jews*. Trans. S. Applebaum. Philadelphia, 1961.

Tischendorf, C. *Novum Testamentum Graece* (Editio octava critica major). 2 vols. Lipsiae, 1869.

Urbach, E. 'Class-status and Leadership in the World of the Palestinian Sages,' *Proceedings of the Israel Academy of Sciences and Humanities* II 4 (1965) 1–37.

Trilling, W. 'Jesusüberlieferung und apostolischen Vollmacht,' *TrierTheolZeit* 71 (1962) 352–368.

Vawter, B. 'The Divorce Clauses in Matt. 5.32,' *CBQ* 16 (1954) 155–167.

Vischer, E. 'Jesus und Paulus,' *TheolRund* 8 (1905) 129–143; 173–188; 11 (1908) 301–313.

Vogelstein, H. 'The Development of the Apostolate in Judaism and Its Transformation in Christianity,' *HUCA* 2 (1925) 99–123.

—— 'Die Entstehung und Entwickelung des Apostolats im Judentum,' *Monatsschr. Geschichte und Wissenschaft des Judentums* 49 (1905) 427–444.

Vogt, E. 'Peace Among Men of God's Good Pleasure (Luke 2.14),' *The Scrolls and the New Testament*, 114–117. K. Stendahl ed. New York, 1957.

Vööbus, A. *Celibacy, A Requirement for Admission to Baptism in the Early Syrian Church* (Papers of the Estonian Theological Society in Exile 1). Stockholm, 1951.

Votaw, C. W. 'The Gospels and Contemporary Biographies,' *AmerJourTheol* 19 (1915) 45–73, 217–249.

Walther, G. 'Uebergreifende Heiligkeit und Kindertauge im N.T.,' *EvangTheol* 25 (1695) 668–674.

Wegenast, K. *Das Verständnis der Tradition bei Paulus and in den Deuteropaulinien* (Wiss. Monogr. z. Alt. u. N.T. 8). Neukirchen-Vluyn, 1962.

Weiss, J. *Der erste Korintherbrief.*[2] (Krit.-exeg. Komm u. d. N.T. 7). Göttingen, 1910.

Wendland, P. *Die Urchristliche Literaturformen* (Handb. z. N.T. 1 Bd. 2. und 3. Teil: *Die hellenistisch-römische Kultur in ihren Beziehungen zu Judenrum und Christentum*) 2, 3 Aufl. Tübingen, 1912.

Wernberg-Møller, P. *The Manual of Discipline* (Studies on the Texts of the Desert of Judah 1). Grand Rapids, 1957.

Wettstein, J. J. *Novum Testamentum graecum . . . cum lectionibus variantibus.* 2 Tom. Amsterdam, 1752.

Wilckens, U. 'Hellenistisch-christliche Missionsüberlieferung und Jesustradition,' *ThLZ* 89 (1964) 517–520.

—— 'Tradition de Jésus at kérygme du Christ: la double histoire de la tradition au sein du christianisme primitif,' *RevHistPhilRel* 47 (1967) 1–12.

Wilder, A. 'Form-history and the Oldest Tradition,' *Neotestamentica et Patristica. Freudesgabe Oscar Cullmann* (Suppl. Nov. Test. 1), 3–13. Ed. W. C. van Unnik. Leiden, 1962.

Winter, P. 'Genesis 1.27 and Jesus' Saying on Divorce,' *ZAW* 70 (1958) 260f.

Wrede, W. *Paul.* Trans. E. Lummis. London, 1907.

Wuellner, W. H. *The Meaning of 'Fishers of Men'* (The New Test. Lib). Philadelphia, 1967.

Zerwick, M. 'De matrimonia et divortio in Evangelio,' *VerbDom* 38 (1960) 193–212.

Zimmerman, H. '*mē epi porneia* (Matt. 19.9)—ein literarisches Problem. Zur Komposition von Matt. 19.3–12,' *Catholica* 16 (1962) 293–299.

Zuntz, G. *The Text of the Epistles. A Disquisition upon the ' Corpus Paulinum'.* London, 1953.

Indices

1. SUBJECTS

asceticism
—— at Corinth 83f.
—— Paul's preference for 84, 86
—— Jesus' view 120
—— Luke's, regarding marriage 129f., 141
commands of the Lord
—— surreptitiously mixed with new sayings 142f.
—— in the form of 'abstracts' of larger accounts 109, 126, 128f., 131, 133, 140
—— having a specific legal jurisdiction 98f., 142
—— Paul keeps separate from his own commands 93, 98f., 100f., 141f.
—— set aside by Paul in context of mission strategy 25, 27, 32f., 36, 139f., 144
—— actual wording of, presupposed in 1 Cor. 9.14 40, 78f.; in 1 Cor. 7.10f. 133f.
—— a source of danger to the Church 33, 39, 68f., 76f., 139
—— Paul not accused of disobeying 39
—— Paul's reverence for 76, 99, 141, 145
—— Matthew and Luke restricting scope of 70–74, 76
—— Paul appears to contradict divorce prohibition 91–93, 101, 147
—— Paul carefully follows, regarding divorce and remarriage 98f.
'concession' as a legal category 87, 121
divorce
—— being sought by a woman at Corinth 90
—— required after adultery 91, 114
—— 'absolutely prohibited' by Jesus an error 127
—— prohibition of, really a ban on remarriage 128f., 140
eschatology
—— esch. horizon of Jesus' mission instructions 56–58
esch. basis of Jesus' view on marriage 117

Essenes
—— support for travelling brothers 45, 54f., 68
—— view of marriage and divorce 115–120, 131
form-criticism, weakness of 61n.
Griesbach hypothesis 66n., 131n.
Hermas, Shepherd of 91, 92, 127
hospitality, original intention of support instructions 45, 67f.
Luke
—— reworks the mission instructions 45f., 47, 56, 59f., 71f.
—— attitude toward support for apostles 71–74, 76
—— attitude toward marriage 127f.
Mark
—— agreements against 49f.
—— attitude toward support for apostles 74f.
—— use of Q 50n., 63f.
—— special treatment of the mission of the Twelve 50, 50n., 65f., 78
—— version of divorce debate 'artificial' 103, 111f., 121f., 127f.; didactically oriented 105f.
marriage
—— right to, among apostles 6
—— not highly regarded at Corinth 84
—— Paul has no high view of 85f.
—— a 'concession' not a 'command' of Paul's 87f.
—— a means of saving nonbelievers 94f., 97
—— after death of first spouse 88f., 134f.
—— after divorce, not allowed by Paul 97, nor Jesus 113f., nor Essenes 116f.
—— eschatological horizon of Jesus' view regarding 117, not romantic 118ff.
—— historic basis of Matthew's account of Jesus' debate regarding 123–125, 131

Matthew
—— placing of mission instructions not in Mark's order 51f.
—— attitude toward support for apostles 70, 76
—— version of Pharisees' question on divorce more original 111
—— gives a more authentic account of divorce debate 112–115, 122, 124
—— use of Jesus' teaching regarding divorce 125f.
mission instructions
—— eschatological character of 56–58
—— received consensus concerning 41f., 48f., 62
—— items prohibited to take along 43–45 and the Essene practice 45
mission of the Twelve, historical basis of 53n., 63
Paul
—— order of arguments in support of apostles 17–20, 140
—— reliance on teachings of Jesus 3f., 146
—— the 'Pauline regime' in the Gentile mission 8f., 9n.
—— non-obligation toward command of the Lord 20, 27, 32, 35f.
—— general missionary procedure 25, 31–36
—— financial arrangements with churches 28–33, 36f.
—— relativism of, under the demands of the mission 33–36, 144
—— accused of duplicity 38f.
—— allusiveness when citing sayings of the Lord 80, 133, 146–150
Peter 6f., 37, 47, 69
Pharisees
—— views on payment for teaching Torah 12, 54f., 61, 70

—— debate on divorce 111, 115, 131
Philippian church supporting Paul 29
privilegium paulinum 96f.
Q
—— mission instructions in, 42f., 46, 48, 49, 62, 66f., 139f.
—— divorce prohibition in, 108f., 126, 129
redaction-criticism and the Gospel tradition 143
rhetorical character of 1 Cor. 9, 23, 33
support for apostles
—— not a new regulation at Corinth 5, 11f., 27
—— Paul not accepting it 13–16, 27, 30f., 139
—— Paul's accepting support while concealing the fact 22, 27f., 37ff.
—— in Synoptic mission instructions 45, 56, 67
—— disapproved of in Pharisaic circles, see Pharisees
—— caution regarding, in *Pseudo-Clementine Homily* 69f.
—— not favourably regarded by Matthew 70, 76 or Luke 71–74, 76, 139
—— no restrictions placed upon by Mark 74f.
—— transferred to resident bishops 77f.
Thomas, Gospel of 47
Two-Document Hypothesis 66n., 106n., 110, 123n.
Ur-Markus 63n.
workman/wages metaphor 9
workman saying 56, 60, 78f.
Zadok's saying opposing payment for teaching 54

2. NAMES

Abrahams, I. 53

Aland, K. 43

Albertz, M. 104, 105, 117

Allegro, J. M. 17

Allmen, J. J. von 84, 87, 88, 90, 96, 97

Allo, E. B. 5, 16, 22, 23, 79, 83, 84, 86, 88, 90, 92, 93, 94, 96, 98, 99, 133

Allon, G. 12

Avi-Jonah, M. 55

Bacher, W. 87

Bacon, B. W. 45, 63, 66, 104, 108, 112

Balcomb, R. E. xxviii

Baltensweiler, H. 110

Barrett, C. K. 5, 9, 37

Bauer, J. B. 6

Bauer, W. 10, 14, 24, 59, 73, 84

Baur, F. C. xviii, xix, xxvi, xxvii, 51, 67, 131

Beare, F. W. 29, 42, 43, 44, 48, 49, 53, 62, 104, 122, 133, 143

Behm, J. 8, 28, 30

Bentz, O. 17

Billerbeck, P. 10, 12, 13, 43, 54, 111, 113

Black, M. 62, 74

Blank, J. xxxi, 20

Blass, F. 10, 99

Blinzler, J. 126

Bonsirven, J. 11, 110

Bornkamm, G. 4, 25

Bousset, W. xviii, xxii

Boyce, J. 143

Brown, F. 119

Brown, J. P. xxix, 53, 63, 80

Brüchner, M. xxiii

Buber, S. 13

Buchanan, G. W. 118

Bultmann, R. xvii, xviii, xxi, xxii, xxiii, xxiv, xxv, xxvii, 7, 9, 10, 17, 23, 42, 43, 60, 64, 65, 79, 100, 103, 104, 105, 106, 107, 108, 122, 123, 126, 127, 143, 148, 150

Burchard, C. 94

Burkitt, F. C. 143

Burton, E. xxxii

Buswell, G. 143

Butler, B. C. 42, 47, 105

Byron, B. 110

Cadbury, H. J. 145

Campenhausen, H. von 11, 13, 19, 79, 84, 88, 91, 94, 97, 99, 130

Carrington, Ph. xxiii

Case, S. J. xx

Cerfaux, L. xxviii, 99

Chadwick, H. 25, 39, 88

Charles, R. H. 111

Cohen, B. 89, 94

Coiner, H. G. 110

Collins, J. J. 5

Congar, X. 29, 30, 32

Considine, T. P. 94

Conzelman, H. xxvii, 45, 46, 60, 72, 73, 143, 144

Cowling, C. C. 143

Cross, F. M., 116, 117, 118, 120

Cullman, O. xxviii, xxxi

Dalman, G. 54

Daniel, C. 126

Daube, D. 5, 10, 11, 12, 13, 17, 18, 25, 60, 87, 89, 94, 97, 105, 108, 117, 119, 121, 122

Dauvillier, J. 110

Davies, P. E. 31

Davies, W. D. xvii, xxii, xxxi, xxxii, 18, 79, 100, 104, 121, 125

Degenhardt, H. J. 73, 74

Deissmann, A. xxv

Delling, G. 85, 86, 92, 95

DeWette, W. M. L. 67

Dibelius, M. xxi, xxiii, xxvii

Diderichsen, B. K. 130

Didier, G. 5, 24, 25, 27

Dodd, C. H. xxiii, xxxii, 18, 80

Dubarle, A. M. 110

Dulau, P. 93, 94, 97

Dupont-Sommer, A. 58, 117

Easton, B. S. 60

Eissfeldt, O. 120

Ellis, E. E. 143, 149

Fannon, P. xxix

Farmer, W. R. 51, 67, 131, 143

Fascher, E. 60

Feilding, C. R. 133

Feine, P. xix, 8, 28, 30

Flusser, D. 17
Foerster, W. 57
Ford, J. M. 95
Fridrichsen, A. xxvi, xxvii, 9
Furnish, V. P. xviii, xix, xx, xxii, xxiii, xxiv, xxv, xxvi

Gärtner, B. xxvii, 17
Georgi, D. 9, 11, 12, 15, 24, 25, 29, 32, 37
Gerhardsson, B. xxviii, xxix, 3, 8, 17, 18, 20, 21, 32, 79, 80, 98, 99, 142, 145, 146, 149
Glombitza, O. 29
Grant, F. C. 143

Hadas, M. 145
Haenchen, E. 73
Hahn, F. 42, 43, 44, 48, 49, 78
Harnack, A. von 9
Heitmüller, W. xviii, xxi, xxv
Herford, R. T. 54
Héring, J. 5, 22, 79, 84, 86, 87, 94, 96, 99, 133
Hermesdorf, B. H. D. 29
Higgins, A. J. B. xxviii
Holmes, B. T. xxviii
Holm-Nielsen, S. 57, 58
Holtzmann, H. J. xx, 143
Hummel, R. 104, 106, 107
Hurd, J. C. 9, 19, 30, 39, 84, 88, 89, 90, 91, 94

Jackson, F. J. xxvii
Jellicoe, S. 43
Jeremias, J. 5, 60, 73, 83, 94, 97, 99
Jolowicz, H. F. 92, 97, 108
Jüngel, E. xxix

Kähler, E. 84, 86
Käsemann, E. 5, 24, 29, 126, 143
Kilpatrick, G. D. 42, 52, 125
Klostermann, E. 7, 42, 43, 49, 51, 52, 59, 60, 104, 105, 107, 108, 122, 126, 130
Knox, W. L. 19, 42, 43, 44, 48, 49, 52, 53, 108, 126
Koester, H. 9, 61, 149
Kümmel, W. G. xviii, xxix, 8, 28, 30, 86, 134

Lagrange, M. J. 62, 105, 107, 111
Lake, K. xxvii

Lang, F. 89
Lattey, C. xxviii
Lauterbach, J. Z. 13
Lehmann, M. R. 110, 113, 128
Leipoldt, J. 86, 130
Lietzmann, H. (W. G. Kümmel) 5, 11, 14, 22, 84, 86, 89, 94, 95, 99, 100, 133
Lightfoot, J. B. 84, 93, 94, 97, 108, 133
Lohman, T. xxviii
Lohmeyer, E. (W. Schmauch) 105, 106, 108, 109, 112, 113, 114, 122, 125, 127

Machen, J. G. xxvi
Maddox, R. J. 58
Mahoney, A. 110
Manson, T. W. 43, 44
Mantel, H. 126
Margot, J. C. 110
Marsh, J. 64
Marxsen, W. 143
Matheson, G. xxv
Maurer, C. 23, 24, 29
Menoud, Ph. H. 84, 85, 95, 134
Metzger, B. M. 43n.
Milik, J. T. 116
Moe, O. xxviii
Montefiore, C. G. 42, 44, 45, 52, 53, 63, 107, 111, 122
Moore, G. F. 12, 13, 53, 92, 111, 115, 126
Morris, L. 29
Munck, J. xxii

Neirynck, F. 129
Neugebauer, F. 143
Nineham, D. E. 143
Norquist, N. L. xxix

Oesterle, G. 95
O'Hagan, A. 44
O'Rourke, J. J. 97, 110

Paret, H. xviii, xix, xxv
Petrie, S. 63
Preisker, H. 5, 24, 60

Quasten, J. 69
Quesnell, Q. 126

Rabin, C. 116, 117
Rahtjen, B. D. 29

Rex, H. H. 84, 87, 91
Resch, A. xxii, xxix, xxx, 150
Richards, H. J. 110
Riesenfeld, H. xxvii, xxviii, xxix 142
Rigaux, B. xxix, 98
Ringgren, H. 58, 116, 118
Robertson, A. (A. Plummer) 5, 8, 14,
  17, 22, 23, 24, 79, 84, 86, 89, 90, 91
  93, 94, 96, 97, 99, 133

Sanday, Wm. 143
Schlatter, A. 24
Schlier, H. xxxii
Scmidt, K. L. 145
Schmithals, W. xxiv, xxix, 5, 29
Schoeps, H. J. xxi, xxii, 9, 99
Schrage, W. 86, 134, 146
Schürer, E. 12, 55
Schweitzer, A. xviii, xix, xx, xxii, xxiv
Seeberg, A. xxiii, xxviii
Selwyn, E. G. xxiii, xxiv
Sevenster, J. N. 86
Smith, M. 145
Stählin, G. 14, 15
Stanley, D. M. xxix
Stendahl, K. xxvii, xxviii, xxix, 9, 57,
  105, 142, 143
Strack, H. L. 13
Strecker, G, 42, 52, 53, 104, 108, 113,
  122
Streeter, B. H. 42, 48, 49, 50, 51, 52,
  62, 63, 64, 103, 107, 111, 122, 123,
  143

Suggs, M. J. 31

Taylor, V. 42, 43, 44, 61, 64, 65, 66,
  74, 104, 107, 108, 111, 122, 133
Tcherikover, V. A. 92
Throckmorton, B. H. 57
Trilling, W. 143

Urbach, E. 12, 28, 55

Vawter, B. 110
Vischer, E. xxv
Vogt, E. 57
Votaw, C. W. 145

Walther, G. 95
Wegenast, K. xxix
Weiss, J. xxv, 5, 8, 11, 15, 16, 79, 80,
  88, 90, 91, 92
Wellhausen, J. 143
Wendland, P. 145
Wilckens, U. xxii
Wilder, A. 143
Windisch, H. 15
Winter, P. 119
Wrede, W. xx, xxi, 24
Wuellner, W. H. 58

Zerwick, M. 110
Zimmerman, H. 109, 122
Zuntz, G. xxxii, 10

3. SCRIPTURE

Genesis
  1.27 116, 119
  2.18 119
  2.24 119f., 128, 132

Exodus
  27.7 128
  32.6 7

Deuteronomy
  4.5 34
  24.1 111, 116
  25.4 10f.
  25.8 10
  25.9 10
  25.10 10
  34.1 126

1 Kings
  4.20 7

2 Kings
  4.29 44

1 Samuel
  8 87
  12.3 72
  12.22 94
  30.16 7

2 Samuel
  11.11 7

Esther
  4.14 94

Jonah
  3.9 94

Joel
  2.14 94

Malachi
  1.6ff. 120
  2.11ff. 120
  2.13ff. 119, 120
  3.6ff. 120
  3.13ff. 120

Matthew
  4.19 58
  4.23 52
  5.32 108, 110, 114f., 126–129, 131, 133
  9.35 52
  9.37 43
  9.38 52, 56
  10 42, 49, 51
  10.1 52
  10.1–16 41, 50, 62
  10.2–4 52
  10.5f. 52
  10.6 52
  10.7 52f.
  10.7f. 49, 53, 65
  10.8 53, 69, 80, 139
  10.8f. 79
  10.9 56, 78
  10.9f. 49, 55f., 60
  10.9–16 64
  10.10 12, 56, 77, 79, 140
  10.11 66
  10.11ff. 56
  10.12f. 56
  10.13 56
  10.14 57, 66
  10.14f. 56
  10.15 66
  10.16 46, 53, 58f.
  15.24 52
  19.3 104, 109, 115
  19.3–9 102, 115f., 120, 122, 127f., 131f.
  19.3–12 103, 110, 126
  19.4–6 113
  19.5 122
  19.6 133
  19.7–9 103
  19.8 105
  19.9 104, 107–110, 113, 115, 125, 127, 130, 133
  19.10–12 125
  19.12 126
  19.29 130
  22.1–10 60
  22.5f. 130
  22.20 130
  22.23–33 107, 120

(Matthew, continued)
   22.30 130
   28.19 53
   28.19f. xxx

Mark
   1.17 58
   3.14 49
   6 48, 66, 71
   6.7–11 41, 62, 63
   6.8 75
   6.8f. 50
   6.9f. 50
   6.12 65
   10.2–4 105
   10.2–9 108
   10.2–12 102, 123, 131
   10.3 103
   10.4 103
   10.4–12 103
   10.7 105
   10.9 133
   10.11f. 107, 127, 128, 131, 133
   10.29 130
   12.18–27 107, 120
   12.25 130

Luke
   2.14 57
   9.1ff. 49, 53
   9.1–5 41, 48, 50, 71
   9.1–6 51
   9.2 65
   9.2–5 62
   9.3 44, 49
   9.3–5 51
   9.4 66
   9.5 66
   10.1ff. 49, 53
   10.1–12 41f., 46, 50, 62, 64
   10.2–12 64
   10.3 43, 46, 59, 72
   10.4 43f., 56
   10.4ff. 51
   10.5f. 66
   10.5–7 46
   10.5–12 46, 60
   10.7 46, 60, 140
   10.8 47, 140
   10.9 59
   10.10f. 66
   10.10–12 57
   10.11 59f.

   10.12 66
   10.18 46
   12.19 7
   14.15–24 59
   14.18ff. 130
   14.20 130
   14.22 60
   16.18 108, 115, 128f., 131,,133f.
   18.29 130
   20.27–40 107, 120
   20.34–36 129, 134
   22.35 46, 130, 72

Acts
   1.74ff. 130
   6.1 xxii
   10 47
   15 19, 110
   15.1 12
   16.4 19
   20.35ff. xvii, 73

Romans
   3.5 10
   6.19 10
   7.1 96
   8.1 10
   10.12 34
   14 35
   14.17–19 33
   15.8 150
   15.16 17
   15.27 11, 29
   16 28
   16.1f. 8
   16.23 28

1 Corinthians
   1.7 8
   1.11f. 7, 90
   1.26 30
   3.16 17
   4.5 87
   4.7 8
   4.14 99
   4.15 11
   4.17 xxviii
   5.1ff. 126
   5.9 30, 94
   6.9f. 85
   6.12ff. 34, 85, 88
   6.13 85
   6.15ff. 85, 95, 132, 147

(1 Corinthians, continued)
6.19   17
7.1   83f.
7.1–6   134
7.2   99
7.2ff.   85, 88
7.3f.   85, 90
7.5   86, 90, 99
7.6   87, 121
7.7   88, 134
7.8f.   83, 88, 135
7.10f.   xvii, xxxii, 81, 83, 89, 96ff.,
   101f., 108, 128f., 132f.
7.10–16   110
7.11a   91f., 97f., 101
7.12   99, 101, 110
7.12–16   83, 93f., 97f., 132, 141,
   147, 149
7.14   95, 142
7.15   94, 96, 99
7.16   94, 97
7.17   99
7.17–24   34, 83
7.18f.   134
7.20–24   39
7.21   96
7.25   98, 100f., 148
7.29   99
7.29–31   134
7.31   24, 99
7.32–35   84
7.39   96
8   5f., 16, 20
8–9   47
8–10   27, 47
8.1ff.   83
8.11f.   33
8.12   16
8.13   4f., 21
9   4ff., 12, 15f., 18, 25, 27, 29f., 36–
   39, 74, 76, 78
9.1   4
9.1ff.   5f.
9.1–23   33
9.4   7, 16, 79
9.4ff.   6f.
9.4–12   4
9.4–15   5, 27, 140, 146
9.4–18   3
9.5   6f., 18, 37
9.6   8, 28
9.7–11   9, 12, 79
9.8ff.   11, 16

9.11   11, 29
9.12   11, 13f., 16, 18, 21, 31
9.13   16, 79, 80
9.14   xvii, xxxii, 3, 14, 41, 78f.,
   101, 139
9.14–27   5
9.15   13f., 24
9.15–23   21
9.18   13, 24
9.19–23   25, 27f., 35, 39
9.22   33f., 39
10   5, 8
10.7   7
10.25–31   39
10.27   46f., 95, 140
11   5
11.23ff.   xvii, xxv, xxx, xxxii
12.1ff.   83
12.13   34
14.33–36   34
14.37   xvii, xxxii
15.1ff.   xxvi
15.15   23
15.18   23
15.31   23
15.50   134
16.1 ff.   83

2 Corinthians
2.17   15
2.17   31
5.16   xxxi
10–13   7, 19, 80
11.7   80
11.7ff.   22, 37, 73
11.8f.   29
11.9   30
12.13   15, 38
12.14   30
12.16   22, 39
12.16–18   8
13.3   xxxii

Galatians
1–2   xviii, xxv, xxvi
1.2   37
1.15   24
1.17   24
2.12   37
3.5   10
3.27f.   34
3.28   134
4.4   150

(Galatians continued)
5.6 34, 134
6.2 xxxii
6.6 29
6.15 34, 134

Philippians
2.25–30 29
4.10–20 29
4.15 29, 31, 38
4.15–17 29
4.17 29

1 Thessalonians
2.5 31
2.5–10 15
2.6 30
2.9 8, 22, 30
4.13 93
4.15f. xvii, xxxii
5.6 93

1 Timothy
5.17 78

Philemon
1 8
23 8

1 Peter
3.1f. 95
3.1–7 86

OTHER ANCIENT SOURCES

Christian
Didache
11.1–6 77
13 60, 77f.

Ignatius, *ad. Trall.*
2.1 10

Hermas, *Shepherd* Mand.
4.1.6 91

Apost. Constitutions II
4.25 78

Ptolemy *ad Flor.*
4.1–9 121

Gospel of Thomas
14 47

Tertullian *ad Uxorem*
1.3 88

Athenagoras *Leg. pro Christ.*
33 135

Irenaeus *adv. Haer.* IV
15.2 101

Pseudo-Clementine Homilies III
71 70

Clement Alex. *Strom.* III
12.81.1 88
12.87.1 130

Jewish
2 Esdras
6.32 86

Test. Naph.
8.8 86

Josephus
    c. Ap. 2.199 119
        4.233 10
    J.A. 4.253 111
        18.21 118
    B.J. 2.120f. 118
        2.124–127 45
        2.160f. 116, 118f.

Damascus Document (CD)
IV 14 116
IV.16f. 116
IV.17f. 116
IV.20f. 116
V.8–11 116
XIII. 17 117

Scroll of the Rule (1 QS)
IV.6f. 57
V.15 128
VI. 19–22 54
IX.14f. 58

Habbakuk Commentary (1 QH)
V.8 58

Mishnah Aboth
2.6 53
3.13 53
4.5 54

Mishmah Gittin
  5.9   53
  9.3   97
  9.10 111

Mishnah Demai
  3.4   53

Mishnah Shebuoth
  5.9   53

bBerakoth
  28a   55

bKethuboth
  17a   128

bNedarim
  37a   54f.
  62a   54

pNedarim
  38c   54

bBechoroth
  29a   54

bYebamoth
  78a   95

Aboth de R. Nathan
  12   54

Tanchuma
  119a   12

Pagan
Cicero *Laelius de amicitia liber*
  16.58   29